中國餐點
CHINESE SNACKS

WEI-CHUAN'S COOK BOOK 味全食譜

Edited by Miss Huang Su Huei 黃淑惠編著

Assisted by Mr. Lee Mu Tsun 李木村協著

Translated by Miss Nina Simonds 席妮娜翻譯

明朝夜宴圖　曾后希作

The explanation of the cover page
Night Feast of Ming Dynasty
by a famous artist, Tseng-Ho-hsi

　　自從民國六十一年二月發行中國菜後；許多讀者曾要求發行中、英文對照本，但由於編排等原因，遲遲未能實現，迄今經過多次增修及創新，海內外讀者建議出版中、英文對照本的更是絡繹不絕。

　　為答謝讀者關愛的熱忱，並為便於參閱，乃經深入研究及考慮之後，決定在版面清晰及經濟適用的原則下，出版中、英文對照本。在內容方面力求充實，使它合於讀者的要求，如有疏誤之處，敬請不吝指正。又最近市面發現有盜印本，不但由舊版翻印，且色彩模糊，請讀者購買時倍加留意，以免誤購。

Since the publication of the first English edition of "Chinese Cuisine" in February 1972, I have received overwhelming public demand for a Chinese-English bilingual edition. After repeated revisions and additions of the original edition, we have been able to meet the unending stream of requests from readers both at home and abroad.

To respond to such a warm reception by the readers, I have decided after careful research and consideration to put out a Chinese-English bilingual version to be used as a practicul cooking guide. It is hoped this volume will meet the needs of the readers in every respect. Your comments on the contents and the techniques are most welcomed and appreciated. I would also like to call to the attention of the readers the fact that recently pirated editions of this cookbook have appeared on the market. They can be detected by the inferior color printing. Your attention to this matter shall be appreciated.

黃淑惠 Huang Su Huei　October 1976

中國餐點
CHINESE SNACKS

● 麵點類　NOODLE SNACKS

● 米點類 RICE SNACKS

● 湯點類 SOUPS

● 飯　類 RICE

● 米粉類　RICE NOODLES

● 沙河粉類　VERMICELLI

● 粥　類　CONGEES

● 食品加工類　PROCESSED FOODS

● 其他類　OTHER KINDS

（共計185種）　　　　　　　　　　　　　**(Total 185 Courses)**

本書所用量器容量參照說明

Reference for the exposition on the weights and measures used in the book

1 杯 (1 飯碗)
1 Cup (1C.)
236 C.C.

1 大匙 (1 湯匙)
1 Tablespoon (1T.)
15 C.C.

1 小匙 (1 茶匙)
1 Teaspoon (1t.)
5 C.C.

台斤 Catty	英兩 Ounce	公分 Gram	磅 Pound
1	21	600	$1\frac{1}{3}$
	1	28.6	0.063

Seasoning for Chinese cooking

We frequently use 5 kinds of seasonings in cooking, such as salt, MSG, pepper, sugar and sesame-oil. Besides, wine, vinegar, cornstarch, fryoil etc. are also necessary.

做中國菜・點必備調味品

做菜時常用五味即鹽（或醬油）、味精、胡椒、麻油、糖，除此之外，酒、醋、太白粉、炸油，也是廚房不可缺少的必備品。

Soy sauce

Sesame oil

Vinegar

Cornstarch

Salt

MSG

Rice wine

Sugar

Black pepper

Fried oil

Instruments for Chinese cooking

Cleavers, chopping block, spatula, strainers, wok and steamers are basic instruments from which a wide variety of delicious foods can be made using roasting, frying, steaming or stewing techniques. Other tools such as a wooden bar for rolling dumplings, a sifter and hand-mixer are also employed in making Chinese snacks.

做中國菜・點必備用具

僅刀、菜板、鍋鏟、漏杓、炒鍋、蒸籠等數樣用具，足夠做炒、炸、蒸、燉、燴…等等多種美味菜餚，唯做點心得另備趕麵桿、篩子、打蛋器等。

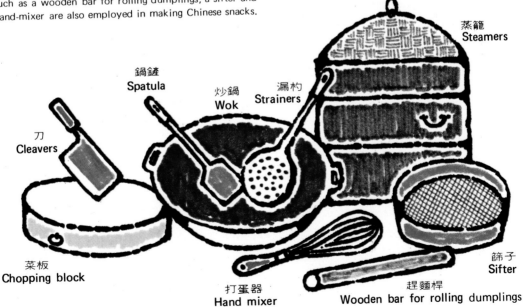

蒸籠
Steamers

鍋鏟
Spatula

炒鍋
Wok

漏杓
Strainers

刀
Cleavers

菜板
Chopping block

打蛋器
Hand mixer

趕麵桿
Wooden bar for rolling dumplings

篩子
Sifter

烹飪慣用語說明

烹調在我國向無份量之規定，亦無一定之時間，全憑經驗由己去摸索所得。本書盡其所能的把材料、佐料之份量及所需時間簡要例出，為使能更進一步了解起見，茲將調理時之工作要點及慣用詞大略說明如次：

Culinary idioms

In Chinese cuisine, cooking is a very subjective art; there are no definite quantities of any ingredient, nor any exact time limit for cooking any recipe. We encourage you to develop all of this personally, through trial and error. We have listed the basic information for the preparation of all dishes, as well as the ingredients involved, however we encourage you to revise according to your own taste. In order that you may further understand the practice, we give the significant points and explain some expressions, used often in Chinese cooking.

清洗材料
材料洗淨需瀝乾水份。

CLEANING
Clean the ingredients before using, then drain and dry thoroughly.

炒
把食物置炒菜鍋內，翻攪至熟了，即曰炒。

STIR-FRYING
To put the material into a very hot pan over high heat and turn over and over, until done.

炒菜是速成之菜，故炒菜時宜將各項佐料調在碗內使用時，較方便。

Stir-frying is a very quick process. So it is advisable to prepare all of the sauces in advance, including the corn-starch and water used to thicken the final sauce.

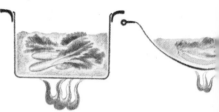

炒一盤菜，如遇使用多種材料，因其各材料性質不同，有些材料需經過泡油，煮熟或分開炒熟後再使用。

When several kinds of ingredients are used in cooking, the difference in tenderness of each ingredient will sometimes require that material to be cooked in oil, boiled or fried before mixing whichever method is used, the ingredient must be precooked till tender.

炸
把食物投入多量的沸油中炸熟謂炸。

DEEP-FRYING
To immerse the food in deep, hot oil.

先將材料調上味，並視其種類，裹上麵糊。

Prepare the material for frying, first the food must be soaked in the prescribed sauce, then it must be covered with the proper flour mixture.

油的份量要多注意，如果要出炒鍋之六分

There should b of oil in the pan to cover the However if to be fried, is w

蒸
所謂蒸是把材料放蒸籠內，下放沸水，藉水蒸汽的熱力把食物蒸熟。

STEAMING
To put the material in a "steaming cage". which is then put in a pan containing boiling water inside.

先將水放入外鍋燒開。
Frist, put water in the pan and allow it to come to a boil.

宜水燒開後才把食物放入蒸
Then place food in cage and put boiling water.

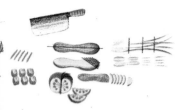

材料

配材料要切成同樣形狀，粗、細、薄要均一，則燒出來的菜着嫩度會一致美觀。

TTING

ingredients must be cut into the same size shape, so that the cooked food will look form and have the same tenderness.

醃

鷄、肉、魚、蝦等要事先調上味，必要時，如能拌入蛋白及太白粉，則可增加其香嫩。

PRE-CONDITIONING

Chicken, pork, fish and shrimp must be soaked in the prescribed sauces (soy sauce, wine or cornstarch) to increase tenderness and deliciousness of food.

熱鍋

炒、煎、炸時，先空鍋燒熱，再倒進油，可防材料黏鍋。

HEATING THE PAN

The pan must be thoroughly heated before adding oil and then thoroughly lubricated with oil so that material will not stick.

以上準備妥當，將鍋燒熱後放油再入葱、薑、蒜等使其香味滲入油中，再把所要炒的材料及調在碗內的調味料倒入鍋內炒拌，操作簡便迅速，且可防止火候過久。

When the preliminary preparation is finished, heat the pan and pour in oil. Add the onion, ginger or garlic and stir so that the oil will pick up its flavor. Then add the ingredients, with a few drops of wine, if desired, to enhance the flavor of the food. Add the sauce and stir-fry until all is mixed together. This entire process must be short and quick so that the food will not overcook.

當臨起鍋時，淋下數滴油，可增加菜着之光澤，並有保溫之功效。

At this point, you may sprinkle a few drops of fried oil on the food. This will help to increase the brilliancy of the food and keep it warm.

食物爲準，但要
水份多，則以不超
泡沫溢出危險。

ains much water, the
ld not occupy more
% of the pan, so
e oil will not splash

炸時先將油燒沸，如遇不容易炸熟者，將鍋暫時離火，以中溫或低溫，但撈出時要大火，並視其材料決定所需要的時間。

First boil the oil; remove the pan from the fire and when the oil has cooled to medium temperature, insert the material into the pan. Replace the pan over medium heat and cook until near-tender. Then turn heat to high and cook over high heat until done. This seals the flavor and ensures that the material will be completely cooked and crispy on the outside.

下鍋時如能同時下鍋，則撈出時宜一次撈起，所炸出來的東西才會一致。

All material put into the oil together, at the same time, must be removed at the same time, to maintain uniformity.

溜、燴：汁或湯注入鍋中燒開，隨即加入經過、炒、炸，或煮熟之食物勾成濃稠狀，其湯汁有，糖醋汁、茄汁、醬汁、白汁、奶汁等。

燒、燜：將水醃滿食物，燒開後，加入調味料用中火或小火，將食物煮軟。

煮：將食物放入多量的水內，燒煮熟。

拌：凡不必再加熱，涼着或生着切了，拌上佐料即可吃的均是涼拌。

燻：用糖、木屑或茶葉上架鐵絲網盛放食物，四週窄蓋緊，加熱使煙與熱力慢慢把物烤熟或烤至上了茶煙之色與香味即曰燻。

烤：加熱在食物之四週，把食物炙熟者曰烤。

MIX-BOIL

To first put the sauce or soup into the pan by itself and allow it to boil. Then add the food. The amount of cornstarch in the sauce should be to your own taste; add more if desired. There should not be too much sauce.

MIXING

If no cooking is required, just mix together the ingredients after cutting. If ingredients have been precooked, allow to cool, then mix together; add sauce and serve.

SMOKING

To put food in an oven, or cover, on a grill over a fire. Then throw sugar, wood powder, or tea into the fire or oven so that the fumes will smoke the food and give it flavor.

ROASTING

To cook or bake food in the oven with all of the ingredients, until done.

FRYING

To cook food on each side until golden, in a little bit of oil.

胃燉與蒸略同，外鍋內放水，內鍋
入食物及水或湯（注滿過食物）置
火經過長時間，至食物煮軟，做出
勻湯汁，非常澄清。

WING

ing is similar to steaming; put water in the
pan and the material to be heated with water
ock to cover, in the inner pan. Cook over
derate fire until food is tender. Soup prepared
ay is very clear and clean.

發麵製作圖解説明

　　凡製饅頭，包子類需先發麵，個人發麵方法不同，現歸三大類供讀者參考，若參照此法屢次研習實驗，綜合各法領悟心得後，可抉擇自己認爲最好的發麵法。

發麵一

　麵粉（6杯）……1斤　　　　　猪油………2大匙

① ⎧ 糖……………¼杯
　⎨ 温水………1¾杯
　⎩ 酵母………1大匙

■ 做法簡便，較適合於家庭中製作。
■ 發好的麵泡孔較大。

先將糖放進温水内，待溶化洒入酵母。

搁置10分鐘，上浮一層白沫。

把篩過麵粉、猪油及備好的①料攪拌。

用手搓匀。

Dissolve sugar in warm water, add yeast.

Let the liquid stand for ten minutes. The yeast will foam into a head and rise to the top.

Sift flour, add shortening and mix together with ingredients prepared in step 1.

Knead dough into ball.

發麵二

① ⎧ 麵種………3兩
　⎨ 麵粉………2杯
　⎩ 水…………½杯

② ⎧ 碱粉…………1小匙
　⎪（發好的①料酸則用碱粉，否則免）
　⎨ 蛋白2個或水…¾杯
　⎪ 糖……………¼杯
　⎩ 猪油…………2大匙

③ ⎧ 麵粉………3杯 ⎫ 篩
　⎨ 　　　　　　　⎬ 過
　⎩ 發粉………1½大匙 ⎭

■ 製作方法較複雜。
■ 適用於餐舘及專門製造業者。
■ 發成的麵，既細緻且味甘美，效果

將①料拌和。

用手搓匀。

上蓋濕布8～10小時

發到2～3倍，此謂「老麵」。

Combine the ingredients in ① and mix.

Knead dough until smooth and elastic.

Place dough in a clean bowl and cover with damp cloth.

Let dough (A) rise fo 8-10 hours until it ha doubled or tripled bulk.

發麵三

① ⎧ 麵粉………1斤
　⎩ 發粉………2大匙

② ⎧ 糖……………¼杯
　⎨ 猪油…………2大匙
　⎩ 温水………1¾杯

■ 做法便捷，可在短時間製作完成
■ 發成之麵效果稍差。

Leavened Dough III

① ⎧ 6　C. flour
　⎩ 2　T. baking powder

② ⎧ ¼ C. sugar
　⎨ 2　T. shortening
　⎩ 1¾ C. warm water

■ Although this recipe is quick and simple and can be made in a short period of time, the result is a bread worthy of praise.

Illustrated Instructions for Making Leavened Dough (Basic Yeast Dough)

In order to make plain steam rolls, buns and breads of this kind, it is necessary to begin with leavened dough (basic yeast dough). Although your own recipes may not be the same, the following three recipes offer tested alternatives. You may compare and collate these recipes and experiment with them often, or follow a given recipe, one chosen by you as the best recipe for making leavened dough.

Leavened Dough I

① 6 C. flour
¼ C. sugar
1¾ C. warm water
1 T. yeast

2 T. shortening

- Good leavened dough has large bubbles.
- This recipe is best for home cooking.

出太硬或太軟時，
入入水或麵粉。

搓成軟硬適中之麵糰。

麵糰放入清潔盆裡，
上蓋濕布。

置2～4小時發到2
～3倍時即可使用。

emove dough from owl. Add flour or ater if necessary.

Knead dough until smooth and elastic.

Place dough in a clean bowl and cover with a damp cloth.

Let dough rise (in a warm place) for 2-4 hours until it has doubled or tripled in bulk.

Leavened Dough II

① 3 oz. dough starter
2 C. flour
½ C. water

② ¾ C. of 3 egg whites or water
¼ C. sugar
2 T. shortening
1 t. baking soda (omit if dough A is not sour.)

③ 3 C. flour
1½ T. baking powder

- The result is a bread which is light and delicate with a delicious flavor.
- This recipe is more complicated and is best suited for use in restaurants and specialty shops.

碱粉用少許水溶化
將②料全部攪勻。

把③料過篩入②料内。

全部攪拌。

倒出與老麵揉成軟硬
適中之麵糰。

ssolve baking soda in ater (only a small mount of water is cessary). Add to the gredients in ② and x.

Sift and add ingredients in ③.

Mix thoroughly.

Remove, add (A) and knead dough until smooth and elastic.

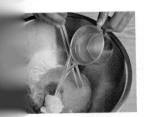   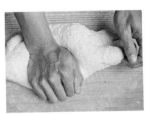

將②料備好。

把①料過篩入②料内。

全部攪拌。

倒出揉成軟硬適中之
麵糰即成。

Prepare the ingredients in ②.

Sift the ingredients in ① then add to ingredients in ②.

Mix together.

Knead dough until smooth and elastic.

中國餐點內容簡介

中國餐點的內容分爲麵點、米點、湯點、飯類、麵類、米粉類、沙河粉類、粥類、以及食品加工類等，其中包括年節應景點心、廣東飲茶點心、宴席常用點心、宵夜點心、家常餐點等，彙集全國各地區之簡餐、點心，風味齊全，範圍廣泛，旣可供正餐，亦可當副食，對於家庭主婦、經營餐舘者、小食店、學校教學、福利社及食品加工業者，皆可作爲參考之用。

Brief Explanation of Chinese Snacks

Chinese snacks can be divided into several sections: noodle snacks, rice snacks, soups, rice dishes, noodle dishes, rice noodles, vermicelli, congees, processed foods, as well as foreign snacks. The selections in this book include snacks eaten for the major yearly festivals, Cantonese tea snacks, banquet snacks, bedtime snacks and everyday simple meals.

"Chinese Snacks" is a wide collection of simple meals and snacks which reflect the regional flavors and styles of cooking in China and can be used as a reference for the housewife, restaurant owner, small food stand operator, cooking schools, food factories, and food processing industries.

年節應景點心

春節—即農曆元旦，我國傳統有食年糕之習俗，寓有「年年高昇」之意。南方多用米磨製而成，北方多用黃米、黍米碾成。例如：

甜年糕------（第48頁）
蘿蔔糕------（第49頁）
臘味蘿蔔糕（第49頁）
發糕--------（第43頁）
碗粿--------（第44頁）

吃的方式爲煎、蒸、炸等。又北方習俗在接財神之後吃餃子，有「招財進寶」之意，餃子又稱「元寶」（參考第16頁、17頁），南方尚有食臘腸、臘肉之習（參考第147頁、148頁）。

Snacks for the Major Yearly Festivals

Lunar New Year Festival — On New Year's Day of the lunar calendar, it is a traditional custom to eat New Year's cake with the hope that each year will bring much peace.

In southern China the cake is made from rice powder, while in the north ground millet is used. Examples:

Sweet New Year's
  Cake . . . . P. 48
Steamed Turnip
  Cake . . . . P. 49
Steamed Turnip Cake
  with Sausage . . . P. 49
Steamed Rice
  Cupcakes . . . . . P. 43
Steamed Rice
  Pudding . . . . . . P. 44

Frying, steaming and deep-frying etc. are different ways of preparing the snacks. In northern China it is a custom to eat dumplings during the lunar new year after welcoming back the "God of Wealth" and expressing the wish for new wealth and riches. Dumplings are also called "ingots" (see P. 16 17). In the south, it is also a custom to eat Chinese Sausage and Spicy Dried Pork (see P. 147,148)

元宵節—也稱「燈節」即上元節，在此「天官賜福、燈綵處處」之時，應景點心是湯圓，北方人稱「元宵」（參考第65頁至67頁），花燈之下，合家圍坐吃元宵，其樂也融融。

During the **Lantern Festival,** when "Riches given by heaven and brightly colored lanterns are everywhere," Sweet Rice Ball Soup is eaten. Northern Chinese also call them "ingots" (see p. 65—67).
It is truly a joyous occasion when the family all gathers together under colored lanterns and eats sweet rice balls.

端午節—每年農曆五月初五，爲了紀念憂國憂民，投汨羅江殉國的愛國詩人—屈原，舉行龍舟競渡，這天每家每戶掛艾葉、懸菖蒲、繫香囊、飲雄黃，以驅五毒，防百病。古時以竹筒裝米投入江中送給屈原食用，慢慢演變成粽子，分有甜、鹹及鹹粽，各地口味及取材均不相同（參考第46頁、47頁）。

Dragon Boat Festival — the fifth day of the fifth lunar month, is a day to be concerned over the fate of the nation. On this day boat races are held to commemorate the ancient poet Chu Yuan who died for his country by throwing himself into the Mi Lo River. During this holiday, each family hangs up tea leaves, sweet flag or calamus, wraps sachets, and drinks realgar to prevent snake and insect poisoning.
Originally, rice wrapped in bamboo leaves were thrown into the river to feed the spirit of Chu Yuan. Today, these rice snacks are called "jungdz" and are separated into sweet, salty and differing tastes according to regional ingredients and flavoring (see P. 46,47).

中秋節—每逢農曆八月十五日，中秋佳節來臨，人們最主要的慶祝活動是合家團圓賞月，品嚐月餅，傳說明朝初年，朱洪武、劉伯温等爲號召群衆，消滅韃子，在月餅中夾藏紙條，作爲聯絡暗記，從此有食「月餅」的風俗。月餅的種類很多，本書內有粤式、蘇式（參考本書第33、34頁）。

Mid-Autumn Festival — 15th day of the eighth lunar month. The most important activity during the Mid-Autumn Festival is gathering together with family and friends to gaze at the moon and eat moon cakes.

According to legend, in the beginning of the Ming dynasty, Chu Kung-wu and Liu Po-wen summoned the people to unite and destroy the Tartars. Pieces of paper were hidden inside moon cakes as a secret signal to keep in contact. From this, the custom of eating moon cakes began. There are many varieties of moon cakes; this book includes Cantonese and Soochow styles (see P. 33, 34).

廣東飲茶點心

廣東飲茶盛行於香港及國內外各地，其營業項目包括很廣，其中較著名的有下列：

Cantonese Tea Snacks

Cantonese "Yam Cha" is not only popular in Hong Kong, but also in foreign countries. The range of items served is endless, but some of the more famous snacks are listed below:

Various dishes over rice, noodle dishes and congee.

　　營業方式與眾不同，由服務生推出裝滿各式點心的輪車，由客人自由挑選喜愛的點心，一邊品飲茗茶，一邊談天說地，氣氛甚為融洽。時間由清晨至中午者稱「上午茶」，午後至黃昏者稱「下午茶」，夜晚亦有，上圖為飲茶時的現場情況。

　　The snacks served in restaurants and those eaten at home are not quite the same. In the restaurant, waitresses wheel a cart filled with a variety of snacks and guests freely pick their favorite ones, while chatting, eating and drinking tea in a bustling atmosphere.

　　From early morning until noon is considered "morning tea". Afternoon until dusk is called "afternoon tea", and evening tea follows the same pattern.

宴席常用點心

　　正式宴席雖以菜爲主，但是點心仍極具重要性，尤其是講究的宴席，在進行當中必有二道鹹點，而在接近尾聲時，尚有甜點、甜湯等，雖然目前逐漸簡化，常將鹹點移至最後，把鹹、甜點、甜湯同時上桌，或將三種內減少爲一或二種，但一席宴席內至少得有甜點或鹹點，茲列舉本書正式宴席常用甜點、鹹點、甜湯：

Banquet Snacks and Desserts

　　Although main dishes are the most essential part of a banquet meal, snacks are also considered important. In the middle of a banquet meal there should be two courses of "salty" snacks, and at the end of the meal desserts and sweet soups should be served.

　　Although today, to simplify the meal, "salty" snacks, desserts, and soups are often served together near the end of the meal or combined together into one or two courses, still it is best to serve at least one sweet and salty snack. Examples:

餡：雞肉丁‥‥‥‥‥‥‥１２兩

① 鹽‥１小匙、酒‥２小匙
太白粉‥‥‥‥‥１½大匙
葱、薑末各‥‥‥‥１大匙

② 熟筍丁、洋菇片各‥‥½杯
冬菇（泡軟切丁）‥‥‥６朵

③ 酒‥‥‥‥‥‥‥‥‥‥１大匙
醬油、糖各‥‥‥‥‥‥２小匙
鹽、味精各‥‥‥‥‥‥１小匙
胡椒‥¼小匙、麻油‥½小匙
太白粉‥‥‥‥‥‥‥‥２大匙
水‥‥‥‥‥‥‥‥‥‥１½杯

皮：參照發麵一、二、三

❶餡：雞肉丁調①料醃約２０分鐘後入鍋炒熟盛起，油４大匙燒熱，將葱、薑末炒香，隨入②料炒拌並調③料燒沸，再加炒熟雞丁炒拌即可盛盤待冷。

❷皮：將發好麵塊（參照發麵做法一、二、三），揉成十分光滑，太硬或太軟時酌量加水或麵粉，揉成長條狀，分成２４個小麵糰，用手壓成圓薄片。

❸做法：① 每張圓薄片中央置１份餡包成包子狀（圖１～４）。
② 將每個包子底墊１張６公分四方之白紙或蒸籠內舖上濕布置約１０分鐘後，以大火蒸１０分鐘即成。

雞肉包 Tasty Chicken Buns

材料：２４個 **Makes 24**

Filling:
1 lb. raw, chicken meat
① 1 t. salt, 2 t. rice wine
1⅓ T. cornstarch
1 T. chopped green onion
1 T. chopped ginger root

② ½ C. precooked, diced bamboo shoot
½ C. sliced button mushrooms
6 pre-softened Chinese black mushrooms, diced

③ 1 T. rice wine, 2 t. soy sauce, ¼ t. black pepper
1 t. salt, 1 t. MSG, 2 t. sugar, ½ t. sesame oil
2 T. cornstarch, 1½ C. water

Skin:
1 recipe "Basic Yeast Dough"

❶ Filling:
Dice chicken meat; mix with ① and let soak 20 minutes. Heat pan and 1C. oil until medium hot; add diced chicken meat and stir-fry until color changes; remove and drain. Drain all but 4T. oil from pan; reheat and stir-fry chopped green onion and ginger until fragrant; add ② and briefly stir-fry. Add ③ and when mixture comes to a boil, add chicken meat; stir-fry together and remove. Let cool.

❷ Skin:
Remove risen dough from bowl (see Basic Yeast Dough) and knead on a floured surface until smooth and elastic (about 5 to 7 minutes); if too dry and water, if too sticky and more flour. Let sit 10 minutes and roll into a long roll, divide into 24 pieces, then flatten with palm of hand.

❸ Procedure:
1 Place one portion filling in middle of dough circle (Fig. 1); pleat edges of circle and press firmly (Fig. 2); pleat entire circle in this fashion (Fig. 3), wrap up entire circle and press all edges together to close (Fig. 4).
2 Place filled buns on squares of paper and let rise 10 minutes. Arrange buns in a steamer ½-inch apart and steam 10 minutes over high heat; remove and serve.

1

餡：棗子⋯⋯⋯⋯ 1 斤　　　　糖⋯⋯⋯⋯ $\frac{1}{4}$ 杯　　　皮：參照發麵一、二、三
　　水⋯⋯⋯⋯⋯ 4 杯　　①{ 猪油⋯⋯⋯⋯ 2 大匙

❶餡：①棗子一斤加水（滿過棗子）煮開約２分鐘後將水倒乾以去苦味另加水４杯，用快鍋中火煮２０分鐘
　　　　後去仔，並用篩子過濾以去皮備用（如不易過濾可加些水）。
　　　②過濾後的棗泥很稀，以中火煮到適當的濃度時加入①料即成棗泥（餡）。
❷皮：將發好麵塊（參照發麵做法一、二、三）揉成十分光滑太硬或太軟時酌量加入水或麵粉揉成長條狀，
　　　分切成２４個小麵糰，用手壓成圓薄片。
❸做法①每張圓薄麵片中央置１份餡，包成壽桃形（圖１〜４）另做好葉子（圖５）沾水（圖６），貼在壽桃上
　　　　面（圖７），再以牙刷沾上食用紅色水，用筷子彈動牙刷，噴上顏色（圖８）。
　　　②將每個包子底墊一張６公分四方之白紙或蒸籠內舖上濕布置約１０分鐘後，以大火蒸１０分鐘即
　　　　可。

壽桃 Steamed Long Life Cake　　　　　　　　　材料：２４個 Makes 24

Filling:　　　　　　　　　　　　　　　　　　　　Skin:
1⅓ lbs. dates　　　　①{ ¼ C. sugar　　　　　　1 recipe "Basic Yeast Dough"
4 C. water　　　　　　　{ 2 T. lard or margarine

❶ Filling:
① Place dates in a pan with water to cover; let boil 2 minutes over medium heat; remove and drain. Place precooked dates and 4 C. water in pressure cooker; cook 20 minutes over medium heat (dates should be very soft); (retain liquid). Strain out skin and pits, discard; place date meat and retained liquid in pan.
② Cook fruit and liquid over medium heat until thick; add ① and mix together; let cool.
❷ Skin:
Remove risen dough from bowl (see Basic Yeast Dough) and knead on a floured surface until smooth and elastic (about 5 to 7 minutes); if too dry add water, if too sticky add more flour. Let sit 10 minutes and roll into a long roll, divide into 24 pieces, then flatten with palm of hand.
❸ Procedure:
① Place one portion filling in the middle of dough circle (Fig. 1); wrap up to enclose filling (Fig. 2, 3, 4); make leaves (Fig. 5); dip the leaves into water (Fig. 6), then stick on the bun (Fig. 7); sprinkle red food coloring on top of each bun for decoration (Fig. 8).
② Place filled buns on squares of paper and let rise 10 minutes. Arrange buns in a steamer ½-inch apart and steam 10 minutes over high heat; remove and serve.

餡：① { 紅豆……1斤
 水……10杯 }　② { 猪油……………1杯
 糖………（2杯）12兩 }　　皮：參照發麵一、二、三

❶餡：豆沙（一）紅豆加水（滿過紅豆）煮約2分鐘，將水倒乾以去苦味，另加水10杯以快鍋中火煮約25
　　　分鐘後用篩子過濾去渣（如不易過濾可加些水）其汁放入布袋內擠出水份不要，只要豆沙，
　　　然後加入②料繼續燒煮免蓋鍋，見水份快乾即成（可做豆沙1斤10兩）。

　　　豆沙（二）做法參照豆沙（一）豆沙經煮熟後不須過濾，直接加入②料繼續燒煮免蓋鍋，見水份快乾即
　　　成（可做豆沙3斤）。取豆沙1斤分成24份。

❷皮：將發好麵塊（參照發麵法一、二、三）揉成十分光滑太硬或太軟時酌量加水或麵粉揉成長條狀，分成
　　　24個小麵糰，用手壓成圓薄片。

❸做法：⑴ 每張圓薄麵片中央置一份餡，包成包子狀。
　　　　⑵ 將每個包子底墊一張6公分四方之白紙或蒸籠內舖上濕布置約10分鐘後，以大火蒸10分鐘即
　　　　成。

豆沙包　Sweet Buns with Red Bean Paste　　　　材料：24個　Makes 24

Filling:　　　　　　　　　　　　　　　　　　　　Skin:
① { 1⅓ lbs. red beans
 10 C. water }　② { 1 C. lard or margarine
 2 C. sugar }　1 recipe "Basic Yeast Dough"

◆ Filling:
o make sweet bean paste (1):
　Place beans in water to cover; cook 2 minutes over medium heat; remove and drain (discard water). Place beans and 10C. water in a pressure cooker and cook 25 minutes over medium heat (beans should be very soft). Strain beans and remove skins; discard. Place strained mixture in a cheesecloth and wrap tightly to remove all water; place strained mixture in a pan and add ② . Cook mixture over medium heat until very thick; remove from heat; stir well and let cool.
o make sweet been past (2):
　Cook ① until very thick; add ② and cook again; remove from heat. (An easier method family-style)

◆ Skin:
Remove risen dough from bowl (see Basic Yeast Dough) and knead on a floured surface until smooth and elastic (about 5 to 7 minutes); if too dry and water, if too sticky　　more flour. Let sit 10 minutes and roll into a long roll, divide into 24 pieces, then flatten with palm of hand.

Procedure:
Place one portion filling in the middle of dough circle and wrap up to enclose filling.
Place filled buns on squares of paper and let rise 10 minutes. Arrange buns in a steamer ½-inch apart and steam 10 minutes over high heat; remove and serve.

3

餡：　叉燒肉‥‥‥‥‥‥‥‥‥１２兩

① 醬油…１½大匙、味精…１小匙
蠔油…１½大匙、水……１½杯
糖……１½大匙

② 粟米粉…２½大匙
水………２½大匙

③ 猪油………３大匙
麻油……１½小匙
胡椒………¼小匙

皮：參照發麵一、二、三

❶ 餡　：叉燒肉切１公分四方小薄片（圖１、２、３、４），把①料燒開以②料調成濃汁後，加③料即成餡汁待冷，與切好肉片拌勻成餡。

❷ 皮　：將發好麵塊（參照發麵做法一、二、三）揉成十分光滑，太硬或太軟時酌量加入水或麵粉擱置１０分鐘揉成長條狀，分成２４個小麵糰，用手壓成圓薄片。

❸做法：叉燒肉做法：□1每張圓薄麵片，中央置１份餡，包成包子狀。
　　　　　　　　　　□2每個包子底墊６公分四方之白紙，或蒸籠內舖上濕布置約１０分鐘後，以大火蒸１０分鐘即成。
■叉燒肉做法：請參照第149頁。

叉燒包 Roasted Pork Buns

材料：２４個 **Makes 24**

Filling:
1　lb. roasted pork*

① 1½ T. soy sauce
1½ T. oyster sauce
1½ T. sugar
1　t. MSG
1½ C. water

② 2½ T. cornstarch
2½ T. water

③ 3　T. lard
1½ t. sesame oil
¼　t. black pepper

Skin:
1　recipe "Basic Yeast Dough"

❶ Filling:
Dice roasted pork (Fig. 1, 2, 3, 4); bring ① to a boil; add ② to thicken; add ③ and mix together. Let cool and the add roasted pork.

❷ Skin:
Remove risen dough from bowl (see Basic Yeast Dough) and knead on a floured surface until smooth and elastic (abou 5 to 7 minutes); if too dry and water, if too sticky and more flour. Let sit 10 minutes and roll into a long roll, divide int 24 pieces, then flatten with palm of hand.

❸ Procedure:
□1 Place one portion filling in middle of dough circle; pleat edges of circle and press firmly; pleat entire circle in this fashion wrap up entire circle and press all edges together to close.
□2 Place filled buns on squares of paper and let rise 10 minutes. Arrange buns in a steamer ½-inch apart and steam 10 minute over high heat; remove and serve.

* To prepare roasted pork see P. 149 "Chinese Roasted Pork".

4

餡： 高麗菜………1斤半　　　　鹽…………2小匙　　　皮：參照發麵一、二、三
①{蝦皮…………1兩　　　②{味精………1小匙
　蒜末…………2大匙　　　　胡椒………1小匙
　　　　　　　　　　　　　　麻油………2小匙

❶餡：高麗菜取葉洗淨（圖1），以開水川燙撈起（圖2），入冷水漂涼後稍握乾水份（圖3），切約2公分四
　　方塊（圖4），油4大匙燒熱將①料炒香，隨下高麗菜及②料炒勻即可盛盤待冷（餡）。
❷皮：將發好麵塊（參照發麵做法一、二、三）揉成十分光滑，太硬或太軟時酌量加入水或麵粉揉成長條狀
　　，分成24個小麵欄用手壓成圓薄片。
❸做法① 每張圓薄麵片中央置1份餡包成包子狀。
　　　② 將每個包子底墊一張6公分四方之白紙或蒸籠內舖上濕布，置約10分鐘後以大火蒸10分鐘即
　　　成。

素菜包 Vegetable Buns

材料：24個 Makes 24

Filling:
2 lbs.cabbage
①{¼ C. dried shrimp
2 T. chopped garlic

②{2 t. salt
1 t. MSG
1 t. black pepper
2 t. sesame oil

Skin:
1 recipe "Basic Yeast Dough"

❶ Filling:
Rinse cabbage (Fig. 1); cook in boiling water until soft (Fig. 2) (about 1 minute); remove and plunge into cold water; and drain thoroughly (Fig. 3) and dice (Fig. 4). Heat pan and 4T. oil; stir-fry ① until fragrant; add cabbage, and ② ; stir-fry to mix together; remove and let mixture cool.

❷ Skin:
Remove risen dough from bowl (see Basic Yeast Dough) and knead on a floured surface until smooth and elastic (about 5 to 7 minutes); if too dry add water, if too sticky and more flour. Let sit 10 minutes and roll into a long roll, divide into 24 pieces, then flatten with palm of hand.

❸ Procedure:
① Place one portion filling in middle of dough circle; pleat edges of circle and press firmly; pleat entire circle in this fashion, wrap up entire circle and press all edges together to close.
② Place filled buns on squares of paper and let rise 10 minutes. Arrange buns in a steamer ½-inch apart and steam 10 minutes over high heat; remove and serve.

餡：絞肉‥‥‥‥‥‥‥‥半斤　　　高湯凍‥‥‥‥‥‥½杯　　　皮：參照發麵一、二、三

醬油半大匙、麻油１大匙　　　　　　　　　　　　　　　　　　份量取½即可

① 鹽‥１小匙、葱末１大匙

味精１小匙、薑末半大匙

水‥‥‥‥‥‥‥‥‥‥６大匙

❶ 餡　：絞肉調入①料攪勻並甩打３分鐘成餡。高湯凍切２４小塊。

❷ 皮　：１ 發麵：參照發麵一、二、三。

　　　　　２ 把發好的麵糰，放在板上洒少許麵粉，揉至極光滑（約５分鐘）後，搓成長條，分切２４小塊。

❸ 做法：每小塊用手壓成圓餅狀（圖１），再趕成直徑７公分邊薄中間稍厚之圓片（圖２），把餡置中央，取一塊高

　　　　湯凍放在餡內，包成如圖狀（圖３、４），放進舖好濕布的蒸籠中，水開中火蒸８分鐘至熟，趁熱食

　　　　用，高湯凍溶化滑潤清香，鮮美可口。

■高湯凍做法：雞骨或豬皮加水熬成湯，冷凍即成。

小籠（湯）包 "Little Juicy Steamed Rolls"　　　　材料：２４個 Makes 24

Filling:
⅔ lb. chopped pork

½ T. soy sauce

1 t. salt, 1 t. MSG

① 1 T. sesame oil

1 T. chopped green onion

½ T. chopped ginger root

6 T. water

¼ C. stock aspic*

Skin:
¼ recipe "Basic Yeast Dough"

❶ Filling:

Mix ① with chopped pork; mix ingredients thoroughly, for 3 minutes by lightly throwing mixture against inside of mixing bowl to combine ingredients. Cut jelled stock aspic into 24 pieces.

❷ Skin:

1 Prepare dough according to "Basic Yeast Dough".

2 Lightly flour counter and knead dough for 5 minutes until smooth and elastic; roll to a long roll and cut into 24 pieces.

❸ Procedure:

Flatten each piece of dough (Fig. 1) to a 2-inch circle, middle should be thick and edges thin (Fig. 2); place 1 portion of filling in the middle of dough skin; place 1 piece jelled stock aspic on top (Fig. 3). Using index finger and thumb, gather edges together in small pleats to form an "igloo" shape (Fig. 4). Place each finished roll on a square of paper or place in steamer lined with a piece of cotton soaked in water; stream over medium heat for 8 minutes; remove and serve.

* To make "stock aspic" use chicken bones, pork skin and bones or fish bones to make a soup stock; pour into a shallow pan and chill; use as directed.

餡：五花肉５公分寬（切２４片）１斤半　　鹹菜（切絲）半斤　　　皮：參照發麵一、二、三
　　紅蔥頭片……………………１大匙　　　花生粉……半斤　　　　麻油或沙拉油２大匙
　①｛酒………１大匙、味精……半小匙　　香菜………半杯
　　醬油……半杯、八角………半朵
　　水……１½杯、五香粉……¼小匙
　　糖……１小匙

❶ 餡：油４大匙燒熱，將鹹菜略炒，並加醬油１大匙炒勻盛起，豬油４大匙燒熱，以中火將紅蔥頭炒香，
　　呈金黃色時，放入五花肉略炒，並加①料燒開，改小火燒煮約４０分鐘，再入鹹菜續煮１０分鐘即成。

❷ 皮：①將發好麵塊（參照發麵一、二、三），揉合成軟硬適度的麵糰，並揣至極光滑時分切２４小塊，每
　　　塊壓成直徑５公分之圓餅狀，中間塗抹麻油（圖１），對折成半圓形（圖２），再輕壓，並趕成直徑
　　　７公分、邊薄中厚之半圓餅狀。
　　　②將筷子直剖十字至３公分處插入兩枝牙籤（圖３）沾上食用色素印在割包上（圖４）以增美觀，水開
　　　後以大火蒸５分鐘至熟即可。

❸ 做法：把割包打開依序包入花生粉、五花肉、鹹菜、香菜，即可食用。

■ 蒸時蒸籠內要先舖上濕布再放割包。

割 包 Taiwanese Steamed Rolls   材料：２４人份 Makes 24

Filling:
2 lbs.fresh bacon, cut into 24 pieces
1 T. chopped shallots
① {
1 T. rice wine，½ t. MSG
½ C. soy sauce, ½ star anise
1½ C. water，¼ t. 5-spice powder
1 t. sugar

⅔ lb. Szechuan pickled mustard green, shredded
½ C. crushed peanuts
½ C. coriander

Skin:
1 recipe "Basic Yeast Dough"
2 T. sesame oil or vegetable oil

❶ **Filling:**
Heat pan and 4T. oil; saute chopped shallots until golden brown; add pork pieces and briefly stir-fry; add ① and heat mixture until boiling; reduce heat to low and cook 40 minutes covered. Add shredded pickled mustard green and cook an additional 10 minutes.

❷ **Skin:**
1. Prepare dough according to "Basic Yeast Dough" recipe; roll to a long roll and cut into 24 pieces. Flatten each piece of dough to a 2-inch circle and spread surface lightly with sesame oil (Fig. 1); fold circle to half (Fig. 2).Using tips of fingers lightly press half circle so that it is 2¾ inches in diameter and the edges are thinner than middle.
2. Place each finished roll on a damp cloth in steamer ½-inch apart. On the square end of each chopstick, make two diagonal cuts about 2-inches long from tip and stick two small bamboo pieces in (Fig. 3); dip end in red food coloring and make a stamp on the surface of each roll (Fig. 4). Steam rolls 5 minutes over high heat; remove.

❸ **Procedure:**
Using fingers, open roll on round side; place crushed peanuts, filling and coriander inside; eat immediately.
You may add as much peanuts, filling and coriander as desired.

參照發麵一、二、三 ①{ 肥肉(剁爛)…………3兩(¾杯) } 蒸1分鐘
　　　　　　　　　　 { 糖…………………3兩(¾杯) }

❶參照發麵一、二、三，將麵發好備用。

❷將發好的麵糰取出來，揉成十分光滑太硬或太軟時酌量加水或麵粉，均分成二等份。

❸把麵糰趕成２大薄片，將蒸好的①料均勻的各塗抹在面上，每７公分連續折起就成爲每層麵皮中間有糖
　漿，可做２條，每條切絲，分成１２堆(圖１)，每堆兩端拉長(圖２)盤捲(圖３)成渦形(圖４)。（可做
　２４個）。

❹攤置半小時再上籠蒸約１２分鐘即可。

■絞肥肉需要攪二次或剁成泥狀。

螺絲捲 Steamed Snail Buns ("Lwo-Sz-Juan")　　材料：２４個 Makes 24 buns

1　recipe "Basic Yeast Dough"　　①{ 3　oz. (¾ C.) pork fat, dropped }
　　　　　　　　　　　　　　　　　　{ 3　oz. (¾ C.) sugar　　　　　　 } steam 1 minute before use

❶　Prepare dough according to "Basic Yeast Dough".
❷　Remove risen dough from bowl; knead on floured surface until smooth and elastic (about 5-7 minutes); divide dough into 2 portions.
❸　Using rolling pin, roll each section into large rectangles about 1/5 inch thick; spread surface thinly with ① ; roll up, jelly-roll style, into a roll 2½-inches across. Shred each roll and divide shreds into 12 equal groups (Fig. 1); take each shred group and lightly stretch until shreds are about 6-inches long (Fig. 2). Holding one end of shreds, wrap the other "May-pole" fashion around index and forefinger (Fig. 3); tuck end underneath to form snail shape (Makes 24) (Fig. 4). Place finished buns on squares of paper.
❹　Let rise 30 minutes until springy to the touch; place in a steamer 2-inches apart; steam 12 minutes. Serve hot.

參照發麵一、二、三　　　　　　猪油…………6大匙

❶ 參照發麵一、二、三，將麵發好備用。

❷ 將發好的麵櫃取出來，揉成十分光滑太硬或太軟時酌量加入水或麵粉，分成六等份麵塊。

❸ 每份麵塊再分成二等份（外皮及麵心）。

　外皮部份：趕成１５公分×１５公分之正方形薄片。

　麵心部份：趕成２０公分×１０公分之長方形薄片（圖１），將猪油均勻塗抹後，對折成１０公分×１０公分，再塗一層猪油並對折成爲１０公分×５公分之四層麵塊，然後切成約５公分×０.３公分之長條，（圖２）。

❹ 把麵心拉長放在外皮中間（圖３），包成枕頭狀（圖４），做好６個，擱置約半小時，再上籠蒸約１５分鐘，上桌時可切塊或油炸。

銀絲捲　Silver Thread Loaves ("Yin-Sz-Juan")　材料：6個 Makes 6

1 receipe "Basic Yeast Dough"　　　　　6 T. lard or margarine

❶ Prepare dough according to "Basic Yeast Dough".
❷ Remove risen dough from bowl and knead on a floured surface until smooth and elastic (about 5-7 minutes); divide dough into 6 portions.
❸ Divide each portion into 2 pieces ("A" and "B").
  (a) Using rolling pin, roll out each piece into a square 6" by 6".
  (b) Using rolling pin, roll out each piece into a rectangle 4" by 8" (Fig. 1). Spread surface lightly with melted lard, margarine or sesame oil; fold in half (surface area is now 4" by 4" and oil-less); spread surface again lightly with oil; fold again in half (surface area is now 2" by 4"); shred this rectangle (Fig. 2).
❹ Gather "B" shreds together and stretch slightly so that the ends extend to about ½-inch from the edges of "A" square (Fig. 3). Wrap edges of "A" around "B" shreds and place these 6 dough "packages" on paper with wrapped edges down (Fig. 4). Let rise 30 minutes until springy to the touch. Place each "package" in a steamer 2 inches apart; steam 15 minutes Before serving, cut into thick slices.
■ "Golden Thread" Loaves: Follow recipe for "Silver Thread" Loaves. After steaming, deep-fry in hot oil until golden brown (about 2 minutes); remove, drain, slice and serve.

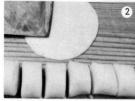

餡：蝦仁 …………… 半斤
　　熟肥肉 ………… 2 兩
　　熟筍 …………… 3 兩

① 鹽 ……………… ¾ 小匙
　 味精 …………… 半小匙
　 糖 ……………… 半小匙
　 胡椒 …………… ¼ 小匙
　 麻油 …………… ¼ 小匙
　 蛋白 …………… 半個
　 太白粉 ………… 1 大匙

皮：
② 澄麵 …………… 1 杯
　 滾水 …………… 1 杯
　 豬油 …………… 1 大匙

❶餡：① 蝦仁切粗粒（大切二，小勿切），入①料攪勻。
　　　② 肥肉、筍各切小片（筍需擠乾水份），加入蝦內拌勻，即成餡，冰涼備用。

❷皮：將②料攪勻（圖1）加豬油 1 大匙，揉勻成麵糰，切成粒狀，刀需抹油壓成圓薄片（圖2），包上餡做
　　　成餃子狀（圖3、4），入蒸鍋大火蒸約4分鐘。

蝦餃 Steamed Shrimp Dumplings

材料：３６個 Makes 36

Filling:
⅔ lb. raw, shelled shrimp
2 oz. pork fat
½ precooked bamboo shoot (3 oz.)

① ¾ t. salt, ¼ t. sesame oil
　 ½ t. MSG, ½ egg white
　 ½ t. sugar, 1 T. cornstarch
　 ¼ t. black pepper

② 1 C. non-glutinous flour ("cheng mien")[1]
　 1 C. boiling water
　 1 T. lard or vegetable shortening

❶ Filling: ① Cut each shrimp into 2 pieces, mix with ① and let soak 20 minutes.
　　② Chop pork fat and bamboo shoot very finely, add shrimp and mix together until all ingredients are thoroughly combined; place in refrigerator to solidify.

❷ Skin: Mix ingredients of ② together (Fig. 1); add 1T. lard and knead into a smooth dough

❸ Procedure:
Roll dough into a long roll and divide into 36 pieces; lightly rub cleaver with an oil-soaked cloth. Place a dough ball on table, cut side down, and place cleaver, flat edge of blade down, on top of ball. Using the pressure of your hand turn the cleaver in a clock-wise direction so that the cleaver blade will flatten and force the dough into a paper thin circle about 2 inches in diameter (Fig. 2); repeat for other pieces. In the center of each circle, place 1 portion (1/36) filling and fold into illustrated shape[2] (Fig. 3, 4). Place filled dumpling in steamer and steam over high for 4 minutes. Remove and serve.

[1] "Cheng mien" is a type of sticky, non-glutinous flour, which may be purchased at a Chinese grocery store.
[2] See P. 17 step ❸ for folding instructions.

10

餡：蝦仁…………6兩　｜鹽………1½小匙　　　皮：餛飩皮……32張
　　里肌肉………6兩　　味精………1小匙
①　肥肉…………2兩　②　糖…………3小匙
　　魚翅…………3兩　　胡椒………¼小匙
　　香菜…………半杯　　麻油………1小匙
　　　　　　　　　　　　太白粉……2小匙

❶ 餡　：將①料各切小丁調上②料用力攪勻至有黏性，即成餡。
❷ 皮　：餛飩皮修成圓形。
❸ 做法：將皮包餡（圖1、2、3），水開以大火蒸約6分鐘，即可供食。
■ 市面賣的魚翅餃，所用餛飩皮呈黃色，是加入雞蛋做成的。

魚翅餃 Shark's Fin Dumplings

材料：32個 **Makes 32**

Filling:
① ½ lb. raw, shelled shrimp
½ lb. pork loin 、 ¼ lb. pre-softened shark's fin*
2 oz. pork fat 、 ½ C. coriander

② 1½ t. salt 、 ¼ t. black pepper
1 t. MSG 、 1 t. sesame oil
3 t. sugar 、 2 t. cornstarch

Skin:
32 won ton skins

❶ Filling:
Dice ingredients in ① ; add ② and mix thoroughly to combine ingredients.

❷ Skin:
Trim won ton skins to circles.

❸ Procedure:
Place a portion of filling in the middle of each won ton skin; fold over to half and using index finger and thumb, bring 2 opposite edges together, while gathering outside edge of skin in little pleats (inside edge is still smooth, but will conform to decreased length of pleated edge); pinch edges to seal (Fig. 1, 2, 3, 4). Repeat for each skin. Place finished pastries in steamer and steam over high heat for 6 minutes; remove and serve.

* To soften dried shark's fin, place in water to cover and heat until just boiling; turn off fire and let soak until water is cool. Scrub surface of shark's fin lightly to remove any filmy covering. Let soak overnight. Repeat procedure 3-4 times changing water each time, until shark's fin is very soft; use as directed.

■ In the above picture, white and yellow won ton skins are shown. To prepare yellow skins, add an egg to won ton dough.

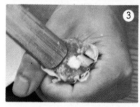

餡：里肌肉‥‥‥‥１０兩　　鹽‥‥‥‥１小匙　、　麻油‥‥‥‥半小匙　　皮：餛飩皮‥‥‥３０張

　　肥肉‥‥‥‥１兩　①　味精‥‥‥半小匙　、　酒‥‥‥‥‥半小匙　　　　紅蘿蔔‥‥‥‥半條

　　冬菇‥‥‥‥４朵　　　糖‥‥‥‥半小匙　、　蛋白‥‥‥‥１個　　　　香菜葉‥‥‥３０片

　　熟筍‥‥‥‥１枝　　　胡椒‥‥¼小匙　、　太白粉‥‥１½大匙

❶ 餡　：里肌肉、肥肉、冬菇均切小丁，筍切小片，加①料順同一方向用力攪勻，並甩打約３～４分鐘成餡

　　　　。

❷ 做法：① 餛飩皮修成圓形（圖１），將餡置當中（圖２）將手合捏，竹匙沾水在餡上抹平（圖３）全部做好（圖４），

　　　　入鍋大火蒸約５分鐘，盛盤。

　　　　② 紅蘿蔔削皮，刨成細末，與香菜葉同擺在燒賣上即可供食。

■ 可將里肌肉取部份改換蝦仁，每只蝦仁切成２或３之粒狀，使用。

燒賣 "Shau Mai"　　　　　　　　　　　　　材料：３０個 **Makes 30**

Filling:

10 oz. pork loin

1　oz. pork fat

4　pre-softened Chinese black mushrooms

1　precooked bamboo shoot

　　　⎧ 1　egg white

　　　⎪ 1　t.　salt

　　　⎪ ½　t.　MSG

　　　⎪ ½　t.　sugar

① ⎨ ¼　t.　black pepper

　　　⎪ ½　t.　sesame oil

　　　⎪ ½　t.　rice wine

　　　⎩ 1½ T.　cornstarch

Skin:

30 won ton skin

½　medium sized carrot

½　C. coriander

❶ Filling:

Dice pork loin, pork fat, pre-softened black mushrooms and bamboo shoot; add ① to diced ingredients and mix well. Throw mixture against inside of bowl for 3-4 minutes so that ingredients are thoroughly combined; separate to 30 portions.

❷ Procedure:

1 Trim won ton skins to round circles (Fig. 1); place 1 portion filling (1/30) in center of won ton skin (Fig. 2). Taking skin between index finger and thumb, gather edges together to make a waist; use a spoon dipped in water to press down filling so that it is compact and has a smooth top (Fig. 3), finish remaining shau mai in this fashion (Fig. 4); place each finished shau mai in a steamer about ½-inch apart. Steam 5 minutes over high heat; remove.

2 Shred carrot; take a leaf of coriander and place on each steamed "shau mai", also sprinkle shredded carrot and serve.

■ To make shrimp "shau mai", substitute shrimp for pork loin and cut each shrimp into 2-3 pieces.

餡：里肌肉‥‥‥‥‥‥４兩　　　鹽‥‥‥‥半小匙 、 麻油‥‥‥‥半小匙　　皮：餛飩皮‥‥‥３０張
　　蝦仁‥‥‥‥‥‥‥２兩　①味精‥‥‥¼小匙 、 酒‥‥‥‥‥半小匙
　　肥肉‥‥‥‥‥‥‥半兩　　　糖‥‥‥‥¼小匙 、 蛋白‥‥‥‥半個
　　熟筍‥‥‥‥‥‥‥半枝　　　胡椒‥‥‥¼小匙 、 太白粉‥‥２小匙
　　　　　　　　　　　　　　　鶉蛋‥‥‥‥‥‥‥‥‥‥‥‥３０個

❶ 餡　：里肌肉、蝦仁、肥肉均切小丁，熟筍切小片加①料順同一方向用力拌合，並甩打約３～４分鐘成
　　　　餡分成３０份，鶉蛋煮熟去殼備用。
❷做法：１ 餛飩皮修成圓形，每張餛飩皮放一個鶉蛋（圖１），上置１份肉餡（圖２）將手合捏，竹匙沾水在
　　　　　餡上抹平（圖３）翻過來（圖４）全部可做３０個。
　　　　２ 水開入鍋大火蒸約５分鐘即成。

鶉蛋燒賣 Quail Eggs Shau Mai　　　　　材料：３０個 Makes 30

Filling:
⅓ lb. pork loin
⅛ lb. raw, shelled shrimp
½ oz. pork fat
½ precooked bamboo shoot

① ½ t. salt 、 ½ t. sesame oil
　¼ t. MSG 、 ½ t. rice wine
　¼ t. sugar 、 ½ egg white
　¼ t. black pepper 、 2 t. cornstarch
30 quail eggs

Skin:
30 won ton skin

❶ Filling:
Dice pork loin, shrimp, pork fat and bamboo shoot; add ① and mix well. Throw mixture against inside of bowl for 3-4 minutes so that ingredients are thoroughly combined. Separate mixture into 30 equal portions; cook quail eggs in boiling water until hard-boiled (about 5 minutes); remove, drain and remove shell.

❷ Procedure:
1 Trim won ton skins to round circles; place a quail egg in center of won ton skin (Fig. 1), then add 1 portion filling on top (Fig. 2). Taking won ton skin between index finger and thumb, gather edges together to make a waist; use a spoon dipped
2 in water to press down filling so that it is compact and smooth (Fig. 3); place open side down (Fig. 4) in a steamer 1½ inches apart. Steam 5 minutes over high heat; remove and serve.

餡：	蝦仁‥‥‥‥１０兩		酒‥‥‥‥‥半小匙	皮：	麵粉‥‥‥‥２½杯		炸扁魚干‥‥少許
	肥肉‥‥‥‥‥１兩		鹽‥‥‥‥‥‥１小匙		滾水‥‥‥‥‥半杯		葱‥‥‥‥‥‥少許
①	熟筍‥‥‥‥‥１枝	②	味精‥‥‥‥‥半小匙	③	冷水‥‥‥‥‥¼杯	④	紅蘿蔔‥‥‥少許
	葱末‥‥‥‥‥１大匙		糖‥‥‥‥‥‥２小匙		豬油‥‥‥‥‥１大匙		蛋皮‥‥‥‥‥少許
	薑末‥‥‥‥‥１大匙		胡椒‥‥‥‥‥¼小匙				
			麻油‥‥‥‥‥¼小匙				
			太白粉‥‥‥‥１大匙				

❶ 餡 ：將①料中蝦仁切粗丁粒，肥肉切碎，筍切小片(擠乾水份)與葱薑末加入②料攪勻成餡。

❷ 皮 ：麵粉２杯(留半杯黏手時用)將③料內滾水沖入攪拌，再入冷水及豬油拌勻，揉成麵糰分成３０個
　　　　小麵塊，用麵桿趕成直徑６公分薄圓片。

❸ 做法：皮包上餡(圖１、２、３)，在四邊角上以④料(切細)裝飾(圖４)入鍋大火蒸約５分鐘即成。

四方餃 "Four-Flavor" Dumplings — 材料：３０個 Makes 30

Filling:

① {
¾ lb. raw, shelled shrimp
1 oz. pork fat
1 precooked bamboo shoot
1 T. chopped green onion
1 T. chopped ginger root
}

② {
½ t. rice wine, 1 t. salt
½ t. MSG, 2 t. sugar
¼ t. black pepper,
¼ t. sesame oil
1 T. cornstarch
}

Skin: 2½ C. flour

③ {
½ C. boiling water
¼ C. cold water
1 T. lard
}

④ {
2 T. chopped, sauteed dried brill fish *[1]
2 T. chopped green onion
2 T. chopped carrot
2 T. chopped egg sheets (see p. 119)
}

❶ Filling:
Rinse and devein shrimp; cut each into 3 sections; dice pork fat and bamboo shoot; add chopped onion and ginger and mix with ② . Throw mixture against inside of the bowl for 3-4 minutes so that ingredients are thoroughly combined.

❷ Skin:
Save ½C. flour to dust on hands when kneading. Add boiling water to flour (2C.) and mix; add cold water and lard and knead into a smooth dough; roll into a long roll and cut into 30 sections. Using a rolling pin; roll each section into a thin 2-inch circle; repeat 30 times for other pieces.

❸ Procedure:
Place 1 portion (1/30) of filling in center of each circle: gather opposite edges together and pinch together at midpoint; repeat procedure for opposite unfolded side (Fig. 1, 2, 3). Sprinkle ingredients of ④ one in each hole (Fig. 4); place in steamer ½-inch apart; steam 5 minutes over high heat. Serve.

*[1] See P. 142 for instructions for brill fish.

14

餡：┌ 絞肉……半斤 、扁魚乾…半兩
　①│ 荸薺……6個 、紅葱頭…5粒
　　│ 紅蘿蔔…½條 、葱末…1大匙
　　└ 蝦仁……2兩 、薑末…1大匙

　②┌ 酒……半小匙 、胡椒…¼小匙
　　│ 鹽……1小匙 、麻油…¼小匙
　　│ 味精…半小匙 、太白粉…1大匙
　　└ 糖……2小匙

皮：┌ 麵粉…2½杯
　③│ 滾水……半杯
　　│ 冷水……¼杯
　　└ 猪油…1大匙

❶ 餡　：將①料中荸薺、紅蘿蔔剁碎，擠出水份，蝦仁剁碎扁魚乾炸呈金黃色，撈出壓碎，紅葱頭切薄片
　　　炸至金黃，然後調入②料攪勻即成餡。

❷ 皮　：麵粉2杯(留半杯黏手時用)將③料內滾水冲入攪拌，再入冷水及猪油揉成麵欓，分成30個小麵
　　　塊，用麵桿趕成直徑6公分圓薄片。

❸ 做法：皮包上餡，做成鳳眼形狀(圖1、2、3、4)蒸約5分鐘即成。

鳳眼餃 "Phoenix-Eye" Dumplings

材料：30個 **Makes 30**

Filling:
- ⅔ lb. chopped pork
- 6 water chestnuts (4 oz.)
- ⅓ medium-sized carrot
- ① 2 oz. raw, shelled shrimp
- ½ oz. dried brill fish ("bien yu gan")
- 5 shallots
- 1 T. chopped green onion
- 1 T. chopped ginger root

②
- ½ t. rice wine
- 1 t. salt
- ½ t. MSG
- 2 t. sugar
- ¼ t. black pepper
- ¼ t. sesame oil
- 1 T. cornstarch.

Skin:
- 2½ C. flour
- ③ ½ C. boiling water
- ¼ C. cold water
- 1 T. lard

❶ Filling:
Chop water chestnuts and carrot until fine; drain; chop shrimp. Heat pan and 1C. oil until medium hot; deep-fry brill fish over low heat until golden brown; remove, drain and chop until fine. Reheat oil and stir-fry shallots until golden brown; mix ① and ②. Throw mixture against inside of bowl for 3-4 minutes to combine thoroughly.

❷ Skin:
Save ½C. flour to dust on hands when kneading. Add boiling water to flour (2C.) and mix; add cold water and lard and knead into a smooth dough; roll into a long roll and cut into 30 sections. Using a rolling pin; roll each section into a thin 2-inch circle; repeat 30 times for other pieces.

❸ Procedure:
Place 1 portion (1/30) of filling in middle of skin; gather opposite edges together and pinch at midpoint to join. Gather outside edges and press together to form crescent-shape (Fig. 1, 2, 3, 4). Place filled dumplings in a steamer and steam 5 minutes over high heat. Serve.
The desired shape is similar to that of an eye; specifically a phoenix's eye, hence the name "Phoenix-Eye" dumplings.

餡：絞肉⋯⋯⋯⋯9兩　　① 鹽⋯⋯⋯⋯1小匙　　皮：② 麵粉⋯⋯⋯⋯2½杯
　　韭黃（切碎）⋯⋯3兩　　　味精⋯⋯⋯⋯半小匙　　　　滾水⋯⋯⋯⋯⅔杯
　　筍（切小片）⋯⋯3兩　　　麻油⋯⋯⋯⋯3大匙　　　　冷水⋯⋯⋯⋯⅓杯
　　　　　　　　　　　　　胡椒⋯⋯⋯⋯¼小匙　　　麵粉（備黏手時用）⋯半杯

❶ 餡　：將絞肉再剁碎，拌入①料攪勻，加入切好之韭黃與筍拌勻即為餡。

❷ 皮　：麵粉盛入盆內，用滾水沖燙，再加冷水，揉成麵櫃，擱置約１０分鐘，搓成長條，再分成３６個，用趕麵棍趕壓成約１０公分×５公分橢圓薄片之麵皮。

❸ 做法：1　將餡放入麵皮中間（圖１），先對摺（圖２），再把兩邊捏緊（圖３），使成長形餃子狀（圖４）。
　　　　2　油燒熱，餃子順序排列在鍋底，以小火煎約１分鐘，淋入熱水約半杯，並將鍋蓋蓋緊，燜煮約４分鐘，等水乾後，再淋入熱油１大匙，使餃子的底面煎呈金黃色餡熟即可鏟出。

蒸餃：參照鍋貼之材料與做法，做成餃子狀（５０個）取潔淨之白布１塊，用水濕透後鋪在蒸籠內，把包好之餃子排於白布上面，連籠放入滾水鍋上，以大火蒸約８分鐘，食時沾醬油、醋、薑與麻油（均適量）。

鍋貼 Golden Fried Meat Dumplings　材料：３６個 Makes 36

Filling:
⅔ lb. chopped pork
¼ lb. chopped Chinese chives*
1 C. chopped bamboo shoot

① 1 t. salt
½ t. MSG
3 T. sesame oil
¼ t. black pepper

Skin:
② 2½ C. flour
⅔ C. boiling water
⅔ C. cold water
½ C. flour(to prevent sticking during kneading)

❶ Filling: Chop pork; add ① and mix well; add chopped Chinese chives and bamboo shoot. Stir ingredients until mixed well and separate into 36 portions.

❷ Skin:
Place flour in bowl; add boiling water and cold water; knead into a smooth dough; let rest 10 minutes; roll out into a long roll and cut into 36 sections. Using a rolling pin, roll sections to ovals 4-inches by 2-inches.

❸ Procedure:
1　In the middle of each skin, place 1 portion filling (Fig. 1); fold in half (Fig. 2) and pinch edges to seal (Fig. 3, 4)
2　Heat pan and 4T. oil; line pan with dumplings, flat side down. Turn heat to low and fry 1 minute until golden brown; add ½C. hot water and cover. Cook 4 minutes until almost all water has evaporated; add 1T. oil and invert dumplings, fried side up onto serving plate. Serve with soy sauce, sesame oil and worcestershire sauce, for dipping. (For a variation, add chopped garlic to soy sauce).
*　If unavailable, substitute green onions.

Steamed Dumplings ("Jeng Jaudz") Follow the materials and Procedures of "Golden Fried meat Dumplings" to make 50 dumplings; Moisten a cotton cloth and use to line steamer; place dumpling in steamer and steam 8 minutes over high heat; remove and serve with soy sauce, seasame oil and worcestershire sauce.

餡：┌包心菜⋯⋯⋯⋯６兩　　　　絞肉⋯⋯⋯⋯⋯⋯⋯⋯⋯６兩　　皮：②┌麵粉⋯⋯⋯⋯⋯⋯⋯⋯３杯
　　鹽⋯⋯⋯⋯⋯半小匙　　　┌鹽⋯⋯¾小匙、胡椒⋯¼小匙　　　　└冷水⋯⋯⋯⋯⋯⋯⋯¾杯
　　韮菜⋯⋯⋯⋯⋯２兩　　①│味精⋯半小匙、薑末⋯１大匙　　　　麵粉（備黏手時用）⋯半杯
　　　　　　　　　　　　　　└麻油⋯３大匙

餡　：包心菜剁碎，加鹽半小匙拌醃，約１０分鐘後，擠出水，韮菜切碎，絞肉再剁一剁，一起調入①
　　　料攪拌均勻，即爲餡。

皮　：麵粉盛入盆內，加冷水拌合，再揉成麵糰，軟硬要適中，取出放在板上，揉至十分光滑，然後擱
　　　置約１０分鐘，搓成長條，切成５０個小塊，分別趕成圓薄片，即餃子皮。

做法：１餡放置皮中間，將麵皮合捏，將一邊麵皮推出一摺（圖１）捏緊（圖２）如此反覆將一邊捏完，另
　　　端捏緊（圖３）再邊推邊捏（圖４）至全部捏合即成餃子。

　　　２半鍋水燒開，放入餃子，用湯杓順着鍋邊推動，以免粘住，蓋上鍋蓋，以大火煮至燒沸，加入
　　　冷水半杯，再煮開，依法續加二次，即可撈出置盤，吃時可沾醋、醬油及麻油（均適量）。

水餃 Boiled Meat Dumplings ("Shwei Jaudz")　　　　材料：５０個 Makes 50

Filling:
½ lb. cabbage
½ t. salt
2 oz. Chinese chives

① ½ lb. chopped pork
¾ t. salt
½ t. MSG
3 T. sesame oil
¼ t. black pepper
1 T. chopped ginger root

Skin:
② 3 C. flour
¾ C. cold water
½ C. flour (to prevent sticking during kneading)

● Filling:
Chop cabbage until fine; add ½ t. salt; mix together and let sit 10 minutes; drain water and chop Chinese chives and chopped pork; mix all ingredients with ① .

● Skin:
Place flour in bowl; add water and knead into a smooth dough; let rest 10 minutes; roll into a long roll and cut into 50 pieces. Using a rolling pin, roll each piece into a thin 2-inch circle.

● Procedure
In the center of each dough wrapper, place 1 portion (1/50) filling; fold in half and moisten edges with water. Using index finger and thumb, bring 2 opposite edges together, gathering outside edge in little pleats (Fig. 1) (inside edge is still smooth, but will bend to conform to decreased length of pleated edge; pinch pleats together (Fig. 2); pinch edge to seal (Fig. 3,4). Repeat procedure for other dumplings.
Boil 10C. water; add 1/3 of dumplings and stir so that dumplings don't stick together; cover and let water boil again; add ½C. cold water and cover. When water boils again, add another ½C. water; let boil, remove and drain. Repeat for other dumplings and serve with soy sauce, sesame oil and worcestershire sauce.
This is the traditional method of cooking "jaudz". An easier method is to cook dumplings in boiling water to cover for 4 minutes, covered; over low heat, remove, drain and serve.

餡：味全瓜仔肉……1½罐　　皮：麵粉…………2½杯
　　（冰凍）　　　　　　　　　滾水…………¾杯
　　　　　　　　　　　　　　　冷水…………¼杯

❶ 皮 ：將麵粉用滾水沖燙，並用筷子攪拌，再加入冷水，揉合成軟硬適度之麵糰。

❷做法：①將麵糰揉成長條狀，分成２０個，用手按一下，再趕成圓薄片（圖１），包入瓜仔肉餡（圖２），
　　　　　並在摺口處捏緊（圖３），再用手輕按一下（圖４），全部做好備煎。

　　　　②油６大匙燒熱，放入餡餅，煎約４分鐘，至兩面均呈金黃色時取出，趁熱供食。

■肉餡亦可用絞肉６兩摻和鹽½小匙、麻油１大匙、葱末２大匙、味精少許代用之。

餡 餅 Chinese Meat Pies

材料：２０個 **Makes 20**

Filling:
1½ cans Wei-Chuan pickled cucumbers and meat*

Skin:
2½ C. flour
¾ C. boiling water
¼ C. cold water

❶ Skin:
Add boiling water to flour; mix and add cold water; knead into a smooth dough.

❷ Procedure:
① Roll dough into a long roll and cut into 20 pieces; flatten each piece with palm of hand into a 3-inch circle (Fig. 1). Place 1 portion (1/20) of filling in center (Fig. 2); gather edges of dough circle together and pinch to seal (Fig. 3); roll into a ball and flatten (Fig. 4). Repeat for other pieces.

② Heat pan and 6T. oil; place pies in oil and fry for 2 minutes on each side until golden brown; remove, drain and serve.

* If unavailable, substitute 6 oz. chopped pork; add ¾ t. salt, 1T. sesame oil, 2T. chopped green onion and a dash of MSG; mix thoroughly and use as directed in recipe, but increase frying time to 3 minutes on each side.

麵粉…………2½杯　　　　冷水…………¼杯
滾水…………¾杯　　　　麻油…………1大匙

❶ 麵粉沖入滾水，用筷子攪勻再加冷水拌勻，揉合成麵糰，放置２０分鐘謂之「醒麵」。
❷ 將麵糰置板上，揉至十分光滑，分成２０小塊，每塊用手掌心壓扁，每二塊疊在一起，中間塗抹油（圖１），再趕成圓薄餅（圖２）。
❸ 鍋燒熱，將麵餅置鍋（不需擦油），以慢火烙烤約２０秒，翻面再烙２０秒後取出（圖３），揭開成兩張荷葉餅（圖４）。
■ 烙餅時只要把餅烙熟即可，烙好荷葉餅一張張疊於盤內，並用白布蓋住，以免冷後轉硬。

荷葉餅 "Lotus Pad" (Mandarin) Pancakes　　　材料：２０張　Makes 20

2½ C. flour　　　　　¼ C. cold water
¾ C. boiling water　　1 T. sesame oil

❶ Place flour in a bowl and add boiling water; mix until smooth and add cold water; mix again until smooth; set for 20 minutes. Further knead on a lightly oiled surface until smooth and elastic; roll into a long roll and cut into 20 pieces.

❷ Flatten each piece with palm of hand into a 4-inch pancake; spread surface of a pancake lightly with sesame oil; place another pancake on top of oiled one (Fig. 1); press together and roll again to a 6-inch paper-thin pancake (Fig. 2). Repeat for other pieces.

❸ Heat pan until medium hot; fry pancake over low heat about 20 seconds until small, golden bubbles appear on fried side (while frying, constantly twirl pancakes in a clockwise direction, using tips of fingers, to fry evenly); invert and repeat procedure (Fig. 3); remove and separate pancakes (Fig. 4); fold into fourths and arrange on serving plate. Cover with a damp cloth to keep warm and moist*.

◀ These pancakes may be served with "Moo Shi Rou" ("stir-fried pork and eggs") or with Peking Duckling, green onions, and hoisin sauce.

* To reheat pancakes, steam 15 seconds and cover with a warm cloth to keep moist.

19

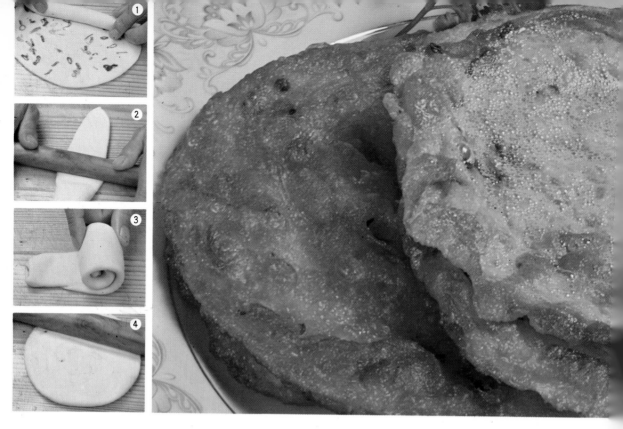

麵粉…………… 1 杯
滾水………… ⅓ 杯

① ┌ 葱末…………… 1 大匙
　 │ 豬油或沙拉油…半大匙
　 └ 鹽……………… 半小匙

❶ 麵粉盛入盆內，徐徐冲下開水，並用筷子攪拌，使麵粉浸得均勻，即用手揉合並加少許冷水，揉成軟度
　 適中之麵櫥擱置１５分鐘。

❷ 將麵櫥分成６塊，每塊用手掌壓扁，再用趕麵桿趕壓成圓薄片，塗上①料由邊捲成圓筒狀（圖１），再略
　 趕扁（圖２），由邊捲成螺絲狀（圖３），平放趕成直徑１０公分圓薄片（圖４）。

❸ 油４大匙燒熱，將做好麵餅，煎至兩面呈金黃色取出，也可放入蛋一起煎。

葱 油 餅　Chinese Onion Crepes

材料：６ 片 **6 crepes**

1　C.　flour
⅓　C.　boiling water

① ┌ 1　T.　chopped green onion
　 │ ½　T.　lard or shortening
　 └ ½　t.　salt

❶ Place flour in a mixing bowl; add boiling water and mix well (add a little cold water if dough is too dry); knead into a smooth
　 dough and let sit 15 minutes.

❷ Roll dough into a long roll and cut into 6 pieces; using a rolling pin, roll each section into a 4-inch circle; brush surface lightly
　 with ① and roll up jelly roll-style (Fig. 1) and flatten(Fig. 2); fold over into a square(Fig. 3). Lightly flatten and turn over or
　 side so that snail shape is formed; flatten to a 4-inch circle (Fig. 4); repeat procedure for each dough piece.

❸ Heat pan and 4T. oil; fry on both sides until golden brown; remove and serve.

■ "Onion Crêpes" may be eaten as a snack or served with hot "Do Jiang" for breasfast.

① 麵粉⋯⋯⋯⋯⋯4杯　②麵粉⋯⋯⋯⋯⋯1杯
　滾水⋯⋯⋯⋯⋯1杯　　沙拉油⋯⋯⋯⋯¼杯
　蛋⋯⋯⋯⋯⋯2個

❶「水油皮」：將麵粉備好在盆內，冲入滾水攪拌待冷，雞蛋打好，放入揉成軟硬適度之麵糰分切為2。

❷「油心」：將②料拌合成麵糰，分切為2。

❸「水油皮」包「油心」包好(圖1)，用手壓一下趕成圓薄片，由邊捲成長筒狀(圖2)，並由兩端盤捲成渦形(圖3)，再用手壓扁趕成20公分之圓薄片(圖4)如此可做成二大薄片。

❹平底鍋或煎鍋略燒熱，餅置上，注意火候，不要烙焦，蓋鍋用小火二面烙熟(約三分鐘)對切六片盛盤。

■此種家常餅可代米飯，燒煮幾道菜一起配食之。

家常餅 Family Cake

材料：2 片 **Makes 2**

① { 4 C. flour
　　1 C. boiling water 　② { 1 C. flour
　　　　　　　　　　　　　　¼ C. salad oil

　　2 eggs

❶ Skin:

1. Place flour in a mixing bowl; add boiling water and mix well. Let cool slightly and add eggs one at a time; mix to a smooth dough and cut into half. (A).

2. Mix ingredients of ② and cut into half. (B).

❷ Procedure:

1. Place each piece of (B) dough in center of (A) dough; gather edges to enclose (B) dough and pinch to seal (Fig. 1). Flatten each piece to a circle 1/6-inch thick; beginning from furthest edge, roll up circle (Fig. 2); flatten lightly and fold piece sideways into a roll (Fig. 3). Flatten again and roll each piece to a 7-inch circle (Fig. 4).

2. Heat pan and lay one cake flat in pan (no oil); cover and cook for 1½ minutes over low heat; flip cake over and cook another 1½ minutes; remove and cut into 6 slices. Repeat procedure for other cake.

■ Serve with stir-fried meats and vegetables.

① ⎰ 雞蛋‥‥‥‥5個
　⎱ 黃砂糖‥ 1 ½ 杯

② ⎰ 奶水(小1罐)‥‥¾杯
　｜ 香草片(壓碎)‥‥1粒
　｜ 碱粉‥‥‥‥‥1小匙
　⎱ 猪油(溶化)‥‥‥½杯

③ ⎰ 麵粉‥‥‥‥‥‥‥‥‥2杯
　⎱ 發粉‥‥‥‥‥‥‥‥‥1大匙
　　玻璃紙直徑３５公分
　　(或牛皮紙、白報紙預先抹油)

❶先將①料盛於乾淨容器內，打到起泡至糖完全溶化約５分鐘(圖１)再加入②料續打１分鐘(圖２)，成蛋液。

❷③料過篩放入打好的蛋液內，攪拌均勻，即為麵糊。

❸將紙舖於蒸籠內、倒入麵糊(圖３)水開大火蒸３０分鐘即成(圖４)。

■蒸籠直徑２５公分，蒸時宜將蒸籠內留四邊縫以備透水蒸氣。

■如無碱粉可免用，但稍感覺粘膩。

馬拉糕 Steamed Sponge Cake ("Ma-La-Gau")

材料：1 籠 **Make 1**

① ⎰ 5　eggs
　⎱ 1½ C. brown sugar

② ⎰ ¾　C. evaporated milk
　｜ 1　t.　vanilla extract
　｜ 1　t.　baking soda
　⎱ ½　C. melted shortening

③ ⎰ 2　C. flour
　｜ 1　T. baking powder
　⎱ 1　　12-inch circle heavy-duty cellophane or brown paper

❶ Grease a 10-inch tube pan or line with greased cellophane or brown paper.
❷ Beat ① until thick and lemon colored (about 5 minutes) (Fig. 1); add ② (Fig. 2) and beat mixture 1 minute.
❸ Sift ingredients of ③ and fold into egg mixture.
❹ Pour batter into lined steamer (Fig. 3); place in steamer and steam 30 minutes over high heat (Fig. 4); remove and cut into slices; serve.

■ You may also use a bamboo steamer itself as a container instead of cake pan; line with oiled brown wrapping paper and follow recipe.

紅葱頭(切片)⋯⋯4大匙
「炸油」⋯⋯⋯⋯⋯1杯
瘦絞肉⋯⋯⋯⋯⋯4兩
①{ 醬油⋯⋯⋯⋯⋯1大匙
   味精⋯⋯⋯⋯⋯¼小匙

②{ 蛋(半斤)⋯⋯⋯⋯5個
   糖⋯⋯⋯⋯⋯⋯1½杯
   麵粉⋯⋯⋯⋯⋯1½杯

圓形玻璃紙
(直徑３５公分１張)

❶「炸油」燒熱，用慢火將紅葱頭炸至金黃色撈起，留油２大匙，將絞肉炒勻，隨加①料炒乾備用。

❷將②料用打蛋器，用力打至起白泡，２０分鐘(圖１、２、３)即可加入篩過麵粉，輕輕攪勻成麵糊（圖４）。

❸將玻璃紙剪成圓形，舖於蒸籠內，倒入一半麵糊抹平，以大火蒸約８分鐘取出，洒上一半的紅葱頭及肉末，並將另一半麵糊倒入抹平，剩下的紅葱頭及肉末洒在上面續蒸８分鐘即成。

■蒸籠直徑２５公分，蒸時宜將蒸籠內留四邊縫，以備透水蒸氣。

鹹蛋糕 "Salty Egg Cake"　　　　　　　　　　材料：1 籠 Make 1

4　T. shallots, minced
1　C. oil
⅓　lb. chopped pork (as lean as possible)
①{ 1　T. soy sauce
   ¼　t. MSG

②{ 5　eggs
   1½ C. sugar
   1½ C. sifted flour

1　12-inch circle heavy-duty cellophane

❶ Heat pan and oil until medium hot; saute shallots until golden brown and fragrant; remove and drain.　Remove all but 2T. oil from pan; reheat and stir-fry chopped pork until color changes; add ① and stir-fry together; remove. (the mixture is topping).

❷ Beat ② until fairly stiff (about 20 minutes by hand with wire whisk) (Fig. 1, 2, 3); fold in flour (A) (Fig. 4).

❸ Line a 12-inch circular pan with cellophane; pour ½ (A) mixture into pan and spread evenly over bottom of pan. Place pan in steamer and steam 8 minutes, remove and sprinkle ½ of topping on top. Portion rest of (A) evenly over steamed cake. Sprinkle rest of topping over top; return to steamer and steam 8 minutes. Cut into slices and serve.

餡：
① ┌ 椰茸⋯⋯⋯1½杯　　皮：參照發麵一、二、三　　豬油⋯⋯⋯⋯⋯⋯⋯⋯⋯2大匙
　　│ 細糖⋯⋯⋯⋯1杯　　　　　　　　　　　　　　紅綠木瓜絲⋯⋯⋯⋯⋯⋯2大匙
　　└ 奶油(溶化)⋯¼杯　　　　　　　　　　　　　　玻璃紙⋯⋯⋯30公分×30公分
　　　　　　　　　　　　　　　　　　　　　　　　　(或濕布)

❶ 將①料全部拌勻即為餡，分12等份。

❷ 參照發麵一、二、三，將麵發好備用。

❸ 將發好麵糰揉成十分光滑太硬或太軟時酌量加水或麵粉，分切2份趕成40公分×15公分，將1份餡
　平均洒在中央⅓麵塊處(圖1)，再將左邊⅓處覆蓋中間再洒上1份餡(圖2)最後將右邊⅓處覆上(圖3
　放橫再趕開，如此重複3次，最後趕成20公分四方塊，下面舖上玻璃紙，上洒紅綠木瓜絲(圖4)置3
　分鐘待其醒發，大火蒸30分鐘，至熟切塊即成。

椰茸千層糕 Coconut Layer Cake

材料：2籠 Makes 2

Filling
① ┌ 1½ C. flaked coconut
　│ 1　C. confectioners' sugar
　└ ¼ C. melted butter

Skin:
1　recipe "Basic Yeast Dough"

2　T. lard or margarine
2　T. candied red papaya shreds
1　10-inch square heavy-duty cellophane

❶ Mix ingredients of ① ; separate into 12 (filling).
❷ To prepare dough follow directions for "Basic Yeast Dough".
❸ Remove risen dough from bowl and knead until smooth and elastic; cut into half. Using a rolling pin, roll each ha
into a 6 x 14-inch rectangle; spread filling in the middle of rectangle (Fig. 1). Mentally divide rectangle into thirds ar
fold over left side and spread surface with filling (Fig. 2); fold over remaining side (Fig. 3) and turn strip to the horizonta
Roll out into a 6 x 14-inch rectangle; spread filling in middle and repeat folding and rolling process two more times
make a 7-inch layered square. Place square on a piece of cellophane and sprinkle top with papaya shreds (Fig. 4); l
rise 30 minutes and place in steamer; steam 30 minutes over high heat; remove and cut into slices; serve.

	雞蛋（大）⋯⋯⋯ 5 個		麵粉⋯⋯⋯⋯⋯⋯ 1 ½ 杯		果醬⋯⋯⋯⋯⋯⋯⋯ 1 杯
①	糖⋯⋯⋯⋯⋯⋯ ⅔ 杯	②	香料⋯⋯⋯⋯⋯⋯ 少許	玻璃紙⋯⋯⋯⋯⋯ 3 張
	奶水⋯⋯⋯⋯⋯ 3 大匙			（30公分×30公分）

● 先將①料在乾淨容器內，打至起泡，約２０分鐘（打到３～４倍高），再加入奶水打約２分鐘。

● 將麵粉篩過連同香料，放入打好的蛋液內，輕輕地拌合，即爲蛋麵糊。

● 每張玻璃紙上，倒入蛋麵糊，四面抹平（薄薄一層）（圖1），即以大火蒸５分鐘，待凉後，可在玻璃紙背面，刷上少許水（圖２），則玻璃紙能輕易撕起（圖３）。

● 蒸好的蛋糕，塗一層果醬（草莓、橘子任選）捲好並以原有玻璃紙包好固定形狀（圖4），２０分鐘後切塊。

如意龍鳳捲 Chinese Jelly Roll　　　　材料：３條 Makes 3

	5 large eggs		1½ C. flour	1 C. strawberry or raspberry jam
①	⅔ C. sugar	②	1 t. vanilla extract	3 sheets heavy-duty cellophane or wax paper
	3 T. evaporated milk			12-inches square

● Place ① in mixing bowl; beat until stiff (about 20 minutes by wire whisk); add evaporated milk and vanilla extract; beat 2 additional minutes.

● Sift flour; fold lightly into egg mixture.

● Place cellophane to line a 15-inch steamer; pour cake batter into steamer and spread into a thin cake (Fig. 1). Steam 5 minutes (cake should be springy and dry when done). Remove and let cool. Add a little water to cellophane surface to facilitate removal (Fig. 2); peel away cellophane (Fig. 3).

● Spread cooked cakes with jam; roll each cake half to middle; wrap rolled halves in cellophane and let rest 20 minutes (Fig. 4); unwrap and cut halves into slices; serve.

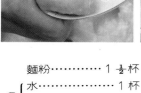

麵粉·········· 1½杯   細砂糖········ 4大匙

①{ 水·············· 1杯   「炸油」·········· 8杯

    鹽·············· 半小匙

    蛋（4個）········ 1杯

❶ 麵粉篩過二次，蛋打散。

❷ ①料煮開，放入篩過麵粉（圖1），待稍冷，將蛋液分次加入（圖2）至蛋和麵糰全部混勻（圖3）。

❸ 「炸油」略燒熱（小火）湯匙沾油把麵丸一個一個（圖4）放入油內俟全部放入後改中火，臨起鍋前改大火，前後炸１０分鐘；撈起，滾細砂糖即可食用。

■ 「炸油」最好用乾淨油，炸出來顏色才好看，依個人的喜愛，鑲上各種不同的果醬。

白糖沙翁 Jam Puffs   材料：１６個 Makes 16

1½ C. flour   4 T. granulated sugar

①{ 1 C. water   8 C. oil for frying

    ½ t. salt

    4 eggs

❶ Sift flour twice; lightly beat eggs.

❷ Heat ① until boiling; slowly add to flour (Fig. 1) and mix until smooth; let cool and add eggs one at a time (Fig. 2) beat lightly into a smooth paste (Fig. 3).

❸ Heat pan and oil until medium hot; dip spoon in oil; add egg balls one by one (Fig. 4). Deep-fry over medium heat unt balls have expanded; turn heat to high and cook until golden (combined frying time should be about 10 minutes); remove drain and dust with sugar. Serve with jam or jelly of choice.

①
糖	$\frac{2}{3}$杯
猪油	1 大匙
雞蛋	1 只
清水	3 大匙

②
麵粉	2 杯
發粉	1 小匙

白芝麻	半杯
「炸油」	8杯

❶ 將①料攪拌均勻，倒入篩過之②料（圖１）略為攪拌，輕揉成麵糰，分切成１６個（圖２），揉成球形，沾些水（圖３）再滾芝麻備炸（圖４）。

❷ 「炸油」燒熱，投入麵球，慢火炸至裂開後，改大火炸至金黃色撈出，待冷後香甜而酥。

開口笑 "Open Mouth Laughs"

材料：１６個 Makes 16

①
- ⅔ C. sugar
- 1 T. lard or margarine
- 1 egg
- 3 T. water

②
- 2 C. flour
- 1 t. baking powder

- ½ C. sesame seeds
- 8 C. oil for frying

❶ Mix ingredients of ① until thoroughly combined; sift ② and add to ① (Fig. 1). Knead to a soft dough and cut into 16 pieces (Fig. 2); roll each piece into a ball and dip in water (Fig. 3); roll in sesame seeds (Fig. 4).

❷ Heat pan and oil until medium hot; deep-fry balls over low heat until they expand and open; turn heat to hgih and deep-fry until golden brown; remove, drain and let cool. Serve.

①	麵粉‥‥‥‥‥‥‥‥2杯	黑芝麻‥‥‥‥‥‥‥$\frac{1}{4}$杯	「炸油」‥‥‥‥‥6杯
	細砂糖‥‥‥‥‥‥‥$\frac{1}{3}$杯	豆腐(壓碎)‥‥‥‥‥$\frac{1}{2}$杯	
	鹽‥‥‥‥‥‥‥‥‥$\frac{1}{8}$小匙	雞蛋1個(或奶水4大匙)	

❶將①料篩過後加入黑芝麻拌勻，再加豆腐及雞蛋，揉成十分光滑之麵糰，如太硬或太軟時，酌量加入水或麵粉揉成軟硬適中之麵糰，擱置半小時（俗稱醒麵）。

❷將麵糰趕成大薄片(越薄越脆)，再切成長5公分，寬2公分之長方形，中間切三條刀痕(圖1)每片再由一端向中間穿過拉直(圖2、3、4)。

❸「炸油」燒熱，將巧果用小火炸3分鐘，再改大火炸1分鐘，呈金黃色撈起待冷，香脆可口(分4次炸)。

■將巧果裝入玻璃罐內，蓋緊可保持數星期之久。

巧 果 Ch'iao Gwo

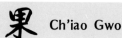

材料：１５０片 **150 strips**

①	2　C. flour	¼　C. black sesame seeds	6　C. oil for frying
	⅓　C. powdered sugar	½　C. bean curd (crushed)	
	⅛　t. salt	1　egg (or 4 T. milk).	

❶ Sift ① ; add sesame seeds and mix together; add bean curd and egg mixture; knead into a soft dough, if too dry or moist, add water or more flour. Knead until soft; let sit for 30 minutes.

❷ Roll dough into a thin sheet (the thinner it is, the more crisp); cut into rectangles 2"x1"; in the middle of each rectangle cut 3 slits (Fig. 1); pull one end of the rectangle through the middle (Fig. 2, 3, 4).

❸ Heat oil; deep-fry "ch'iao gwo" over low heat for 3 minutes; turn heat to high and continue to fry for 1 minute until golden brown; remove and let cool. When crisp it's ready to eat.

■ If Chiao Gwo are kept in a tightly sealed glass container, they will keep fresh for several weeks.

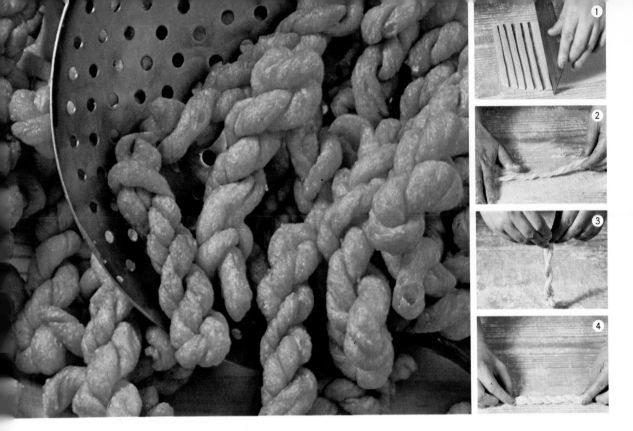

①
- 麵粉‥‥‥‥‥‥‥２杯
- 糖粉‥‥‥‥‥‥‥⅔杯
- 鹽‥‥‥‥‥‥‥‥¼小匙
- 小蘇打‥‥‥‥‥‥⅓小匙

- 雞蛋‥‥‥‥‥‥‥１個
- 水‥‥‥‥‥‥‥‥２大匙
- 「炸油」‥‥‥‥‥‥６杯

❶①料篩過二次後，隨加雞蛋、水揉成十分光滑之麵糰，如太硬或太軟時，酌量加入水或麵粉，揉成軟硬適中之麵糰，擱置半小時(俗稱醒麵)。

❷將麵糰趕成長方形狀(２４公分×１５公分×0.5公分)，麵皮分切２４條（圖１）。

❸每條麵條左手拉住一端，用右手輕壓另一端，向前搓滾(圖２)，將兩端捏合（圖３），再搓成麻花狀（圖４）。

❹「炸油」燒熱，中火將麻花炸４分鐘，呈金黃色撈起待冷，香脆可口。

■將麻花裝入玻璃罐內蓋緊，可保持數星期之久。

如意麻花 Round Pretzels   材料：２４條 24 strips

①
- 2 C. flour
- ⅔ C. powdered sugar
- ¼ t. salt
- ⅓ t. baking soda

- 1 egg
- 2 T. water
- 6 C. oil for frying

❶ Sift ingredients in ① twice; add egg, water and mix into a soft dough; if dough is too dry or too moist, add more water or flour; knead until dough is smooth; let sit 30 minutes.

❷ Roll dough into a paper-thin sheet (5″ x 8″ x ⅛″); cut sheet into 24 pieces (Fig. 1).

❸ Take each piece, using left hand lightly stretch piece while right hand keeps other end of dough firmly pressed on table; twist dough between fingers of left hand (Fig. 2); bring both ends of piece together (Fig. 3), and twist so that ends are connected into a circle (Fig. 4).

❹ Heat oil for deep-frying; deep-fry pretzels over medium heat for 4 minutes; when golden brown, remove; drain and cool; serve.

■ If kept in tightly sealed glass container, pretzels will keep fresh for several weeks.

①{ 麵粉（半斤）…３杯
　 發粉………１大匙
　 蛋…………４個

②{ 「炸油」………………６杯
　 糖……………………１杯
　 麥芽糖………………¾杯
　 水……………………¼杯
　 檸檬汁（或醋）……½大匙

③{ 炒熟白芝麻…半大匙 } 或花生粉１杯
　 葡萄乾………２大匙

❶蛋打散放入過篩之①料內拌合，並揉成軟硬適當之麵糰(黏手時洒上乾麵粉)放置２０分鐘，（俗稱醒麵）。

❷將麵糰切成二塊，逐塊趕成厚０.２公分之大方形薄片，再切成３公分寬之麵片，繼而切成絲（圖１）。

❸「炸油」燒熱，中火炸呈淡黃色撈出盛於鍋內。

❹將②料以中火燒開後改小火熬煮２分鐘至糖完全溶化時，即可淋澆在炸過之麵條上（圖２）迅速拌勻後，（圖３）倒入鋁盤內壓成厚４公分四方大塊（圖４），再洒上③料待冷切塊即成。

■麥芽糖可用蜂蜜取代，但份量需加倍，燒煮時間加長，用筷子沾糖汁放入水內成珠狀即可。

薩其馬 "Sa-Ji-Ma"

材料：１５塊 **Makes 15**

①{ 3 C. flour
　 1 T. baking powder
　 4 eggs

②{ 6 C. oil for frying
　 1 C. sugar
　 ¾ C. maltose*
　 ¼ C. water
　 ½ T. lemon juice or vinegar

③{ ½ T. sesame seeds
　 2 T. raisins

❶ Sift ingredients of ① ; add eggs and knead into a smooth dough; let stand 20 minutes.

❷ Cut dough into half and using a rolling pin, roll out each half into a rectangle 1/6-inch thick. Cut into 1-inch strips and shred strips (Fig. 1).

❸ Heat oil for deep-frying; add shreds and deep-fry for 45 seconds over medium heat until golden brown and expanded; remove and drain; place in a large mixing bowl.

❹ Place ② in a pan and cook 2 minutes over medium heat (sugar should be dissolved); pour mixture onto fried noodle (Fig. 2) and toss lightly to coat noodles (Fig. 3). Pour onto a greased cookie sheet and press noodles into a compact rectangle 1-inch high (Fig. 4); sprinkle with ③ and let cool; cut into 15 squares; serve.

*If unavailable, instead of honey, but use double and cook longer; let chopsticks dip some cooked honey into water if honey become small hall, Remove.

餡：豆沙半斤（１杯）　皮：│麵粉…………３杯　　糖…………⅓杯　、奶水……３大匙
　　「炸油」………８杯　①│發粉……２小匙　②│鹽…………⅓小匙　、水…………半杯
　　　　　　　　　　　　　　　　　　　　│豬油………１大匙
　　　　　　　　　　　　　　　　　　　　（或白油、沙拉油）

❶餡：豆沙分成２４份，揉搓成圓球狀備用。
❷皮：１①料用篩子篩過加②料，拌合成麵糰。
　　　２將麵糰揉至極光滑後，揉成長條狀，分切成２４塊。
❸做法：每只小麵塊，壓成直徑５公分圓形麵皮，豆沙置中央（圖１），包成圓球狀（圖２），再按扁成直徑
　　　　５公分，厚１公分圓餅狀約１０分鐘，以小火將做好圓餅入鍋（圖３）炸６分鐘，改大火炸１分
　　　　鐘，呈金黃色撈起即成（圖４）

油香餅 Tasty Fried Bean Cakes　　材料：２４個 Makes 24

Filling:
1　C.　red bean paste*
8　C.　oil for frying

Skin:
①{ 3　C.　flour
   2　t.　baking powder

②{ ⅓　C.　sugar
   ⅓　t.　salt
   1　T.　lard or vegetable shortening
   3　T.　evaporated milk
   ½　C.　water

❶ Filling:
Cut red bean paste into 24 pieces; roll to round balls.
❷ Skin:
Sift together ingredients of ① ; add ② and mix together to make a dough.
Knead dough until smooth, roll into a long roll and cut into 24 pieces.
❸ Procedure:
Roll each piece into a ball and flatten to a 2-inch circle; in the center of each dough circle, place a piece of red bean filling
(Fig. 1); gather edges of dough circle to completely enclose filling; pinch to seal securely (to ensure cake will not open during
deep-frying). Roll each piece into a ball (Fig. 2) and flatten to a 2-inch circle (piece should be about 1/3-inch thick) let circles
rest covered under a damp cloth for 10 minutes. Heat pan and oil until medium hot; over low heat, deep-fry cakes for 6
minutes (Fig. 3); turn heat to high and fry an additional minute until golden brown; remove, drain and serve (Fig. 4).
See P. 3 "Sweet Buns with Red Bean Paste" for directions on preparation of red bean paste.

餡：┌麥芽糖（或蜂蜜）２大匙
①│糖粉……………………¾杯
 │奶油……………………２大匙
 └麵粉……………………３大匙

皮：┌麵粉…２杯
②│豬油４大匙
 └水…８大匙

③┌麵粉１½杯
 └豬油６大匙

❶餡：麥芽糖加熱軟化後加入篩過之糖粉，並將奶油、麵粉依序加入揉勻，搓成長條切２０塊。
❷皮：[1]將②料拌勻揉成麵糰分成２０個即成「水油皮」。
　　　[2]將③料拌勻揉成麵糰分成２０個即成「油心」（圖１、２）。
❸做法：
[1]「水油皮」包「油心」包好（圖３），用手壓薄，再用木桿趕長，由邊捲成筒狀放直再趕長，再由邊捲成圓狀。（請參照本書腊味蘿蔔餅圖片說明）。
[2]將以上做好麵塊，逐塊壓扁，將餡包好，趕成直徑５公分薄餅（圖４），置於烤盤以３５０度烤１０分即成。

太陽餅　Sunshine Cakes

材料：２０個 Makes 20

Filling:
① ┌ 2 T. honey or maltose
　│ ¾ C. confectioners' sugar
　│ 2 T. butter
　└ 3 T. flour

Skin:
② ┌ 2 C. flour
　│ 4 T. lard
　└ 8 T. water

③ ┌ 1½ C. flour
　└ 6 T. lard

❶ Filling:
Briefly heat honey or maltose until soft; remove from heat. Sift confectioners' sugar and add butter; cream together and ad honey and flour. Knead into a smooth dough and roll to a long roll; cut into 20 pieces.

❷ Skin:
Mix ingredients of ② and roll into a long roll; cut into 20 pieces (A).
Mix ingredients of ③ and roll into a long roll; cut into 20 pieces (B) (Fig. 1, 2).

❸ Procedure:
[1] Flatten (A) pieces; place (B) pieces in center of (A) pieces and wrap edges to enclose (B) (Fig. 3).
[2] Lightly flatten each piece and place a portion of filling in center of skin; gather edges to enclose filling; pinch to seal. Using rolling pin, roll each into a 2-inch flat circle (Fig. 4). Place cakes on a cookie pan; preheat oven to 350°; bake sheets 1 minutes; remove and cool; serve.

餡：鹹蛋黃(生)……２０個　皮：①{麵粉………４杯　發粉……１大匙　奶粉………½杯　②{蛋………３個　糖粉……１¼杯　③{奶油………⅓杯　鹽………½小匙　蛋黃………１個

❶ 餡　：鹹蛋黃盛於烤盤內，以３５０度烤１５分鐘。豆沙分成２０份，把烤好的蛋黃包成圓球狀。

❷ 皮　：[1]將①料過篩３次。
　　　　　[2]把②料用打蛋器攪打１０分鐘至糖粉溶化後加入③料，再拌入已篩過的①料輕攪，分成２０塊
　　　　　小麵糰。

❸ 做法：模型內洒入少許麵粉(圖１)將皮壓成直徑１０公分圓形麵皮，把豆沙球(餡)包好，裝入模型內壓
　　　　　緊，印好花樣(圖２、３、４)置烤盤上，面擦蛋黃，放進烤箱用４００度烤３０分鐘，呈金黃色即成。
■家庭如無模型，包好餡後壓成直徑８公分之扁圓形，可任意劃花紋。

廣式月餅 Cantonese Moon Cakes　　　　材料２０個 **Makes 20**

Filling:
20 "salty egg yolks"
(see p.169)
4 C. red bean paste
(see p. 3)

Skin:
① { 4 C. flour
1 T. baking powder
½ C. milk powder
② { 3 eggs
1¼ C. sugar
③ { ¾ C. butter, melted
½ t. salt
1 egg yolk

❶ Filling: Bake "salty-egg yolks" at 350°F for 15 minutes; remove and let cool. Separate red bean paste into 20 portions; roll each portion into a ball and using thumb, press to make a shallow "well" or indentation in center of each piece; place "salty egg yolk" in center and press bean paste around yolk; roll each piece into a ball.

❷ Skin: [1] Sift together ingredients of ① 3 times.
[2] Lightly beat the ingredients of ② about 10 minutes until sugar has dissolved; add ③ and mix well. Fold in sifted ① and lightly mix into a soft dough; divide dough into 20 pieces.

❸ Procedure:
Lightly press each dough piece to a 4-inch circle; place filling in center of dough and gather edges of dough to completely enclose filling; press edges to seal and roll each piece into a ball. Lightly flour inside of moon cookie press (Fig. 1); place dough ball in cookie press and using palm of hand, flatten dough to conform to shape of cookie press (Fig. 2, 3, 4). Bang sides of press lightly to dislodge pressed cookie; place each pressed cookie on an ungreased cookie sheet; brush top lightly with a beaten egg yolk. Preheat oven to 400°F; bake cookies for 30 minutes until golden brown; remove and serve.

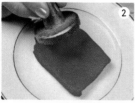

餡：豆沙（1斤）2杯　　皮：

① 麵粉‥‥‥‥‥2杯
　猪油‥‥‥‥‥4大匙
　水‥‥‥‥‥‥8大匙
　糖‥‥‥‥‥半大匙
　鹽‥‥‥‥⅓小匙

② 麵粉‥‥‥‥‥1杯
　猪油‥‥‥‥‥4大匙

③ 食用紅粉‥‥‥適量
　水‥‥‥‥‥‥適量
　紗布20公分×20公分‥1塊

❶ 餡　：豆沙分成20份，揉成圓球狀備用。
❷ 皮　：參照P.39臘味蘿蔔餅「皮」做法説明。
❸ 做法：將以上做好的麵塊，壓成直徑5公分之圓形麵皮，把豆沙球（餡）置中間包好，用手壓成直徑5公
　　　　分之扁圓形（圖1），用印花模型沾③料（圖2）在光滑面加蓋紅色花樣，（圖3、4）排在烤盤上放
　　　　進烤箱以350度烤20分鐘即成。
■家庭如無印花模型可用筷子沾③料印在月餅上。

酥皮月餅 Flaky Moon Cakes　　材料：20個 Makes 20

Filling:
2　C. red bean paste*[1]

Skin:

① { 2　C. flour
4　T. lard or vegetable shortening
8　T. water
½　T. sugar
⅓　t. salt

② { 1　C. flour
4　T. lard or vegetable shortening

③ { drop of red food coloring
a few drops of water
1　piece cotton cloth 20 Cm. x 20 Cm.

❶ Filling:
Cut filling into 20 pieces; roll to round balls.
❷ Skin:
Refer P. 39 Turnip cakes' skin procedures.
❸ Procedure:
Roll each piece of skin to a ball and roll into a 2-inch circle; place 1 piece of red bean filling in center of each dough circle and
gather edges to completely enclose white bean filling in dough piece; press edges to seal; lightly press down piece with palm of
hand to form a 2-inch circle (Fig. 1). Place each finished cake on an ungreased cookie sheet and using a stamp*[2] dip in ③
(Fig. 2) make a design on each cake (Fig. 3, 4). Preheat oven to 350° and bake for 20 minutes until dough is flaky; remove
and serve.
*[1] See P. 3 "Sweet Buns with Red Bean Paste" for directions for making red bean paste.
*[2] If stamp is unavailable, use the end of a chopstick, dipped in food coloring, to make a decorative design on each cake.

餡：豆沙(半斤)1杯　　皮：┌麵粉⋯⋯⋯2杯　　　②┌麵粉⋯⋯⋯⋯1杯
　　「炸油」⋯⋯8杯　　　　│豬油⋯⋯4大匙　　　　│豬油⋯⋯⋯4大匙
　　　　　　　　　　①│水⋯⋯⋯8大匙　　　　└白芝麻⋯⋯⋯1杯
　　　　　　　　　　│糖⋯⋯⋯半大匙
　　　　　　　　　　└鹽⋯⋯⋯⅓小匙

❶餡：將豆沙分成２４份，揉成圓球狀備用。

❷皮：參照Ｐ.39臘味蘿蔔餅「皮」做法說明。

❸做法１將以上做好的麵塊，壓成直徑５公分之圓形麵皮，把豆沙球(餡)置中間包好(圖１)，用手壓成直徑５公分之扁圓形(圖２)，兩面沾水(圖３)，再沾芝麻(圖４)。

　　　２烤法：烤箱先燒熱至３５０℉，把芝麻餅置烤盤，放進烤箱上層，烤約２０分鐘即成。

　　　３炸法：油４大匙燒熱，中火先將芝麻餅兩面煎呈金黃色，使表皮固定，前後煎約１分半鐘取出。「炸油」燒熱，再以中火炸６分鐘，臨起鍋改大火炸一分鐘撈出即可，炸前先煎，則表皮不致膨脹爆裂。

芝麻脆餅 Crunchy Sesame Cakes

材料：２４個 Makes 24

Filling :
1 C. red bean paste*
8 C. oil for frying

Skin:
①{
2 C. flour
4 T. lard or vegetable shortening
8 T. water
½ T. sugar
⅓ t. salt
}

②{
1 C. flour
4 T. lard or vegetable shortening
1 C. white sesame seeds
}

❶ Filling:
Divide red bean paste into 24 pieces; roll to round balls.

❷ Skin:
Refer P. 39 Turnip cakes' skin procedures.

❸ Procedure:
1 Roll each piece of skin to a ball and roll into a 2-inch circle; place 1 piece of filling in middle of each dough circle and gather edges to completely enclose filling; press edges to seal (Fig. 1); lightly press down piece with palm of hand to form a 2-inch circle (Fig. 2); dip each circle in water (Fig. 3) and roll in sesame seeds (Fig. 4).

2 Heat pan and 4T. oil ; over medium heat, fry both sides of cakes until golden (total frying time should be about 1½ minute); remove.

3 Heat oil for deep-frying until medium hot; add cakes and deep-fry for 6 minutes over low heat; turn heat to high and cook an additional minute until skin is flaky; remove, drain and serve.

* See P. 3 "Sweet Buns with Red Bean Paste" for directions for making red bean paste.

餡：①{絞肉……………4兩
蝦仁（切丁）………2兩
冬菇（泡軟切碎）…1朵

②{鹽…………半小匙
味精………半小匙
糖…………1大匙
胡椒………¼小匙
麻油………1大匙
太白粉……1小匙
水…………1小匙

③{葱末………………3大匙
蒜末………………1大匙

④{韭菜（切碎）………1杯
炸扁魚干（切碎）3大匙
「炸油」……………8杯

皮：⑤{麵粉……2杯
豬油…4大匙
水……8大匙
鹽……⅓小匙

⑥{麵粉……1杯
豬油…4大匙

❶餡：油4大匙燒熱，中火將③料炒香，隨入①料炒熟，並調②料再加④料拌勻即成餡，冰冷備用。

❷皮：參照 P.39 臘味蘿蔔餅「皮」做法説明。

❸做法 ①將以上做好麵塊，逐塊趕壓成直徑8公分圓形薄片，中間放2小匙餡後，折半成半圓形，皮邊做花後（請參看咖哩酥餃圖片説明），兩角疊合在一起（圖 1、2、3、4）。

②「炸油」略燒熱，將韭菜酥餅，用小火炸6分鐘，臨起鍋改大火炸1分鐘即起。

韭菜酥餅 Flaky Vegetable Turnovers

材料：20 個 **Makes 20**

Filling:
① { ⅓ lb. chopped pork
⅙ lb. raw, shelled shrimp (diced)
1 pre-softened Chinese black mushroom (chopped)

② { ½ t. salt, ½ t. MSG
1 T. sugar, ¼ t. black pepper
1 T. sesame oil, 1 t. cornstarch
1 t. water

③ { 3 T. chopped green onion
1 T. chopped garlic

④ { 1 C. Chinese chives, cut into 1/8-invh section
3 T. chopped, fried brill fish* ("bien yu gan")
8 C. oil for frying

Skin:
⑤ { 2 C. flour
4 T. lard or vegetable shortening
8 T. water, ⅓ t. salt

⑥ { 1 C. flour
4 T. lard or vegetable shortening

❶ Filling:
Heat pan and 4T. oil; stir-fry ingredients of ③ over medium heat until fragrant; add ① continue to stir-fry until meat changes color; add ② and let thicken. Add ④ and mix well; remove and let cool.

❷ Skin:
Refer P. 39 Turnip cakes' skin procedures.

❸ Procedure:
Flatten skin piece lightly with palm of hand and using a rolling pin, roll to a 3-inch circle. Place 2t. filling in center of circle and fold over skin to half; pinch edges to seal; taking corners of half circle, press together to overlap. Using index finger and thumb, fold edge into pleats as shown in, pictures (Fig. 1, 2, 3, 4); repeat process for each turnover. Heat oil for deep-frying until medium hot; add turnovers and deep-fry over low heat for 6 minutes; turn heat to high and cook an additional minute until turnovers are golden brown; remove, drain and serve.

* See P. 143 step ❶ "Frog's Legs Congee" for directions concerning fried brill fish.

餡：紅豆沙（半斤）1杯　　皮：

餡：紅豆沙（半斤）1杯
鹹蛋黃‥‥‥‥3個
「炸油」‥‥‥‥8杯

皮：
① 麵粉‥‥‥‥‥2杯
猪油‥‥‥‥‥4大匙
水‥‥‥‥‥8大匙
糖‥‥‥‥‥半大匙
鹽‥‥‥‥‥⅓小匙

② 麵粉‥‥‥‥‥‥‥1杯
猪油‥‥‥‥‥‥4大匙

❶ 餡：紅豆沙分成24份，搓圓，鹹蛋黃分切24份，壓扁。（豆沙做法，請參照本書豆沙包）。

❷ 皮：參照 P.39 臘味蘿蔔餅「皮」做法説明。

❸ 做法：將以上做好小麵塊，壓成直徑5公分圓形麵皮，先放鹹蛋再置豆沙（圖1）包成圓球狀（圖2）用刀
片在光滑面劃3刀成6等份（圖3、4）不可觸及豆沙。「炸油」略燒熱，將牡丹甜酥（切口向上）用
小火炸15分鐘待開花，改大火炸1分鐘即起。

■如無鹹蛋黃，可免用。

牡丹甜酥 Sweet Pastry Flowers

材料24個 **Makes 24**

Filling:
1 C. red bean paste *¹
3 precooked "salty egg yolks" *²
8 C. oil for frying

Skin:

①
2 C. flour
4 T. lard or vegetable shortening
8 T. water
½ T. sugar
⅓ t. salt

②
1 C. flour
4 T. lard or vegetable shortening

❶ Filling:
Cut red bean paste into 24 pieces; roll into round balls. Cut "salty egg yolks" into 24 pieces; mash each piece finely.

❷ Skin:
Refer P. 39 Turnip cakes' skin procedures.

❸ Procedure:
Roll each piece into a ball and flatten to a 2-inch circle; place 1 portion "salty egg yolk" and red bean paste in center (Fig. 1). Gather edges of dough to completely enclose filling; pinch edges securely to seal. (to ensure ball will not open during frying); roll piece to a ball (Fig. 2). Using the tip of a razor, make 3 diagonal cuts on the smooth side of ball through skin (don't cut into red bean paste) (Fig. 3, 4). Place finished pastries in strainer or slotted spoon for deep-frying. Heat pan and oil until medium hot; ease pastries on slotted spoon into hot oil and deep-fry over low heat until they "blossom" (about 15 minutes); turn heat to high and cook an additional minute; remove, drain and serve.

*¹ See P. 3 "Sweet Buns with Red Bean Paste" for directions for preparation of red bean paste.
*² See note on P.162 "Salty Egg"; if unavailable, omit.

餡：紅豆沙（半斤）‥‥‥ 1 杯
　　「炸油」‥‥‥‥‥ 8 杯

皮：① {
麵粉‥‥‥‥‥‥‥ 2 杯
豬油‥‥‥‥‥‥ 4 大匙
水 ‥‥‥‥‥‥ 8 大匙
糖‥‥‥‥‥‥ 半大匙
鹽‥‥‥‥‥‥ $\frac{1}{3}$ 小匙
}

② {
麵粉‥‥‥‥‥‥‥ 1 杯
豬油‥‥‥‥‥‥ 4 大匙
}

❶ 餡：紅豆沙分成 2 4 份，每份壓扁成直徑 3 公分之圓餅狀備用。（豆沙做法請參照本書豆沙包）。
❷ 皮：參照 P.39 臘味蘿蔔餅「皮」做法説明。
❸ 做法 1 將以上做好麵塊切成兩半（圖 1）每一半從切口處壓扁成直徑 5 公分之圓餅（圖 2），把餡夾在中間
　　（兩半切口有線紋處向外）（圖 3），兩片邊捏緊並做花（圖 4）（請參照本書咖哩酥餃 圖 片説明）。
　　 2 「炸油」略燒熱，將豆沙酥餅，用小火炸 6 分鐘，臨起鍋時改大火炸 1 分鐘即起。

豆沙酥餅 Flaky Red Bean Turnovers

材料：2 4 個 Makes 24

Filling:
1　C.　red bean paste*
8　C.　oil for frying

Skin:
① {
2　C.　flour
4　T.　lard or vegetable shortening
8　T.　water
½　T.　sugar
⅓　t.　salt
}

② {
1　C.　flour
4　T.　lard or vegetable shortening
}

❶ Filling:
　Cut filling to 24 pieces; roll into balls.
❷ Skin:
　Refer P.39 Turnip cakes' skin procedures.
❸ Procedure:
1 Divide each dough piece into half (Fig. 1); with cut edge up, press each piece to a 2-inch circle (Fig. 2). Place 2 circles together with cut surface on the outside; place a portion of filling in the center of the 2 circles (Fig. 3) and pinch outside edge to seal two circles together. Using index finger and thumb, fold outer edge into pleats as shown in picture (Fig. 4); repeat procedure for each turnover. (see p. 41)
2 Heat oil for deep-frying until medium hot; add dumplings and deep-fry over low heat for 6 minutes; turn heat to high and cook an additional minute until turnovers are golden brown; remove, drain and serve.
* See P. 3 "Sweet Buns with Red Bean Paste" for directions for preparation of red bean paste.

餡：蘿蔔（絲）…1斤4兩　臘腸（細丁）…3兩　肥肉（剁爛）…5兩

① ｛鹽………1小匙　味精……1小匙　胡椒……¼小匙　麻油……半大匙

皮：② ｛麵粉………2杯　猪油……4大匙　鹽……⅓小匙　水………8大匙

③ ｛麵粉………1杯　猪油……4大匙　「炸油」……適量

❶ 餡：① 蘿蔔絲加鹽1小匙醃15分鐘，擠乾水份盛盤。油1大匙燒熱，將臘腸丁炒香盛起候冷。
　② 將剁爛肥肉、蘿蔔絲及①料拌勻後，把炒好的臘腸丁也倒入拌和即成餡。

❷ 皮：① 「水油皮」：將②料拌合成麵糰，揉至極光滑並揉成長條狀分切成20份。
　② 「油心」：將③料拌合成麵糰，揉至極光滑並揉成長條狀分切成20份。
　③ 「水油皮」包「油心」包好用手壓薄再用木桿趕長（圖1），由邊捲成筒狀（圖2），放直再趕長（圖3），再由邊捲圓筒狀（圖4）。

❸ 做法：① 將做好的麵塊壓成直徑5公分之圓形麵皮包上餡，用手壓成直徑5公分之圓餅狀。
　② 「炸油」燒溫先由餅底向下，（油宜滿過餅⅔處）慢火半煎炸約8分鐘，翻面中火再炸8分鐘至兩面呈金黃色，餡熟了即成。

臘味蘿蔔餅 Turnip Cakes　材料：20個 Makes 20

Filling:
1 lb. shredded turnip
3 oz. Chinese pork sausage, diced
5 oz. chopped pork fat

① ｛1 t. salt
1 t. MSG
¼ t. black pepper
½ T. sesame oil

Skin:
② ｛2 C. flour
4 T. lard or margarine
⅓ t. salt
8 T. water

③ ｛1 C. flour
4 T. lard or margarine
3 C. oil for frying

❶ **Filling:** 1 Add 1t. salt in shredded turnip, let stand 15 minutes; remove and squeeze to remove all water.
2 Heat pan and 1T. oil; stir-fry sausage ½ minute; remove and cool.
3 Mix pork fat, turnip, sausage and ① until combined thoroughly.

❷ **Skin:**
1 Mix together the ingredients of ② to make a smooth dough (A); knead briefly until very smooth; roll into a roll and cut into 20 pieces.
2 Mix together ingredients of ③ to make a smooth dough (B). Roll into a long roll and cut into 20 pieces.
3 Flatten (A) pieces; place (B) pieces in center of (A) pieces and wrap edges to enclose (B); lightly flatten. Using rolling pin, roll out to a ¼-inch thick rectangle (Fig. 1). Beginning at top edge, roll up rectangle to a thin, baton-shape (Fig. 2); turn piece to the vertical and roll out to a ¼-inch rectangle (Fig. 3); roll up once again to form a square shape (Fig. 4). Repeat for all pieces.

❸ **Procedure:**
1 Flatten skin lightly and roll into a 2-inch circle; place 1 teaspoon of filling in center of skin and gather edges to enclose; pinch to seal. Lightly flatten filled cakes; repeat for all other pieces to make 20 cakes.
2 Heat oil until medium hot; place turnip cakes in oil (oil should cover 2/3 of cakes); cook over low heat for 8 minutes; turn cakes over, cooked side up and fry an additional 8 minutes; turn heat to high and deep-fry until golden brown; remove, drain and serve.

餡：里肌肉…4兩　①{醬油…半大匙　太白粉1小匙　蝦仁……2兩　鷄肝……1個　「炸油」10杯　②{鹽…1小匙、麻油…1小匙　醬油1大匙、胡椒…½小匙　味精半小匙、太白粉半大匙　糖…1小匙、水……4大匙　皮：蒸熟芋頭12兩　③{豬油……5大匙　太白粉…3大匙　鹽………½小匙　糖………1大匙

❶ 餡：
  1 里肌肉切小丁拌上①料調勻，蝦仁、鷄肝亦切小丁。
  2 油4大匙燒熱，將里肌肉、蝦仁、鷄肝各料炒熟，入酒半大匙調入②料拌勻，冰涼備用。
❷ 皮：蒸熟芋頭，趁熱放在板上，用刀壓爛(圖1)，調入③料揉勻，搓長條分切爲24個小芋粒。
❸ 做法：
  1 將小芋粒按扁(黏手時洒上太白粉)即可將肉餡放在當中捏合(圖2、3、4)。
  2 「炸油」燒熱，中火炸1分鐘再改大火炸1分鐘，呈金黃色即成。

荔浦芋餃 Fried Taro Cakes

材料：24個 Makes 24

Filling:
① {
4 oz. pork loin
½ T. soy sauce
1 t. cornstarch
2 oz. raw, shelled shrimp
1 chicken liver
10 C. oil for frying

② {
1 t. salt , 1 t. sesame oil
1 T. soy sauce , ¼ t. black pepper
½ t. MSG , ½ T. cornstarch
1 t. sugar , 4 T. water

Skin:
③ {
1 lb. peeled taro root
5 T. lard or margarine
3 T. cornstarch
½ t. salt
1 T. sugar

❶ Filling:
1 Dice prok loin; mix with ① ; rinse and devein shrimp, drain and dice. Dice chicken liver.
2 Heat pan and 4T. oil; separately stir-fry prok, chicken liver and shrimp until color changes; add ½T. rice wine and ② ; toss lightly to mix together and remove.
❷ Skin:
1 Cut taro into 1/3-inch thick slices; steam 30 minutes until soft; keep covered.
2 Mash hot taro slices (Fig. 1); mix with ③ and knead into a smooth dough; roll into a long roll and cut into 24 pieces.
❸ Procedure:
Roll each piece into a ball (add cornstarch if too wet) and flatten with palm into a 3-inch circle; place 1 portion (1/24) filling in center and fold into half to form semi-triangular shape; pinch edges to seal (Fig. 2, 3, 4). Heat oil for deep-frying; drop taro cakes into hot oil and deep-fry 1 minute over medium heat; turn heat to high and cook 1 minute; remove and drain; serve.
■ You may substitute pre-softened Chinese black mushrooms for liver.

餡：絞肉……8兩　｜ 鹽……1 小匙　　　　　｜ 太白粉…1 大匙　　皮：｜ 麵粉……2 杯　　　　｜ 麵粉……1 杯
　　洋葱丁…半杯　①｜ 味精…半小匙　②｜ 水………1 大匙　　　　｜ 豬油…4 大匙　　④｜ 豬油…4 大匙
　　咖哩粉1 大匙　　｜ 糖……1 大匙　　　　　　　　　　　③｜ 水……8 大匙　　　　｜「炸油」…8 杯
　　　　　　　　　　｜ 水………半杯　　　　　　　　　　　　｜ 鹽……⅓ 小匙

❶ 餡　：絞肉調太白粉1 大匙，油6 大匙燒熱，將絞肉炒熟盛起，餘油炒香洋葱，隨入咖哩粉同炒，再將炒
　　　　好肉及①料放入燒開，以②料勾汁後，淋上1 大匙熟油即成餡，冰冷備用。
❷ 皮　：參照 P.39 腊味蘿蔔餅「皮」做法説明。
❸ 做法：⬝1⬝將以上做好麵塊逐塊趕壓成直徑8 公分中間稍厚的圓形薄片，中間放2 小匙餡折半成半圓形，
　　　　　　用食指與姆指，由一端向前折0.5 公分捏緊（圖1），再由捏緊½ 處向前折0.5 公分捏緊（圖2）
　　　　　　，如此反覆做全部做完（圖3、4）。
　　　　⬝2⬝「炸油」燒熱，小火炸6 分鐘，臨起鍋時改大火炸1 分鐘即起。

咖哩酥餃 Curry Dumplings

材料：24 個 **Makes 24**

Filling:
8 oz. chopped pork
½ C. minced onion
1 T. curry powder

① ｛1 t. salt
　 ｜½ t. MSG
　 ｜1 T. sugar
　 ｜½ C. water

② ｛1 T. cornstarch
　 ｜1 T. water

Skin:
③ ｛2 C. flour
　 ｜4 T. lard or vegetable shortening
　 ｜8 T. water
　 ｜⅓ t. salt

4 ｛1 C. flour
　｜4 T. lard or vegetable shortening

8 C. oil

❶ Filling:
Mix chopped pork with 1T. cornstarch. Heat pan and 6T. oil; stir-fry chopped pork until color changes; remove and drain. Reheat pan and remaining oil; add onion and saute until soft; add curry powder and stir-fry until fragrant; add chopped pork, ① and let mixture come to a boil; add ② to thicken and 1T. oil; mix together and set aside to cool.
❷ Skin:
Refer P. 39 Turnip cakes' skin procedures.
❸ Procedure:
Roll each piece into a 2-inch circle (middle should be slightly thick and outside edges thin); place 2t. filling in center of dough circle; fold circle over to half and pinch edges to seal. Using index finger and thumb, fold over edge about 1/6-inch to make a thin pleat (Fig. 1); at halfway point of this pleat, make another 1/6-inch fold (Fig. 2); continue pleating edge; finish pleating edge to opposite edge of skin; repeat process for each dumpling (Fig. 3, 4). Heat oil for deep-frying until medium hot; add dumplings and deep-fry over low heat for 6 minutes; turn heat to high and cook an additional 1 minute until dumplings are golden brown; remove, drain and serve.

41

餡：棗泥‧‧‧‧‧‧‧‧4兩　　皮：
　　熟鹹蛋黃‧‧‧‧‧1個

① { 麵粉‧‧‧‧‧‧‧‧1杯
　　豬油‧‧‧‧‧2大匙
　　水‧‧‧‧‧‧‧4大匙
　　糖‧‧‧‧‧‧‧1小匙 }

② { 麵粉‧‧‧‧‧‧‧‧‧‧半杯
　　豬油‧‧‧‧‧‧‧2大匙
　　「炸油」‧‧‧‧‧‧‧8杯 }

❶餡：棗泥分成１６份，搓圓，熟鹹蛋黃壓碎。

❷皮：1「水油皮」：將①料拌合成麵糰，揣至極光滑。
　　　2「油心」：將②料拌合成麵糰，揣至極光滑。

❸做法 1「水油皮」包「油心」包好用手壓薄，再用麵桿趕成四方薄片，四週厚薄要均一，疊三折再趕，反覆
　　　　做三次（如次數多層數愈多），最後疊三折（圖１），使其成厚１公分，寬６公分長條，用刀切絲（圖２
　　　　）切口向上，每二條拼成一件，成十字形（圖３），用筷子在中央穿洞（圖４）（全部做好有３２件）。
　　　2「炸油」燒熱，中火浸十字麵條３分鐘，待開花後大火炸１分鐘撈起，待冷，將棗泥夾在二只炸好
　　　　十字麵條中，可做１６件，每件菊花酥放上適量鹹蛋黃即成。

棗泥菊花酥 Smashed Date Flower Pastries　　材料：１６個 Makes 16

Filling :
4　oz. smashed pitted dates
1　precooked "salty egg" yolk
(see page 162)

Petal Dough:
① { 1　C. flour
2　T. lard or vegetable shortening
4　T. water,　1　t. sugar }

② { ½　C. flour
2　T. lard or vegetable shortening
8　C. oil for frying }

❶ Filling: Separate dates into 16 pieces; roll into round balls; mash salty egg yolk finely.

❷ Petal Dough: 1 (Dough A) Mix ingredients in ① to make a dough; knead until smooth.
2 (Dough B) Mix ingredients in ② to make a dough; knead until smooth; roll to a big circle.

❸ Procedure:
1 Place dough (B) in the middle of dough (A) circle; wrap edges around, dough (B) piece to completely enclose; press edges to seal. Flatten piece with palm of hand and using a rolling pin, roll out to a square. about 1/8-inch thick; fold square to thirds and roll out. Repeat process 3 more times (you may repeat procedure additional times for additional layers); at last roll piece to a rectangle 2-inches wide and 1/3-inch thick (Fig. 1). Cut rectangle into shreds 1/8-inch wide (Fig. 2). Placing cut edge surface-side up, twist dough piece to a half-turn. Place one strip on top of another to form a cross (Fig. 3), using the square end of a chopstick, make an indentation in center of dough cross (Fig. 4) to secure dough pieces more firmly together; repeat procedure to make 32 crosses.

2 Heat oil for deep-frying; over medium heat, deep-fry crosses for 3 minutes until they "blossom"; turn heat to high and cook an additional minute until golden brown; remove and drain; let cool. Place one portion of smashed date filling in center of 16 of the crosses; top with another "flowercross" to make a sandwich; sprinkle salty egg yolk on the top of each pair and serve.

$$①\begin{cases}在萊米 \cdots\cdots\cdots\cdots\cdots\cdots 半斤\\水 \cdots\cdots\cdots\cdots\cdots\cdots\cdots 1\frac{1}{2}杯\\糖(紅糖、白糖均可)\cdots\cdots\cdots 1杯\end{cases}$$

$$②\begin{cases}麵粉 \cdots\cdots\cdots\cdots\cdots\cdots 半杯\\發粉 \cdots\cdots\cdots\cdots\cdots 2小匙\end{cases}\}篩過$$

❶ 在萊米洗淨，以適量水(淹蓋米面)浸泡12小時後，倒乾水待用。

❷ 備果汁機，將①料攪打約10分鐘(圖1)，倒入盛②料的盆內攪勻(圖2)，分盛8個小碗內（8分滿）
　 (圖3) 待蒸。

❸ 水燒開將備好小碗排在蒸籠內，蒸約25分鐘，以一枝筷子插入不黏時，待冷即可取出(圖4)。

■ 如使用電鍋可分次蒸，電鍋內放入3杯水。

■ 蒸好發糕冷後容易倒出。

■ 發糕冷後可再蒸或切成片煎來吃。

發　糕　Steamed Rice Cupcakes　　　　　材料：8個 Makes 8

$$①\begin{cases}⅔ \text{ lb. long-grained rice (1½C.)}\\1½\text{ C. water}\\1 \text{ C. sugar (brown or white)}\end{cases}$$

$$②\begin{cases}½ \text{ C. flour}\\2 \text{ T. baking powder}\end{cases}\}\text{Sifted}$$

❶ Rinse rice until water runs clear; drain and let soak 12 hours in water to cover; drain again.

❷ Place ① in electric blender and blend until very fine (about 10 minutes) (Fig. 1). In a mixing bowl, mix blended rice
　 mixture and ② thoroughly (Fig. 2); portion into cupcake tins or finger bowls (Fig. 3).

❸ Place in steamer and steam over boiling water about 25 minutes; test with a chopstick; insert in cake, if chopstick comes
　 out clean, then cakes are done. Let cakes cool and remove (Fig. 4); serve.

◀ If using an electric rice cooker, add 3 cups water to cooker and steam until cooker automatically shuts off.

◀ You may eat steamed rice cakes hot or slice and fry lightly until golden brown.

①	在萊米········· 1 杯		紅葱頭········· 2 粒		②	味精············ ¼ 小匙
	水············· 3 杯		蘿蔔乾········· 1 兩			胡椒············ ½ 小匙
	鹽············· ½ 小匙		絞肉············ 2 兩			鹽············· ¼ 小匙

❶ 在萊米洗淨，以適量水（淹蓋米面）浸泡約１２小時，倒淨水待用。

❷ 將①料放入果汁機內攪細，約打１０分鐘成米漿後，用小火（需不停攪動約３分鐘），煮成濃湯狀。

❸ 紅葱頭切薄片（圖１），蘿蔔乾剁碎（圖２）備用。

❹ 油３大匙燒熱，把紅葱頭炒香，續將絞肉和蘿蔔乾放入炒香，調入②料炒勻備用。

❺ 將米漿分盛在小碗內８分滿（圖３、４），以大火蒸約１５分鐘後，將炒香蘿蔔乾等放於中央再略蒸即可。

碗 粿 Steamed Rice Pudding

材料：6 碗 **6 servings**

①	1 C. long-grain rice	2 shallots	②	¼ t. MSG
	3 C. water	¼ C. dried turnip		½ t. black pepper
	½ t. salt	⅛ lb. chopped pork		¼ t. salt

❶ Rinse rice until water runs clear; drain; let soak 12 hours in water to cover; drain again.

❷ Place ① in electric blender and blend about 10 minutes until very fine (rice paste); stir continually for 3 minut so that rice paste won't stick to pan and burn.

❸ Mince shallots (Fig. 1); chop turnip (Fig. 2).

❹ Heat pan and 3T. oil; stir-fry shallots until fragrant and golden brown; add chopped pork and chopped turnip and stir-fr until fragrant; add ② and mix together (topping).

❺ Portion rice paste into cupcake tins or 4-inch finger or rice bowls (Fig. 3, 4); place in steamer and steam over high hea for 15 minutes; add topping to each cake and steam 3 additional minutes; remove and serve.

餡：蘿蔔絲…………2斤	② { 鹽……………1小匙	皮：
五花肉…………4兩	味精……………1小匙	③ { 糯米粉…3杯 / 麵粉……½杯
① { 蒜白（斜切薄片）…2枝 / 蝦皮………3大匙	胡椒……………⅓小匙	④ { 滾水……⅔杯 / 冷水……⅓杯 / 猪油…1大匙
	青菜葉……………20片 （修成直徑5公分大小圖1、圖2）	

❶ 餡 ：①蘿蔔絲加鹽1小匙，醃15分鐘後擠乾水份，五花肉切絲備用。

②油4大匙燒熱，將肉絲爆香，隨入①料炒香，即可放入蘿蔔絲及②料拌匀起鍋待冷，分20份。

❷ 皮 ：③料篩過後，將④料內滾水沖入攪拌，再加入冷水及猪油拌匀，揉成十分光滑軟硬適度之糯米櫚

（太硬或太軟時酌量加水或糯米粉）分切20小塊。

❸ 做法：每個糯米櫚按扁成圓薄片，黏手時塗油將餡置中央包好（圖3）置於青菜葉上（圖4），大火蒸10

分鐘即可，趁熱食之。

菜包 Steamed Vegetable Dumplings

材料：20個 Makes 20

Filling:
3⅓ lbs. turnip
⅓ lb. fresh bacon
① { 2 stalks fresh garlic, white part only / ¼ C. dried shrimp

② { 1 t. salt / 1 t. MSG / ⅓ t. black pepper
20 water lily leaves ("lian hwa yeh") cut into round circles* (Fig. 1, 2)

Skin:
③ { 3 C. glutinous rice powder / ½ C. flour
④ { ⅔ C. boiling water / ⅓ C. cold water / 1 T. lard

❶ **Filling:**
① Peel turnip; grate until fine; add 1t. salt and let soak 15 minutes; drain. Cut fresh bacon into shreds; chop the white part of garlic stalk.
② Heat pan and 4T. oil; stir-fry meat shreds briefly over high heat; add ① and stir-fry until fragrant; add precooked turnip shreds and ② ; stir-fry to mix together and remove; let cool. Separate into 20 portions.

❷ **Skin:**
Sift ingredients of ③ ; add ingredients of ④ in descending order (mixing well after each addition); knead to a smooth dough and cut into 20 pieces.

❸ **procedure:**
Flatten dough pieces into circles (if sticky, add a little oil); place filling in middle and fold in half; pinch edges to seal (Fig. 3). Place each finished dumpling on a lily leaf (Fig. 4) and place in steamer; steam 10 minutes over high heat; serve.
If lily leaves are unavailable, substitute lettuce or cabbage leaves and use as directed.

① | 圓糯米（３杯）……１斤 | 粽葉…………４０張
| 碱粉………２½小匙 | 粽繩…………２０條

❶米洗淨，浸水１小時，瀝乾水份，加碱粉拌勻。

❷每二張粽葉，折成三角形，裝入３大匙平的糯米，包時要注意每只要留有空隙，不要裝滿，包成粽子狀，以粽繩繫好入快鍋（水要滿過粽子）水開改小火煮約１小時半，待冷即可沾糖或糖漿供食。

■粽子包法：先將兩片粽葉對好（圖１）折成三角形（圖２）放入糯米（圖３），蓋好包成粽子狀（圖４、５），露出葉子折好（圖６）以粽繩繫緊（圖７）用剪刀修去露出粽葉梗（圖８）。

碱　粽　Sweet "Jungdz"

材料：２０個 **Makes 20**

① | 3 C. glutinous rice | 40 bamboo leaves
| 2½ t. baking soda | 20 pieces of string

❶ Rinse rice until water runs clear; let soak 1 hour in water to cover; drain; mix with baking soda (filling).

❷ Place 2 leaves together; fold into a cone shape, (as a make-shift pastry bag), however one top should be longer than the other; add 3T. of filling and fold over long edge of leaf as a cover; wrap securely and bind loosely with string. (Filling will expand with cooking). Place finished jungdz in a pressure cooker* with water to cover and cook 1½ hours over medium heat; remove, drain and let cool. Unwrap and dip in sugar or honey, serve.

* If no pressure cooker is available, place jungdz in a covered pot with water to cover and cook over medium heat for 3 hours.

■ To Fold "jungdz":
Place 2 bamboo leaves together (opposite ends together) (Fig. 1)
Fold leaves to form a cone shape (Fig. 2)
Add filling (Fig. 3)
Fold over leaves to cover top (Fig. 4)
Press stuffed bamboo leaves into pyramid shape (Fig. 5)
Fold bamboo leaf cover to conform to top surface and fold remaining excess to side (Fig. 6)
Use string to wrap around "jundz" (Fig. 7)
Cut away any long leaf edges (Fig. 8)

5 6 7 8

①				②		
尖糯米（３杯）１斤	腿肉…………半斤		醬油…………３大匙	粽葉………２０張		
蝦米…………¼杯	冬菇…………３朵		味精………¼小匙	粽繩………１０條		
鹽…………¾小匙	鹹蛋黃………３個		糖…………¼小匙			
味精………¼小匙			胡椒………¼小匙			
醬油……半大匙			酒…………半小匙			
胡椒………¼小匙			炸香紅葱頭片２大匙			

❶ 糯米洗淨，浸水約１小時後，瀝乾水份，粽葉、粽繩洗淨在開水內煮約５分鐘，取出備用。

❷ 肉切爲２０塊，冬菇切１０塊，以②料拌醃，鹹蛋也分切爲１０塊，此爲「餡」。

❸ 油４大匙燒熱，將蝦米炒香，再下泡好糯米及①料拌炒。

❹ 粽葉折成三角形，包入糯米、肉等餡料，再放少許糯米包成粽子狀，以粽繩繫好，入快鍋（水需滿過粽子）水開煮約２０分鐘即成。

■ 如用普通鍋燒煮時，所需時間約１小時。

肉 粽 Salty "Jungdz"

材料：１０個 **Makes 10**

①
3 C. glutinous rice
¼ C. dried shrimp
¾ t. salt
¼ t. MSG
½ T. soy sauce
¼ t. black pepper

⅔ lb. pork flank (fresh bacon)
3 Chinese black mushrooms, pre-softened
3 salty egg yolks

②
3 T. soy sauce
¼ t. MSG
¼ t. sugar
¼ t. black pepper
½ t. rice wine
2 T. minced and sauteed shallots
20 bamboo leaves
10 pieces of string

❶ Rinse rice until water runs clear; drain and soak 1 hour; drain again lightly. Wash bamboo leaves and cook in boiling water 5 minutes; remove and drain.

❷ Cut pork into 20 pieces; cut mushrooms into 10 pieces; mix meat and mushroom pieces with ② and let soak 20 minutes. Cut salty egg yolks into 10 sections. Equally divide above ingredients into 10 portions (filling).

❸ Heat pan and 4T. oil; stir fry dried shrimp until fragrant; add rice and ① 、Stir-fry over medium heat until dry; remove and separate into 10 portions; let cool.

❹ Place 2 leaves together; fold into a cone shape (as a make-shift pastry bag) however one top should be longer than the other add ½ of a rice portion, pressing rice gently to line cone; add one portion of filling and then cover with the other half of the rice portion. Fold over long end of leaves to form cover and encase rice and filling; wrap and bind with string. Place finished "jungdz" in pressure cooker with water to cover, cook 20 minutes over medium heat. *

＊ If no pressure cooker is available, place jungdz in a pot with water to cover and cook covered over medium heat for 1 hour.

糯米粉⋯⋯⋯6杯　①{ 糖（紅糖、白糖均可）⋯⋯⋯⋯2杯　圓型玻璃紙⋯⋯⋯1張
　　　　　　　　　　滾水⋯⋯⋯⋯⋯⋯⋯⋯⋯⋯⋯2杯　（直徑３５公分）

❶ 先將①料拌勻至糖溶化，再倒入糯米粉內（圖１）拌合至全部均勻即成「糯米漿」（圖２、３）。
❷ 備一蒸籠舖上玻璃紙倒進拌勻糯米漿（圖４），水燒開蒸２小時，筷子插入不黏時即可。
■ 蒸年糕時宜在蒸籠旁插入竹筒，以便透氣容易蒸熟。
■ 糯米漿倒入蒸籠內時，以不超過七分滿為宜，以免蒸年糕時米漿溢出。
■ 蒸籠外切記密封，用濕布塞緊否則不易蒸熟。

甜年糕 Sweet New Year's Cake

材料：1 籠　**Make 1**

6 C. glutinous rice powder　　①{ 2 C. sugar (granulated or brown sugar)　1 12-inch circle heavy-duty cellophane
　　　　　　　　　　　　　　　　　 2 C. boiling water

❶ Mix ① until sugar is dissolved; add glutinous rice powder (Fig. 1) and mix well (Fig. 2, 3). (rice paste)
❷ Line steamer with cellophane; pour rice paste mixture into steamer (Fig. 4). Steam 2 hours over high heat; insert chopstick
　 to test doneness; remove and set aside until cold; tear down the cellophane and let sit 2 days; cut into slices and serve
■ Rice cake will cook much more quickly and evenly if thin batons, sticks or separators are placed between the steamer and
　 cellophane paper as illustrated.
■ If using a bamboo steamer, cover the outside with damp cloths to prevent steam from escaping or use an electric rice
　 cooker.

①	在萊米（１斤）…３杯		③	鹽…２½小匙			圓型玻璃紙…１張
	水……………………３杯			胡椒…１小匙			（直徑３５公分）
②	白蘿蔔絲（圖１）２斤			味精…１小匙			
	水…………………１杯						

❶ 在萊米浸泡水（需淹蓋米面）１２小時後，瀝淨水備用。

❷ 備果汁機，把①料攪細約１０分鐘，即為"米漿"。

❸ 鍋洗淨，倒入②料蓋鍋小火煮２０分鐘，煮到透明且爛（圖２），隨即將③料及米漿倒入（圖３）保持小火，用鍋鏟翻拌至半熟（５分鐘）放入蒸籠或蒸鍋內（圖４），（預先舖好布或玻璃紙）並抹平，蒸４０分鐘，以筷子插入不黏時即成。

臘味蘿蔔糕： 蘿蔔糕內多加臘味（蝦米１兩，紅葱頭３大匙、香腸、臘肉切丁各３兩一起炒香）與③料放進米漿內，其他做法相同。

蘿蔔糕 Steamed Turnip Cake

材料：１籠　**Make 1**

①	3 C. long grained rice	③	2½ t. salt	1	12-inch circle heavy-duty cellophane
	3 C. water		1 t. black pepper		
②	2 lbs. shredded turnip (Fig. 1)		1 t. MSG		
	1 C. water				

❶ Rinse rice until water runs clear; drain and let soak 12 hours in water to cover, drain.

❷ Line steamer with cellophane paper or wet cloth.

❸ Put ① in an electric blender and blend at high speed for 10 minutes until very fine (rice paste).

❹ Heat pan and add ② ; cover and cook 20 minutes over low heat until soft (Fig. 2); add ③ and rice paste (Fig. 3). Stir-fry 5 minutes and continually stir so that mixture doesn't stick to pan and burn; pour into steamer (Fig. 4). Smooth top and steam 40 minutes. Test with a chopstick; insert into cake and if chopstick comes out clean, cake is done. Let cool and cut into slices.

Spicy Steamed Turnip Cake: steamed turnip cake add (10z. dried shrimpchopped, 3 T. chopped fried shallots, ½ lb. Chinese sausage diced, stir-fry) add ③ ; Pour mixture in cake; other procedures are same as above.

49

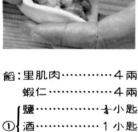

餡：里肌肉…………4兩　　　　葱花………………………1大匙　　　皮：糯米粉…………3杯
　　蝦仁…………4兩　　　　醬油………半大匙、麻油………1小匙　　③　糖…………………半杯
　①｛鹽………………¼小匙　　　①｛鹽………半小匙、胡椒………¼小匙　　　　水…………………1杯
　　酒………………1小匙　　　　味精………半小匙、太白粉……1小匙
　　太白粉………半大匙　　　　糖………¼小匙、水………半杯
　　冬菇(切小丁)…2朵　　　　「炸油」…………………………8杯

❶ 餡 ：里肌肉、蝦仁切約1公分四方丁，全部以①料拌匀，並炒熟盛起，油4大匙燒熱，將葱花、冬菇
　　　　丁炒香，隨加②料燒開，即可放入炒熟的肉丁及蝦丁同炒匀成餡，待冷。
❷ 皮 ：將③料揉合至够光滑並搓成長條狀(圖1)，分成20個小糯米糰(圖2)。
❸ 做法：每個糯米糰按扁成圓薄片(圖3)粘手時塗油，將餡置中央包好(圖4)，以中火炸，見鹹水角浮出
　　　　油面並炸呈金黃色漲大時約需4分鐘即可撈起。

鹹水餃 Golden Dumplings　　　　　　　　　　　　　材料：２０個 Makes 20

Filling:
4　oz. pork loin
4　oz. raw, shelled shrimp
①｛¼　t. salt
　1　t. rice wine
　½　T. cornstarch
　2　pre-softened Chinese black
　　mushrooms, diced
　1　T. chopped green onion

②｛½　t. soy sauce, 1　t. sesame oil
　½　t. salt, ¼　t. black pepper
　½　t. MSG, 1　t. cornstarch
　¼　t. sugar, ½　C. water
　8　C. oil for frying

Skin:
③｛3　C. glutinous rice powder
　½　C. sugar
　1　C. water

❶ Filling: Dice pork and shrimp; mix with ① . Heat pan and 4T. oil; stir-fry meat mixture until color changes; remove and drain.
Reheat pan and 4T. oil; stir-fry chopped green onion and black mushroom shreds until fragrant; add ② and let boil; add pork
loin and shrimp; stir-fry together and remove; let cool.
❷ Skin: Mix together the ingredients of ③ ; knead into a smooth dough; roll into a long roll (Fig. 1) and cut into 20 pieces
(Fig. 2).
❸ Procedure: Taking one of the dough pieces, flatten with the palm on a hard surface (Fig. 3). Using tips of fingers press into
2-inch flat circle, spread fingers with a little oil if dough is very sticky; place a portion (1/20) of filling into the center of dough
wrapper (Fig. 4); fold in half and pinch edges to seal. Heat oil until medium hot; deep-fry ½ of dumplings over medium heat
until they rise to the surface and are golden brown and expanded (about 4 minutes). Remove, drain and repeat procedure for
other dumplings; serve.

①	黑棗…………6個、 桔餅(切片)…3個 紅棗…………6個、 蓮子………12粒 桂元肉……2大匙 (或葡萄乾)	②	糯米……2杯 猪油…2大匙 白糖…3大匙 豆沙……3兩	③	水………1杯 糖………3大匙
				④	太白粉…2小匙 水………2小匙

❶在中碗(或小鋁盆)擦抹猪油1大匙後,把①料整齊排在碗底備用(圖1、2)。

❷糯米洗淨,煮成飯,趁熱拌上②料,取一半先放入已排好的圖案碗內,中間略成凹狀,填入豆沙(圖3),再將另一半糯米飯,舖蓋在豆沙上面(圖4)攤平,蒸約1小時,取出後反扣圓盤內。

❸燒開③料,俟溶化後,以④料勾成糊狀,即澆在八寶飯上面,即可。

■糯米飯燒煮法:

　2杯糯米洗淨加水1½杯浸泡1小時,然後蓋鍋燒沸3分鐘,改用最小火燜煮7分鐘,或用電鍋煮成糯米飯也可。

■①料可依個人喜歡之蜜餞擇色排列成圖案。

八寶飯 8-Treasure Rice Pudding　　　　材料:12人份 **12 servings**

①	6 black dates 6 red dates 2 T. candied red papaya shreds or raisins 3 preserved kumquats, sliced 12 pre-softened lotus seeds *1	②	2 C. glutinous rice 2 T. lard or margarine 3 T. sugar ¼ lb. red bean paste*2	③	1 C. water 3 T. sugar
				④	2 t. cornstarch 2 t. water

❶ Coat a bowl, 7-inches in diameter and 3 inches high, with 1T. oil, or shortening; arrange ingredients of ① in bottom of bowl in a circular fashion as shown in picture (Fig. 1, 2).

❷ Rinse rice with water until water runs clear; let soak 3 hours in water to cover; remove and drain. Place in pan with 1¾C. water; bring water to a boil, cook 3 minutes covered over high heat; turn heat to low and cook 7 more minutes; remove Mix cooked rice with ② ; add ½ rice mixture to prepared bowl; pack down firmly so that rice is higher on sides and there is an indentation in the middle (Fig. 3); fill indentation with red bean paste and add other half of rice mixture (Fig. 4). Pack down again and smooth top. Steam 1 hour over medium heat; remove and demold on serving plate.

❸ Bring ③ to a boil; after sugar has dissolved add ④ to thicken and pour over rice pudding; serve.

*1 Available in dry form at a Chinese grocery store. Lichee nuts, walnuts or almonds may be substituted.
*2 See P. 3 "Sweet Buns with Red Bean Paste" for directions concerning preparation of red bean paste.

豬腸（１２０公分）…１２兩
糯米……………………１２兩
① ｛ 紅葱頭（切片）………２大匙
　　 蝦米……………………２大匙

① ｛ 鹽………半小匙 、 胡椒……半小匙
　　 醬油……２大匙 、 麻油……１小匙
　　 味精……１小匙 、 五香粉…１小匙
　　 糖………１小匙 、 水………１½杯

❶ 用鹽和醋將腸的裏外兩面均搓洗，並以清水沖洗乾淨，瀝乾水份備用。

❷ 糯米浸水約６小時，蝦米泡軟洗淨。

❸ 油４大匙把①料炒香，放入糯米略炒，再入②料炒拌均勻盛出。

❹ 將豬腸一端以繩子綁住（圖１）另端套上漏斗，把豬腸全部推上（圖２），灌入炒好的糯米約６分滿（圖３）
　 每１０公分處用繩子繫緊，即為糯米腸（圖４）。

❺ 鍋內盛糯米腸及水（需淹滿糯米腸）以中火煮４０分鐘後即可切片供食。

糯米腸 Spicy Rice Sausage

材料：６人份 **6 servings**

1 lb. intestinal casing (about 40 inches long)
1 lb. glutinous rice
① ｛ 2 T. minced, sauteed shallots
　　 2 T. dried shrimp

② ｛ ½ t. salt
　　 2 T. soy sauce
　　 1 t. MSG
　　 1 t. sugar
　　 ½ t. black pepper
　　 1 t. sesame oil
　　 1 t. 5-spice powder
　　 1½ C. water

❶ Rub interior and exterior of intestinal casings with salt and vinegar; rinse in cold water; repeat 3-5 times until the intestines are rid of any slimy covering; drain.

❷ Rinse rice until water runs clear; let soak 6 hours in water to cover; drain. Soften dried shrimp in warm water; drain.

❸ Heat pan and 4T. oil; stir-fry ① until fragrant; add glutinous rice and ② ; stir-fry together until dry and remove (filling

❹ Tie off one end of sausage (Fig. 1); attach a funnel to the other end and gather sausage casing on funnel tube (Fig. 2 Stuff casing with filling (Fig. 3), tie off every 4-5 inch (Fig. 4).

❺ Place sausage in pot, cover with water. Cook over medium heat for 40 minutes; remove, drain and serve.

圓糯米（１斤）……３杯　　　　　糖……………１½杯

① { 水………………１½杯
　　酒………………４大匙 }

❶ 糯米洗淨，用水浸泡約１小時後，瀝乾水份，另加①料待蒸。

❷ 電鍋內放水半杯，擺上糯米蒸熟後，續燜２０分鐘取出，趁熱加糖拌勻（圖１）再蒸５分鐘，至糖溶化。

❸ 備鋁盤（２５公分×２０公分×３公分）舖上玻璃紙（圖２），擦少許油（圖３）倒入拌好的糯米飯，用飯勺或湯匙沾水壓平（圖４）待冷切塊即可。

糯米糕 Glutinous Rice Cake

3 C. glutinous rice　　　　　　　　1½ C. sugar

① { 1½ C. water
4 T. rice wine }

❶ Rinse rice until water runs clear; place in pan with 2C. water and let soak 1 hour; drain rice and add ① .

❷ Place mixture in an electric rice cooker* with ½C. water, in bottom of rice cooker, steam until rice cooker automatically turns itself off; let mixture sit covered for 20 minutes. Add sugar immediately and mix thoroughly (Fig. 1); steam an additional 5 minutes until sugar dissolves.

❸ Line an 8" by 8" by 1" cookie sheet with heavy-duty cellophane (Fig. 2), rub lightly with oil (Fig. 3); add rice mixture and using a spoon dipped in water, smooth surface of rice and pack to conform to shape of pan (Fig. 4). Let cool and cut into squares; serve.

* If no rice cooker is available, place rinsed rice and water in a pan; cover and cook over high heat for 3 minutes; turn heat to low and cook an additional 7 minutes. Turn off heat and let rest covered 10 minutes; use as directed.

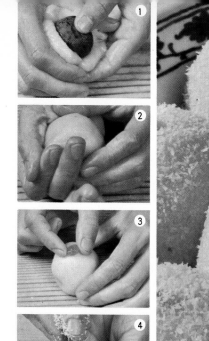

餡：豆沙‥‥‥‥‥ 1 杯　　皮：①{糯米粉‥‥‥‥ 2 杯　　椰茸‥‥‥‥‥‥‥‥半杯
　　　　　　　　　　　　　　　水‥‥‥‥‥‥ $\frac{3}{4}$ 杯　　熟鹹蛋黃‥‥‥‥‥半個

❶　餡　：豆沙分成 1 2 份備用。
❷　皮　：①料拌勻，分成 4 塊，壓成 1 公分厚的薄餅狀，用開水 6 杯煮 5 分鐘至熟撈起瀝乾水份，置於容
　　　　　器趁熱用力攪拌 5 分鐘，取出抹上少許油分切 1 2 塊。
❸做法：每塊皮中間包上 1 份餡(圖 1)包成球狀(圖 2)，上面放少許鹹蛋黃或櫻桃(圖 3)，洒上一層椰茸
　　　　即成(圖 4)。
■糯米慈的餡，可依個人喜好改變，如芝麻餡或花生粉(需加細糖 4 大匙拌勻)等。

糯米慈 Glutinous Rice Snowballs　　　　　　　　材料：1 2個 Makes 12

Filling:　　　　　　　　　Skin:
1 C. sweet bean paste　　①{2 C. glutinous rice powder　　½ C. shredded coconut
　　　　　　　　　　　　　　　¾ C. water　　　　　　　　　　　½ salty egg yolk

❶Filling:
Divide red bean paste into 12 pieces.
Mix ingredients of ① and separate into 12 portions.
❷Skin:
Mix ingredients of ① until smooth and separate into 4 pieces. Flatten each piece until ¼-inch thick. Heat 6C. water un
boiling; add rice pieces and cook 5 minutes until pieces rise to the surface and become a little clear; remove and drain. Pla
rice pieces in a bowl and beat vigorously about 5 minutes; coat hands with oil (to prevent mixture from sticking to hands) a
separate to 12 portions.
❸Procedure:
Take each piece of glutinous rice powder and flatten lightly; place 1 portion of filling in center (Fig. 1) and gather edges
skin to enclose filling; pinch to seal and roll to a ball (Fig. 2). On top of each ball sprinkle a little mashed salty egg yolk
cherry (Fig. 3) and grated coconut (Fig. 4); serve.
■ You may change the filling to crushed peanuts with 4T. granulated sugar or sesame seed filling (See P. 56 for directions

餡：豆沙 …………1 杯　　　皮：糯米粉………2 杯　　　白芝麻……………1 杯
　　　　　　　　　　　　①糖 ………5 大匙　　　「炸油」…………6 杯
　　　　　　　　　　　　水 ……………⅔ 杯

❶餡：豆沙分切１６個。白芝麻洗淨備用。
❷皮：①料拌勻（圖１）板上擦油將拌好①料倒在板上（圖２），揉合夠光滑（圖３），搓長分切成１６個小糯
　　　米糰（圖４）。
❸每個糯米糰按扁成圓薄片，包入豆沙搓成圓球狀，再滾上芝麻。
❹「炸油」略燒熱，中火炸呈金黃色漲大時（５分鐘）即可撈起。

糯米球　Glutinous Rice Balls　　　　　　材料：１６個 Makes 16

Filling:
　1　C.　red bean paste*

Skin:
①　2　C.　glutinous rice powder
　　5　T.　sugar
　　⅔　C.　water

1　C.　white sesame seeds
6　C.　oil for frying

❶ Filling:
Divide red bean paste into 16 portions.
❷ Skin:
Mix ingredients of ① into a smooth dough (Fig. 1); slightly oil table top, place ① on table (Fig. 2), knead until smooth (Fig. 3); roll into a long roll and cut into 16 pieces (Fig. 4).
❸ Procedure:
1　Flatten each piece of dough into a 2-inch circle; place a portion of filling in middle and gather edges of skin to enclose filling; pinch to seal. Roll each filled skin into a ball; dip in water and coat outside with sesame seeds.
2　Heat oil for deep-frying; deep-fry balls over medium heat for 5 minutes until expanded and golden; remove, drain and serve.
　*　See P. 3 "Sweet Buns with Red Bean Paste" for directions concerning preparation of red bean paste.

餡：(尖)糯米⋯⋯⋯⋯⋯半斤 　酒⋯⋯⋯½大匙 　皮：餛飩皮⋯⋯⋯⋯３６張

① { 熟腿肉丁(圖１、２)１杯
　　冬菇丁⋯⋯⋯⋯⋯¼杯
　　蝦米丁⋯⋯⋯⋯⋯¼杯

② { 醬油⋯⋯２大匙
　　鹽⋯⋯⋯½小匙
　　味精⋯⋯１小匙
　　糖⋯⋯⋯１小匙
　　胡椒⋯⋯¼小匙

③ { 葱花(綠色部份)２大匙
　　蛋皮(切碎)⋯⋯２大匙

❶餡：①糯米洗淨用清水浸泡１小時瀝乾水份，加水１¾杯蓋鍋燒沸３分鐘，改用最小火燜煮７分鐘或以
　　　　電鍋煮成糯米飯用筷子撥散。
　　　②油２大匙燒熱，先將①料炒香，下酒½大匙及②料(圖３)並放入糯米飯(圖４)炒拌均勻即為餡，
　　　　盛於盤內待涼。
❷皮：餛飩皮修成圓形。
❸每張餛飩皮放入餡，包成燒賣狀，上洒適量③料蒸３分鐘即成。

糯米燒賣 Glutinous Shau Mai　　　　材料：３６個　Makes 36

Filling:
⅔ lb. glutinous rice

① {
1　C. precooked, diced pork loin (Fig. 1, 2)
¼　C. diced, pre-softened black mushrooms
¼　C. diced, dried shrimp
}

½ T. rice wine

② {
2　T. soy sauce
½　t. salt
1　t. MSG.
1　t. sugar
¼　t. black pepper
}

Skin:
36 won ton skins

③ {
2　T. chopped green onion
2　T. chopped egg sheet*
}

❶ Filling
1 Rinse rice until water runs clear; let soak 1 hour in water to cover; drain. Place rice with 1¾ C. water in a pan and let boil 3 minutes over high heat; turn heat to low and cook 7 more minutes; remove and toss rice lightly to separate grains.
2 Heat pan and 2 T. oil; stir-fry ① until fragrant; add ½ T. rice wine, and ② (Fig. 3); add glutinous rice (Fig. 4) and mix to-gether and remove. Let mixture cool (filling).
❷ Skin:
Trim won ton skins to circles.
❸ Procedure:
1 Place a portion of filling in the middle of each won ton skin; gather edges to make a waist; smooth top of filling with the underside of a spoon and sprinkle ③ on top; place filled shau mai in steamer and steam 3 minutes over high heat; remove and serve.
* See note in P. 14 "Four-Flavor Dumplings" for directions for preparation of egg sheet.

餡：豆沙…半杯　　皮：①{糯米粉……３杯　　青菜葉２４片（３公分直徑）
　　　　　　　　　　　麵粉………½杯
　　　　　　　　　　滾水………１杯
　　　　　　　　　　冷水………⅓杯
　　　　　　　　　　豆沙………半杯

❶餡：豆沙分切２４個。
❷皮：將①料過篩加入滾水燙勻，不燙手時即可加入冷水⅓杯及豆沙半杯（圖１）揉勻（圖２、３），搓成長
　　　條切爲２４小塊（圖４）。
❸將以上做好的麵塊，逐塊壓扁，包入豆沙餡，再壓成直徑３公分圓形之糕餅，用青菜墊底，蒸５分鐘至
　　熟趁熱食之。

豆沙糕餅 Steamed Red Bean Cakes　　　　材料：２４個　Makes 24

Filling:
½　C. red bean paste

Skin:
①{ 3　C. glutinous rice powder
　 ½　C. flour
1　C. boiling water
⅓　C. cold water
½　C. red bean paste

24 leaves of a vegetable (about 1-inch in diameter)

❶ Filling:
Divide red bean paste into 24 portions.
❷ Skin:
Sift ① and add boiling water; mix until smooth and add cold water; mix again and add red bean paste (Fig. 1). Knead mixture to a smooth dough (Fig. 2, 3); roll into a long roll and cut into 24 pieces (Fig. 4).
❸ Procedure:
Flatten each piece of skin to a 1-inch circle; place 1 portion of red bean paste in middle. Gather edges of skin to enclose red bean paste; pinch to seal. Flatten each piece of a 1-inch circle and place on a vegetable leaf: repeat for other pieces and place finished red bean cakes in steamer. Steam 5 minutes over medium heat; remove and serve.

餡：豆沙⋯⋯⋯⋯⋯半斤　　皮：番薯⋯⋯⋯⋯⋯1斤　　白芝麻⋯⋯⋯⋯⋯¾杯
　　　　　　　　　　　　　①｛細沙糖⋯⋯⋯2大匙　　「炸油」⋯⋯⋯⋯8杯
　　　　　　　　　　　　　　｛糯米粉⋯⋯⋯⋯2杯

❶餡：豆沙分成32個丸子
❷皮：番薯去皮，蒸熟壓爛，加①料搓勻，分切成32個。
❸做法：①將「皮」包上「餡」（圖1）揉成長橢圓形（圖2），沾水（圖3）滾上白芝麻（圖4），待炸。
　　　　②「炸油」燒熱，以中火炸成金黃色即成。

軟脆豆沙棗 Sesame-Bean Paste Puffs　　材料：32個 Makes 32

Filling:
⅔ lb. red bean paste*

Skin:
1⅓ lbs sweet potato or taro root
① ｛2 T. confectioners sugar
　 ｛2 C. glutinous rice powder

¾ C. white sesame seeds
8 C. oil for frying

❶ Filling:
Cut red bean past into 32 pieces.
❷ Skin:
Peel sweet potato; cut into 1/3-inch slices; steam 30 minutes until tender; mash thoroughly, and add ① , mix well and knead into a smooth dough; roll into a long roll and cut into 32 pieces.
❸ Procedure:
1 Roll each piece dough into a 2-inch round circle; hollow and place 1 portion (1/32) of red bean paste in center (Fig. 1). Gather edges of dough around filling and pinch to seal; roll into illustrated shape (Fig. 2); repeat to make 32 puffs. Dip finished puffs in water (Fig. 3) and then roll in sesame seeds (Fig. 4).
2 Heat oil for deep-frying; add puffs and deep-fry over medium heat for about 3 minutes until golden; remove drain and serve.
* See P. 3 "Sweet Buns with Red Bean Paste" for directions for the preparation of red bean paste.

花生⋯⋯⋯⋯半斤　　　　糖⋯⋯⋯⋯⋯⋯ 1 杯
清水⋯⋯⋯⋯ 1〇杯

將花生加清水淹蓋花生面（圖 1 ），煮開約 2 分鐘，瀝乾（圖 2 ），除去外膜（圖 3 、 4 ），加入清水 1 〇杯，
用快鍋燒開後，續煮約 3 〇分鐘至爛時，即可加入糖，待溶即爲花生湯。

花生湯 Sweet Peanut Soup　　　　　　材料：1 2 人份 **12 servings**

⅔ lb. unsalted, roasted peanuts (without shells)　　　　　1　C. sugar
10 C. water

Place peanuts in a pan with water to cover (Fig. 1); let boil 2 minutes; remove, drain and let cool (Fig. 2). Remove skins (Fig. 3, 4) and place in a pressure cooker with 10C. water; cook 30 minutes over medium heat* until peanuts are very tender; add sugar and bring liquid to a boil. When sugar has dissolved, pour into a serving bowl and serve.

* If no pressure cooker is available, place mixture in a covered pan and cook 1 hour over low heat.

蓮子·············· 6兩　　　　　　糖················· ⅔ 杯
清水·············· 6杯

❶蓮子用清水浸泡（圖1），泡時須多次換水，除去碱味（圖2、3）。
❷將泡好的蓮子，加清水（圖4），燉約３０分鐘後，放入糖即可。
■有的蓮子滲碱成份多，燉煮時間需縮短。

蓮子湯 Lotus Seed Soup　　　　　材料：１２人份 **12 servings**

½　lb. dried lotus seeds　　　　　⅔　C. sugar
6　C. water

❶ Soak lotus seeds 10 minutes in cold water (Fig. 1); drain and repeat procedure 3 more times (Fig. 2, 3), drain.
❷ Place lotus seeds and water (Fig. 4); steam over boiling water 30 minutes; remove and add sugar. Mix until sugar dissolve serve.
■ Some dried lotus seeds contain baking soda and therefore may be less brittle than others; adjust soaking time accordingly.

燕窩‧‧‧‧‧‧‧‧‧‧‧‧‧‧‧‧ 2 兩 ①{水‧‧‧‧‧‧‧‧‧‧‧‧‧‧‧‧‧‧ 6 杯
冰糖或糖‧‧‧‧‧‧‧‧‧‧ 1 杯

❶ 燕窩加入滾水 6 杯（圖 1）浸泡 1 小時後，瀝乾水份，再加入滾水 6 杯浸泡 1 小時，使其膨脹 2 ～ 3 倍（圖 2），如燕毛多，加入少許油（圖 3），輕攪使燕毛與油附着同時浮出水面，將燕毛挑出，並用水多次漂洗瀝乾（圖 4）。

❷ ①料燒開至冰糖溶化，加入發好燕窩燉或燒煮 1 0 分鐘，趁熱食之。

■ 煮好燕窩也可冰涼食用。

冰糖燕窩 Bird's Nest Soup with Rock Sugar   材料：1 2 人份 **12 servings**

2 oz. bird's nest ①{ 6 C. water
1 C. rock sugar

❶ Rinse bird's nest in 6 cups boiling water (Fig. 1); let soak 1 hour; drain. Add 6 more cups boiling water and let soak until nest is 2 to 3 times bigger than original size (about 1 hour) (Fig. 2). If feathers remain in the nest, add a few drops of oil (Fig. 3); lightly rub oil and feathers together and rinse bird's nest a few times to wash away feathers; drain (Fig. 4).

❷ Heat ① until sugar dissolves; add bird's nest and cook 5 minutes; serve hot or cold.

①{
温水‥‥‥‥‥1½杯
糖‥‥‥‥‥6大匙
香草片‥‥‥‥2粒

雞蛋‥‥‥‥‥4個

②{
水‥‥‥‥‥‥6杯
糖‥‥‥‥‥‥1杯
香草片‥‥‥‥1粒

❶將①料拌勻至糖溶化(圖1),雞蛋打散(圖2),①料與雞蛋全部拌勻(圖3)濾過(圖4)倒入大碗內,用小火蒸15分鐘至蛋剛熟,用小刀在碗內劃刀成1.5公分寬之菱形。

❷將②料燒開輕輕倒入蒸好蛋內即可。

■也可加入其他水菓或白木耳。

芙蓉甜湯 Sweet Custard Soup

①{
1½ C. warm water
6 T.   sugar
2 t.   vanilla extract

4 eggs

②{
6 C.   water
1 C.   sugar
1 t.   vanilla extract

❶ Stir ① until sugar dissolves (Fig. 1). Beat eggs lightly (Fig. 2). Mix ① and eggs (Fig. 3). Strain mixture (Fig. 4); discard matter remaining in strainer and place liquid in a big soup bowl. Place bowl in steamer and steam 15 minutes over medium heat; remove and cut egg custard into ½-inch squares.

❷ Place ② in a pan and heat until boiling; lightly pour mixture into bowl containing custard; serve. (You may add fruit or pre-softened white wood ears, if desired.)

白木耳············半兩　　　①{ 水················6杯
水菓罐頭·········⅓罐　　　　　 冰糖············半斤

❶白木耳沖入熱水（圖１、２），見木耳脹開，即可去蒂撈起（圖３、４）。

❷①料放入白木耳燉煮至冰糖溶化，即可倒入水果罐頭待冷，放冰箱冰涼，加些冰塊，即可供食。

■此甜點也可熱食，水果罐頭種類看個人之喜愛選擇，至於有的白木耳很容易煮爛必要時需先撈出，吃時才加入。

雪白木耳 Sweet Fruit Soup with White Wood Ears

材料：１２人份 **12 servings**

½ oz. white wood ears
⅓ can fruit with syrup*¹

①{ 6 C. water
⅔ lb. rock sugar*²

❶ Rinse wood ears; add hot water to cover wood ears (Fig. 1, 2); let soak until expanded; remove stems and drain (Fig. 3, 4).

❷ Place ① and wood ears in a saucepan; steam until sugar has dissolved. Allow liquid to cool; remove wood ears and temporarily set aside; place liquid in refrigerator. Before serving, add canned fruit with syrup, wood ears and ice cubes, if desired.

*¹ Use canned fruit of choice.

*² If rock sugar is unavailable, substitute 1½C. granulated sugar.

◀ This soup may also be served hot; after steaming, add canned fruit and serve immediately.

洋菜⋯⋯⋯⋯⋯¼兩
水⋯⋯⋯⋯⋯⋯3杯

① { 糖⋯⋯⋯⋯⋯⋯半杯
奶水⋯⋯⋯⋯⋯¼杯
杏仁精⋯⋯⋯半大匙

② { 糖⋯⋯⋯⋯⋯1½杯
水⋯⋯⋯⋯⋯⋯6杯
杏仁精⋯⋯⋯半大匙

❶洋菜洗淨（圖１），加水３杯泡約３０分鐘後燒沸，繼續燒至洋菜完全溶化時，加入①料（圖２）隨即熄火，倒入鋁盤中（圖３），待涼切成小塊。

❷將②料燒開，溶化成糖水，盛於碗中待涼和杏仁豆腐供食。

■食用時，最好加入冰塊及水果罐頭。

杏仁豆腐 Sweet Almond-Beancurd Soup

材料：１２人份 **12 servings**

¼ oz. agar-agar*¹
3 C. water

① { ¼ C. evaporated milk
½ T. almond extract
½ C. sugar

② { 1½C. sugar
6 C. water
½ T. almond extract

1 small can mandarin orange sections preserved in syrup*²

❶ Lightly rinse agar-agar (Fig. 1); add 3C. water and soak 30 minutes; pour mixture into pan and heat until agar-agar dissolves; add ① (Fig. 2). Pour into a 9-inch round pan and let cool; when mixture has set, cut into bite-size pieces (Fig. 3).

❷ Bring ② to a boil and cook until sugar dissolves; pour mixture into serving bowl and let cool; add almond "beancurd" cubes, orange sections and serve.

*¹ If unavailable, use gelatin and follow instructions on package.

*² If unavailable, substitute canned fruit of choice.

■ Before serving, you may also add ice cubes and milk if desired.

餡：黑芝麻⋯⋯⋯⋯ 1 兩
　板油（去膜）⋯⋯ 1 兩
　細砂糖⋯⋯ 2½ 大匙

皮：糯米粉⋯⋯⋯⋯ 1 杯
①　滾水⋯⋯⋯⋯ ¼ 杯
　冷水⋯⋯⋯⋯ 2 大匙

❶ 餡　：黑芝麻篩去砂塵，洗淨，小火炒乾後壓成粉末（圖1），板油剁爛成泥狀與細砂糖，同攪勻成餡（圖2），入冰箱冰約30分鐘，取出分成20份（圖3），並揑圓（圖4）。

❷ 皮　：將①料依次加入揉合，並揑勻成糯米糰分切為20份。

❸ 做法：將每只糯米糰捏成圓薄片，包上餡，做成湯圓，放入開水5杯內煮約5分鐘，見湯糰浮出水面，即可盛碗供食。

■ 餡可改做花生、豆沙等，豆沙餡參考豆沙包。　如無板油可用肥肉代替。

■ 酒釀湯圓：將湯圓煮熟，再加入糖半杯，酒釀3大匙，桔子（罐頭）1杯燒開倒入打散之雞蛋2個即可。

芝麻湯圓 Sweet Rice Balls with Soup

材料：6人份 **6 servings**

Filling:
1　oz. (¼C) black sesame seeds*
1　oz. pork fat
2½ T. confectioners sugar

Skin:
① {
1　C. glutinous rice powder
¼　C. boiling water
2　T. cold water
}

❶ Filling:
Rinse sesame seeds; stir-fry over low heat (no oil) until fragrant (about 30 seconds); grind into a fine powder (Fig. 1). Chop pork fat until fine; mix with black sesame seed powder and sugar until smooth (Fig. 2); place in refrigerator and let cool until solid (about ½ hour); cut into 20 pieces (Fig. 3). roll each piece into a ball (Fig. 4).

❷ Skin: Mix ingredients of ① into a smooth dough; roll into a long roll and cut into 20 pieces;

❸ Procedure:
Roll each piece of skin into a ball; use palm of hand to flatten into a 3-inch circle. Place 1 portion filling in center of "skin" circle and gather edges around filling, pinch to seal. Roll into a ball; repeat for other balls. Bring 5 C. water to a boil; add glutinous rice balls and let cook 5 minutes over medium heat until they rise to the surface; pour soup and balls into serving bowl and serve.

■ You may also substitute peanuts or red bean paste (see p. 3 for making red bean paste) in filling for sesame seeds.

■ **Sweet Rice Balls with Fermented Rice Wine** Follow the above recipe, when the balls rise to the water surface, add ½ C. sugar, 3T. fermented rice wine, 1C. orange sections, and bring mixture to a boil; add 2 beaten eggs, turn off heat. Pour into a serving bowl and serve.

小紅豆⋯⋯⋯⋯⋯ 半斤
水⋯⋯⋯⋯⋯⋯ １０杯

① ⎰ 糯米粉⋯⋯⋯⋯⋯ １杯
　 ⎱ 滾水⋯⋯⋯⋯⋯ ¼杯
　 　 冷水⋯⋯⋯⋯⋯ ２大匙

糖⋯⋯⋯⋯⋯⋯ １杯

❶紅豆加水煮開約２分鐘，將水倒乾以去苦味，另加水１０杯，用快鍋煮約２０分鐘。

❷將①料依次加入揉合，揣至夠光滑，分做成小湯圓（圖１、２、３），用開水煮熟後，連同糖放入紅豆湯內即成。

紅豆圓仔湯 Sweet Rice Balls with Red Bean Soup

材料：６人份　**6 servings**

⅔ lb. red kidney beans
10 C. water

① ⎰ 1　C. glutinous rice powder
　 ⎱ ¼　C. boiling water
　 　 2　T. cold water

1　C. sugar

❶ Place beans, with water to cover, in a pan; cook 2 minutes over medium heat; drain and place in a pressure cooker with 10C. water; cook 20 minutes over medium heat*.

❷ Mix ingredients of ① together and knead into a smooth dough; roll into a long roll and cut into 80 pieces; roll each into a ball (Fig. 1, 2, 3), heat 6 cups water until boiling; add rice balls and cook 3 minutes until they rise to the surface of water; remove and drain. Place rice balls in red bean mixture and add sugar; mix together and bring mixture to a boil; pour into a serving bowl and serve.

* If no pressure cooker is available, place beans and water in a casserole and cook 1 hour covered over medium heat.

餡：絞肉‥‥‥‥‥‥4兩

① 鹽‥‥‥‥‥‥半小匙
味精‥‥‥‥‥‥半小匙
胡椒‥‥‥‥‥$\frac{1}{4}$小匙
麻油‥‥‥‥‥$\frac{1}{4}$小匙
炸香紅葱頭‥‥1大匙
太白粉‥‥‥‥1小匙

皮｛糯米粉‥‥‥‥‥‥2杯
② 滾水‥‥‥‥‥‥$\frac{1}{2}$杯
冷水‥‥‥‥‥‥$\frac{1}{4}$杯

葱段3公分‥‥‥6枝
清水‥‥‥‥‥‥9杯
鹽‥‥‥‥‥2$\frac{1}{2}$小匙
③ 味精‥‥‥‥‥1小匙
胡椒‥‥‥‥‥$\frac{1}{4}$小匙
麻油‥‥‥‥‥$\frac{1}{4}$小匙
唐好菜‥‥‥‥4兩

❶ 餡　：將絞肉調①料拌勻成餡，分成24份備用。

❷ 皮　：將②料依次加入揉合成糯米糰，亦分成24份。

❸ 做法：①將每份小糯米糰用手捏成圓薄片包上1份餡揑圓成鹹圓。
　　　　②油4大匙燒熱，將葱段炒香（圖1），隨下③料燒開，即可放入鹹圓待滾約5分鐘（圖2），見鹹
　　　　圓浮出水面（圖3），加唐好菜（圖4）熄火即可供食。

鹹湯圓 Salty Rice Ball Soup

材料：6人份 **6 servings**

Filling:
⅓ lb. chopped pork
① ½ t. salt
½ t. MSG
¼ t. black pepper
¼ t. sesame oil
1 T. minced, sauteed shallots
1 t. cornstarch

Skin:
2 C. glutinous rice power
② ½ C. boiling water
¼ C. cold water

6 1-inch sections green onion
9 C. water
2½ t. salt
③ 1 t. MSG
¼ t. black pepper
¼ t. sesame oil
⅓ lb. "tang hau tsai" *

❶ Filling: Mix ① and chopped pork until ingredients are thoroughly combined; separate into 24 portions; cut vegetable into 1-inch sec- tions.

❷ Skin: Mix ingredients of ② and knead into a smooth dough; roll into a long roll and separate into 24 pieces; roll each piece into a ball and flatten with palm into 3-inch circle.

❸ Procedure:
1 Place 1 portion filling in center of rice circle and gather edges of circle around filling; pinch to seal; roll into balls.
2 Heat pan and 4T. oil; stir-fry onion sections until fragrant (Fig. 1) and add ③ . Heat liquid until boiling; add glutinous rice balls and let boil 5 minutes over medium heat (Fig 2); when balls rise to the surface (Fig. 3), add green vegetable and let boil again; portion into serving bowls and serve (Fig. 4).

* if unavailable, substitute spinach or watercress.

餡：蝦仁‥‥‥‥‥‥4兩
① 酒‥‥‥‥‥‥¼小匙
　 鹽‥‥‥‥‥‥¼小匙
　 味精‥‥‥‥‥¼小匙
　 太白粉‥‥‥‥半小匙
　 熟筍(切小片)2大匙
　 薑末‥‥‥‥‥1小匙

皮：餛飩皮‥‥‥‥30張
② 高湯‥‥‥‥‥‥6杯
　 酒‥‥‥‥‥‥1小匙
　 鹽‥‥‥‥‥1½小匙
　 味精‥‥‥‥‥1小匙
　 薑絲‥‥‥‥‥1大匙

豆苗或其他青菜4兩
③ 胡椒‥‥‥‥‥¼小匙
　 麻油‥‥‥‥‥半小匙
　 醬油‥‥‥‥‥半大匙
　 葱末‥‥‥‥‥1大匙
　　　　　　　　每人份

❶蝦仁每隻切為3段，調入①料並加筍片、薑末拌勻成「餡」。每張餛飩皮包上適量的餡，即成餛飩。
❷將②料燒開，分別倒入備好③料之湯碗內。
❸燒半鍋水，分別將餛飩及豆苗煮熟，放入做好的湯汁內即成。
■餛飩包法(一)：將餡放在皮中間，折成三角形（圖1）由1公分處向前折（圖2）兩端沾水粘住（圖3、4）。

蝦仁餛飩 Shrimp Won Ton

材料：3人份 3 servings

① ⅓ lb. raw, shelled shrimp
　¼ t. rice wine
　¼ t. salt
　¼ t. MSG
　½ t. cornstarch
　¼ C. bamboo shoot, diced
　1 t. chopped ginger root

② 30 won ton skins
　6 C. stock
　1 t. rice wine
　1½ t. salt
　1 t. MSG
　1 T. shredded ginger root

③ 4 oz. spinach or another green vegetable
　¼ t. black pepper
　½ t. sesame oil
　½ T. soy sauce
　1 T. chopped green onion
　　　Each serving

❶ Rinse and devein shrimp; drain and cut each into 3 pieces; mix with ① ; dice bamboo shoot. Mix shrimp, bamboo shoot and chopped ginger root together thoroughly (filling).
❷ Folding method I: Taking one won ton skin, put a teaspoon of filling in the center (Fig. 1); fold over in half to form a triangle; make another fold ¼ from longest diagonal edge (Fig. 2). Bring the two outside corners together ("¼-fold" should be on inside) and using a drop of water, pinch these 2 edges together to seal (Fig. 3, 4).
❸ Heat ② until boiling; prepare ingredients of ③ and put into each serving bowl; add hot ② mixture to each bowl.
❹ Boil 6 cups water; add won ton and green vegetable; cover. When won tons rise to the surface of the water after an additional boil, remove won-ton with green vegetable; drain and portion into serving bowls.[1] Serve immediately.
[1] Use this method for 3 servings or more.

餡：絞肉‧‧‧‧‧‧‧4兩　　荸薺‧‧‧‧‧‧‧2個　　　　紅葱頭‧‧‧‧‧‧‧‧‧‧‧‧‧‧‧‧‧‧‧‧‧‧3粒
　　　酒‧‧‧‧‧‧‧¼小匙　　薑末‧‧‧‧‧1小匙　　　　　　水‧‧‧‧‧‧‧6杯、味精‧‧‧‧1小匙
　　　鹽‧‧‧‧‧‧‧半小匙　　蒜末‧‧‧‧‧1小匙　　　②　　鹽‧‧‧‧‧1½小匙、胡椒‧‧‧‧¼小匙
①　　味精‧‧‧‧¼小匙　　葱末‧‧‧‧‧1小匙　　　　　　酒‧‧‧‧‧1小匙、麻油‧‧‧‧半小匙
　　　胡椒‧‧‧⅛小匙
　　　麻油‧‧‧⅛小匙　　皮：餛飩皮‧‧‧‧30張　　　　小白菜‧‧‧‧‧‧‧‧‧‧‧‧‧‧‧‧‧‧‧‧4兩
　　　太白粉‧‧‧半小匙

❶ 絞肉調入①料攪勻，再加入荸薺（拍碎握乾水份），及葱、薑、蒜末拌成「餡」。

❷ 每張餛飩皮包上適量的餡，即成餛飩。

❸ 油3大匙燒熱，先炒香紅葱頭（切片），隨入②料燒開，再加餛飩及小白菜（切段）燒沸即可。

■ 餛飩如果份量少，可用此方法燒煮簡單易做。

■ 餛飩包法（二）：將餡放在皮中央（圖1）成凹狀（圖2）姆指與食指捏緊，抽出竹匙（圖3）成餛飩（圖4）。

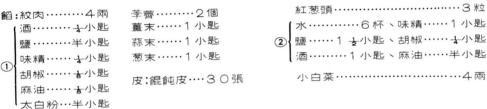

猪肉餛飩 Pork Won Ton

材料：3人份 **3 servings**

⅓ lb. chopped pork	2 water chestnuts, smashed and drained
¼ t. rice wine	1 t. chopped green onion
½ t. salt	② 1 t. ginger root
① ¼ t. MSG	1 t. chopped garlic
⅛ t. black pepper	
⅛ t. sesame oil	30 won ton skins
½ t. cornstarch	

3 shallots, minced
6 C. water
1½ t. salt
③ 1 t. rice wine
1 t. MSG
¼ t. black pepper
½ t. sesame oil
⅓ lb. white Chinese cabbage*

❶ Mix ① with chopped pork; add ② and mix together thoroughly. (filling)

❷ Taking a won ton skin, put a teaspoon of filling in the center; fold over in half to form a triangle; make another fold 1/3 from longest diagonal edge. Bring the two outside corners together ("1/3-fold" should be on inside) and using a drop of water, pinch these 2 edges together to seal. Repeat for other skins.

❸ Heat pan and 3T. oil; saute shallots until golden brown; add ③ and heat liquid until boiling; add won tons and vegetable. Cover and when won tons rise to the surface of the water, after an additional boil, portion into serving bowls and serve.

* White Chinese cabbage ("syau bai tsai") may be purchased at Chinese grocery stores. If unavailable, substitute spinach or watercress.

■ Use this method for 3 servings or less.

■ Folding Method II: Place one teaspoon filling in the middle of won ton skin (Fig. 1). Gather edges of skin to make an indentation in the middle of skin (Fig. 2). Insert chopstick in middle and gather edges of skin together; remove chopstick (Fig. 3). Finished won ton (Fig. 4).

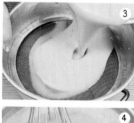

① ⎰ 芋頭………… 1 斤半
　⎱ 水 …………… 7 杯

② ⎰ 冬瓜糖（切碎）…… 3 兩
　⎰ 桔餅（切碎）……… 3 兩
　⎱ 豬油…………… 4 大匙
　⎱ 糖 ……………… 1 杯

❶ 芋頭去皮（圖 1）切片（圖 2）蒸熟，加水 7 杯用果汁機攪細，過濾後備用（圖 3）。
❷ 打好芋頭汁加入②料以小火燒煮約 2 0 分鐘，待成糊狀即成（圖 4）。
■ 芝麻炒香壓碎，紅葱頭切片，用油炒香，依各人喜好酌量加入同煮。

芋　泥　Sweet Taro Soup

材料：１２人份 **12 servings**

① ⎰ 2　lbs. taro root
　⎱ 7　C. water

② ⎰ ¼　lb. chopped candied winter melon
　⎰ ¼　lb. chopped candied orange peel
　⎰ 4　T. lard or margarine
　⎱ 1　C. sugar

❶ Peel taro root (Fig. 1), slice (Fig. 2); steam until tender; place steamed taro root in an electric blender with 7C. water; blend at high speed until smooth; place mixture in a cheesecloth and strain (Fig. 3); retain liquid and throw away mixture left in cheesecloth.

❷ Place retained liquid and ② in a pan; cook 20 minutes over low heat until thick (Fig. 4); serve.

■ You may also add minced, sauteed shallots and stir-fried mashed sesame seeds for extra flavor.

①	炒熟花生米……1 杯 白芝麻…………半杯 水……………… 1 杯	②	水………………6 杯 糖…………… ¾ 杯	③	太白粉………3 大匙 水…………3 大匙 奶水……………半杯

❶將花生去皮(圖1、2),白芝麻炒香(圖3、4)備用。

❷①料加水2杯以果汁機攪細,加②料攪拌燒開,並以③料勾汁即可熄火,最後加入奶水拌勻即成。

■可用花生醬6大匙、芝麻醬3大匙代替①料。

■將花生改用腰果即成腰果奶露。

花生奶露 Nutty-Milk Soup

材料:6人份 **6 servings**

① { 4 oz. (1C.) unsalted, roasted peanuts
½ C. sesame seeds
  1 C. water

② { 6 C. water
¾ C. sugar

③ { 3 T. cornstarch
3 T. water
½ C. evaporated milk

❶ Remove skins from peanuts (Fig. 1, 2); stir-fry sesame seeds over low heat (no oil) until golden (Fig. 3, 4); remove.

❷ Place peanuts, sesame seeds and 1C. water in an electric blender; blend at high speed until smooth, strain mixture into a pan (discard big pieces). Add ② and bring liquid to a boil; add ③ to thicken and turn off fire; add evaporated milk and mix; serve.

■ Substitute cashews for peanuts and prepare recipe as directed above.

黑芝麻或白芝麻……4兩
水……………………1杯

① 水………………5杯
　 冰糖或糖………¾杯
　 醬油…………1大匙

② 太白粉………3大匙
　 水…………3大匙

❶ 芝麻洗淨（圖1、2），小火炒乾至有香味（圖3、4），加1杯水用果汁機攪細。

❷ 將①料燒開，加入攪細芝麻，並以②料勾成薄汁即成。

冰糖芝麻糊 Sweet Sesame Soup

材料：6人份 **6 servings**

4 oz. white (or black) sesame seeds
1 C. water

① 　5 C. water
　　¾ C. rock sugar or fine sugar
　　1 T. soy sauce

② 　3 T. cornstarch
　　3 T. water

❶ Rinse sesame seeds (Fig. 1, 2); heat pan and stir-fry sesame seeds over low heat until dry and fragrant (Fig. 3, 4); place in blender with 1 C. water and blend at high speed until mixture is fine.

❷ Place ① and sesame liquid in a pan; heat until rock sugar has dissolved. Add ② to thicken and pour into serving bowls serve.

①	②	③	④
奶水………半杯 糖…………1 杯 清水………6 杯	太白粉……3 大匙 清水………3 大匙	山渣片………3 兩 糖…………¼ 杯 清水………2 杯	太白粉…1½ 大匙 清水………2 大匙

❶ 山渣放入清水1杯，蒸溶備用（圖1、2、3）。

❷ 將②④各料攪勻待用。

❸ 鍋入①料燒滾，將②料徐徐倒入，再加奶水攪勻，成為奶糊狀，倒在大碗內。

❹ 入③料燒滾，倒入蒸好之山渣攪拌（此為紅色），再徐徐加入④料待滾，即倒在盛奶糊之大碗裡，使其糊成為太極形（如圖）。

山渣奶甜露 Sweet "Yin-Yang" Soup ⟶ 材料：1 2 人份 **12 servings**

① { ½ C. evaporated milk
1 C. sugar
6 C. water

② { 3 T. cornstarch
3 T. water

③ { ¼ lb. dried hawthorn slices
("shan jya pian")*
¼ C. sugar
2 C. water

④ { 1½ T. cornstarch
2 T. water

❶ Add 1C. water to dried fruit slices ("shan jya pian"); steam until fruit slices have dissolved (about 10 minutes) (Fig. 1, 2, 3).

❷ Prepare ② and ④ .

❸ Heat ① until boiling, add ② and stir until thickened; add evaporated milk and mix together; pour into serving bowl.

❹ Heat ③ until boiling; add "shan-jya" mixture (red color); add ④ and stir until thick; pour into bowl and coax liquid into pictured design with a spoon; serve.

■ Design represents "yin-yang"; opposing forces; fire; air; sun: moon; sweet; sour.

* "Shan jya pian" are available in Chinese drugstores. You may substitute "umeboshi" (pickled plums); boil until soft in 1C. water; remove skin and seeds; follow recipe instructions form step ❷. (may add red food coloring).

① 鴨‥‥‥‥1隻3斤
⎰ 蝦米、　筍丁 ⎱
⎨ 冬菇丁、青豆仁 ⎬ 1杯
⎩ 紅蘿蔔丁、火腿丁 ⎭

② ⎰ 糯米‥‥‥‥‥‥1 杯 ⎱
　 ⎩ 水‥‥‥‥‥‥1½杯 ⎭
③ ⎰ 塩‥‥‥‥‥‥半小匙 ⎱
　 ⎩ 味精、胡椒各¼小匙 ⎭

醬油‥‥‥1大匙
「炸油」‥‥6杯

④ ⎰ 葱‥‥‥‥2枝 ⎱
　⎮ 薑‥‥‥‥2片 ⎮
　⎨ 醬油‥‥4大匙 ⎬
　⎮ 糖‥‥‥‥1小匙 ⎮
　⎮ 八角‥‥‥1朶 ⎮
　⎩ 水‥‥‥‥3½杯 ⎭

❶ 糯米洗淨以1½杯水泡約1小時。

❷ 油4大匙燒熱，將①料炒香，隨下②料及③料煮約5分鐘見汁快乾盛起，塞入鴨腹內，以針線或用牙籤將鴨腹縫合。

❸ 用醬油1大匙，將鴨全身抹勻，即投入已燒熱之油鍋內炸呈金黃色撈起，連同④料置快鍋內中火燒煮約1小時，至鴨肉軟，餘汁剩1杯抽出縫線即可盛盤供食。

■ 鴨燒煮時可使用大同鍋（④料內的水改換爲8杯，燒煮時間需1½小時）或烤箱（④料內的水改換爲2杯，宜將鴨炸好後，連同④料先放入有蓋耐熱玻璃碗內，再放入烤箱，燒烤時間需2小時）。

■ 餐廳做法通常將鴨去全骨：先將鴨頭頸剁去，由頸口將皮翻起，順著緊裹在背骨周圍的筋及肉，慢慢用刀割開（圖1）翅膀關節部切開（圖2）腿部關節處及尾端切開（圖3）整隻鴨去骨完成（圖4）。

糯 米 鴨 Eight-Treasure Duckling

材料：6人份 6 servings

1 duckling (4 lbs.)
① ⎰ dried shrimp ⎱
　⎮ pre-softened Chinese black mushrooms ⎮ Combined
　⎨ diced carrot ⎬ ingredients
　⎮ diced bamboo shoot ⎮ should
　⎮ green peas ⎮ equal
　⎩ diced Chinese ham ⎭ 1 cup

② ⎰ 1 C. glutinous rice ⎱
　 ⎩ 1½ C. water ⎭
③ ⎰ ½ t. salt ⎱
　⎮ ¼ t. MSG ⎮
　⎨ ¼ t. black pepper ⎬
　⎮ 1 T. soy sauce ⎮
　⎩ 6 C. oil for deep-frying ⎭

④ ⎰ 2 stalks green onion ⎱
　⎮ (scallion) ⎮
　⎮ 2 slices ginger root ⎮
　⎨ 4 T. soy sauce ⎬
　⎮ 1 t. sugar ⎮
　⎮ 1 star anise ⎮
　⎩ 3½ C. water ⎭

❶ Rinse duckling thoroughly; drain. Rinse rice in cold water until water runs clear; place in 1½C. water and soak 1 hour.

❷ Heat pan and 4T. oil; stir-fry ① over medium heat until fragrant; add ② and ③; saute about 5 minutes until dry (filling). Stuff filling into cavity of duckling, sew up cavity openings with thread or secure closed with toothpicks.

❸ Rub duckling exterior with 1T. soy sauce; heat oil for deep-frying; deep-fry duckling until golden brown; remove and drain. Place duckling in a pressure cooker with ④ *; cook about 1 hour over medium heat. (Meat should be very tender and sauce should be thick and equal to about 1 cup). Remove thread or toothpicks; place duckling on serving plate. Pour sauce over duckling and serve.

* If you have no pressure cooker, reduce water in ④ to 2C. and bake for 2 hours at 350° in a covered casserole.

■ In restaurant, they usually debone duckling, but avoid to piece the skin of duckling. To debone duckling: Cut off head of duckling; roll skin inside out at neck; using blade of cleaver, cut away meat from bones to shoulder (Fig. 1). Cut through skin and meat at shoulder joints (Fig. 2). Lightly cut through meat at leg joint and fold back and dislodge leg sections from carcass (Fig. 3). Debone duckling to tail and turn to right side (Fig. 4).

①		②		③	
米	6杯	里肌肉	3兩	水	1½杯
水	4½杯	冬菇(泡軟)	3朵	鹽	1小匙
紅葱頭	5粒	筍	1枝	醬油	2大匙
蝦米	¼杯	紅蘿蔔	1枝	味精	1小匙
		青豆仁	3兩	胡椒	⅓小匙

❶ 紅葱頭切薄片，米、蝦米洗淨，②料各切小丁備用。

❷ 油4大匙燒熱，將紅葱頭及蝦米炒香(圖1)，加②料、青豆仁(圖2)及③料加入同炒勻後(圖3)，再加①料(圖4)盛內鍋，外鍋放水¾杯以電鍋蒸熟即可。

鹹 飯 Rainbow Rice

材料：6人份 **6 servings**

①		②		③	
6	C. rice	3	oz. pork loin	1½ C.	water
4½	C. water	3	pre-softened Chinese black mushrooms*	1 t.	salt
5	shallots	1	bamboo shoot	2 T.	soy sauce
¼	C. dried shrimp	1	medium-sized carrot	1 t.	MSG
		¼	lb. green peas	⅓ t.	black pepper

❶ Mince shallots; rinse rice until water runs clear; drain. Rinse dried shrimp and dice ingredients in ② .

❷ Heat pan and 4T. oil; stir-fry shallots and diredr shrimp until fragrant (Fig. 1); add ② , green peas (Fig. 2) and ③ . Cover and allow liquid to come to a boil (Fig. 3); add ① (Fig. 4) and let boil 3 minutes covered, over high heat; turn heat to low and cook 7 minutes. Remove and serve.

* Soak Chinese mushrooms in warm water until soft; remove stems, discard and use caps as directed.

蟹(小)⋯6隻2斤半

① { 鹽⋯⋯⋯⋯1大匙
    薑酒⋯⋯⋯2大匙

尖糯米⋯⋯⋯2杯
蝦米⋯⋯⋯¼杯

② { 瘦肉⋯⋯⋯4兩
    芋頭(小)⋯⋯1個
    筍⋯⋯⋯⋯1枝
    紅蘿蔔⋯⋯半條
    冬菇⋯⋯⋯4朵
    毛豆⋯⋯⋯⅓杯
    炸香紅葱頭⋯2大匙

③ { 酒⋯⋯⋯1½小匙
    鹽⋯⋯⋯半小匙
    醬油⋯⋯2大匙
    味精⋯⋯1小匙
    糖⋯⋯⋯1小匙
    胡椒⋯⋯¼小匙
    麻油⋯⋯¼小匙

❶蟹身分切六塊調①料，糯米煮成飯，②料分別切丁，並將芋頭丁入鍋炸香撈起。

❷油4大匙燒熱，先將蝦米炒香，隨入②料炒熟，再放入糯米飯、炸香紅葱頭及③料炒拌均勻盛在盤上。

❸將蟹塊置糯米飯上，入鍋蒸約１５分鐘，即可供食。

■蟹的處理：用筷子直穿至蟹心處(圖１)等蟹不能動時，打開蟹殼(圖２)除腮(圖３)刷淨泥沙(圖４)。

蟹 飯 Rainbow Rice with Crab

材料：6人份 6 servings

6 live hard-shelled crabs
(about 3⅓ lbs.)

① { 1 T. salt
    2 T. ginger wine

2 C. rice
¼ C. dried shrimp

② { 4 oz. pork loin
    1 small taro root*²
    1 bamboo shoot
    ½ carrot
    4 pre-softened Chinese black mushrooms
    ⅓ C. green peas
    5 shallots, minced

③ { 1½ T. rice wine
    ½ t. salt
    2 T. soy sauce
    1 t. MSG
    1 t. sugar
    ¼ t. black pepper
    ¼ t. sesame oil

❶ Clean crab and cut into six sections; mix crab pieces with ① . Rinse rice until water runs clear; drain. Combine rice and 2C. water in a pot; bring water to a boil; cook 3 minutes over high heat. Turn heat to low, cover and cook 7 minutes*¹; dice ingredients of ② ; deep-fry taro root until fragrant; remove.

❷ Heat pan and 4T. oil; stir-fry minced shallots and dried shrimp until fragrant; add ② and stir-fry until bamboo shoot cubes are tender; add precooked rice and ③ ; portion equally on serving plates.

❸ Place crab pieces on top of rice on serving plates; steam 15 minutes; serve.

*¹ 1C. uncooked rice = 2C. cooked rice.

*² If available, substitute sweet potato.

■ To clean crab: Push a chopstick through mouth and down into the heart to kill crab (Fig. 1). When crab stops moving, remove upper shell (Fig. 2). Remove spongey gills (Fig. 3) and rinse inside with cold water, removing dirt and any runny matter (Fig. 4).

白米‥‥‥‥‥2½杯	青菜‥‥‥‥‥半斤	①{ 醬油露‥‥‥‥3大匙 猪油‥‥‥‥‥1大匙
臘腸‥‥‥‥‥3兩		
臘肉‥‥‥‥‥3兩		

❶臘腸、臘肉洗淨（圖1），臘肉除皮（圖2）備用。

❷洗淨白米，加水2½杯，大火燒開蓋鍋以中火煮2分鐘，放進臘腸、臘肉，用小火燜煮8分鐘，即可熄火，繼續燜約10分鐘。

❸青菜取嫩莖，炒熟擺於飯上，臘肉、臘腸切片（圖3、4），澆上①料即可食用。

■金銀肝、臘鴨等，依個人喜愛用之。

臘味飯　Sausage Rice Casserole　　　　材料：12人份 **12 servings**

2½ C. rice	3 oz. "Spicy Dried Pork"*	①{ 3 T. soy sauce 1 T. melted lard
3 oz. Chinese pork sausage	⅔ lb. green cabbage	

❶ Rinse sausage and dried pork; drain (Fig. 1). Remove skin from dried pork (Fig. 2).

❷ Rinse rice until water runs clear; place in earthenware pot or casserole with 2½C. water; cook over high heat until liquid comes to a boil; cover and turn heat to medium; cook 2 minutes. Arrange sausage and pork on top of rice and cover; simmer over low heat for 8 minutes; turn off heat and let sit 10 minutes.

❸ Remove any dead leaves or ends from green cabbage; heat pan and 3T. oil; stir-fry vegetable until tender; remove and arrange on rice, next to sausage. Cut sausage and pork to thin slices and arrange on top of rice (Fig. 3, 4); pour ① mixture over meat, vegetable and rice; serve.

* See P. 148 for directions on the preparation of "Spicy Dried Pork".

濕蹄筋‥‥‥‥‥‥6兩
里肌肉‥‥‥‥‥‥4兩
① 醬油‥‥‥‥1 ½ 小匙
太白粉‥‥‥1 ½ 小匙
麻油‥‥‥‥‥‥半小匙
魚漿‥‥‥‥‥‥2兩
大黃瓜‥‥‥‥‥‥1條

② 高湯‥‥‥‥‥‥6杯
鹽‥‥‥‥‥‥‥2小匙
味精‥‥‥‥‥‥1小匙
糖‥‥‥‥‥‥‥半大匙
③ 太白粉‥‥‥‥4大匙
水‥‥‥‥‥‥‥4大匙

④ 醬油‥‥‥‥‥‥2大匙
黑醋‥‥‥‥1 ½ 大匙
胡椒‥‥‥‥‥¼ 小匙
麻油‥‥‥‥‥‥半小匙
香菜‥‥‥‥‥‥半杯
熱飯‥‥‥‥‥‥6人份

❶ 濕蹄筋切為3公分長段(圖1)。里肌肉切片,拌入①料,再入魚漿拌勻。大黃瓜去皮(圖2)去籽(圖3),切滾刀塊(圖4)。
❷ 濕蹄筋及黃瓜投入②料煮熟,以小火將備好的肉片一片一片放入後,改用大火燒沸,並以③料勾汁,即熄火,加入④料,即為肉粳。
❸ 做好肉粳,酌量淋在飯上即成。
■依個人喜歡,調入辣豆瓣醬或蒜末味道更佳。

蹄筋肉粳飯 Meat Slices with Cucumber over Rice 材料:6人份 6 servings

6 oz. pork tendons *[1]
4 oz. pork loin
① 1½ t. soy sauce
1½ t. cornstarch
½ t. sesame oil
2 oz. (¼C.) fish paste *[2]
1 large cucumber

② 6 C. stock or water
2 t. salt
1 t. MSG
½ T. sugar
③ 4 T. cornstarch
4 T. water

④ 2 T. soy sauce
1½ T. worcestershire sauce
¼ t. black pepper
½ t. sesame oil
½ C. coriander or parsley
6 servings hot, precooked rice *[3]

❶ Cut pork tendons into pieces 1-inch long (Fig. 1); cut pork loin into paper-thin slices; mix with ① ; add fish paste. Remove skin (Fig. 2) and seeds (Fig. 3) from cucumber; cut into chunks (Fig. 4).
❷ Add pork tendons and cucumber pieces to ② ; cook over low heat until cucumber is tender; add pork slices piece by piece, making sure that each slice is thoroughly coated with fish paste; turn up heat to high and cook until pork slices change color; add ③ to thicken. Turn off heat and add ④ (sauce).
❸ Place rice servings on serving plates; portion sauce equally over rice. Serve.
*[1] You may substitute pork loin.
*[2] Follow step ❶ on Page 152 for making fish paste; use as directed.
*[3] See Page 76 step ❶ for directions for cooking rice and quantity.
■ You may add chopped garlice or hot bean paste to ④ for extra flavor.

78

① 雞肉‥‥‥‥‥‥‥‥‥‥ 1 2 兩
　鹽‥‥‥ ¾ 小匙 、 麻油‥‥ ¼ 小匙
　味精‥‥ 半小匙 、 水 ‥‥‥ 3 大匙
　糖‥‥‥ 半小匙 、 太白粉‥ 1 大匙
　胡椒‥‥ ¼ 小匙

金針菜‥‥‥ 半兩
乾木耳‥‥‥ ¼ 兩
青江菜‥‥ 1 2 棵
雞蛋‥‥‥‥ 3 個

② 高湯‥‥‥‥ 6 杯
　鹽‥‥‥‥ 2 小匙
　味精‥‥‥ 1 小匙
　糖‥‥‥‥ 1 小匙

③ 太白粉‥ 4 大匙
　水‥‥‥‥ 4 大匙

④ 蒜末‥‥ 2 大匙
　醬油‥‥ 2 大匙
　麻油‥‥ 半小匙
　胡椒‥‥ ¼ 小匙
　熱飯‥‥ 6 人份

❶ 雞肉切片，調入①料，金針菜（泡軟）去硬梗打結，木耳（泡軟）切半，青江菜煮熟在水裏泡冷撈出，雞蛋打散。

❷ ②料燒沸，將醃好的雞肉一片一片放入後，續入金針、木耳、青江菜燒開，以③料勾成薄糊狀，再把蛋（打散）徐徐倒入，立即熄火，隨入④料，並澆上油 1 大匙即成雞肉粳。

❸ 做好的雞肉粳，酌量淋在飯上即可。

■ 雞胸除骨取肉：在翅膀關節處切開（圖1）將白色筋割斷（圖2）先拉開一邊（圖3）兩邊一起拉（圖4）。

雞肉粳飯 Chicken Slices with Vegetables over Rice 材料：6人份 6 servings

1　lb.　raw, chicken meat
① ¾　t.　salt
　½　t.　MSG
　½　t.　sugar
　¼　t.　black pepper
　¼　t.　sesame oil
　3　T.　water
　1　T.　cornstarch

½　C.　dried tiger lily buds
¼　C.　dried wood ears
12　stalks green cabbage *¹
3　eggs
② 6　C.　stock or water
　2　t.　salt
　1　t.　MSG
　1　t.　sugar

③ {4　T.　cornstarch
　{4　T.　water
④ {2　T.　chopped garlic
　{2　T.　soy sauce
　{½　t.　sesame oil
　{¼　t.　black pepper
6　servings hot, precooked rice *²

❶ Cut chicken meat into paper-thin slices; mix with ① . Remove hard end from tiger lily buds and discard; soak in warm water until soft (about 10 minutes); tie each into a knot. Soak wood ears until expanded; cut into half. Precook green vegetable; remove and plunge into cold water; drain, beat eggs lightly.

❷ Let ② come to a boil; add chicken slices, one piece at a time; add tiger lily knots, wood ear halves, precooked vegetable; bring liquid to a boil; add ③ to thicken. Slowly add eggs in a thin stream; turn off heat and add ④ ; gently mix together (sauce).

❸ Place rice servings on individual plates; portion sauce equally over rice. Serve.

*¹ Green cabbage is the pictured vegetable and may be purchased at a Chinese grocery store. If unavailable, substitute spinach or watercress.

*² See Page 76 for directions for cooking rice and quantity.

■ To debone chicken breast: (Fig. 1) Fold under skin to expose shoulder joints. (Fig. 2) Cut through skin and meat at shoulder joints. (Fig. 3) Pull meat from each side at shoulder joint down to mid-section of carcass. (Fig. 4) Gather 2 side pieces in one hand and continue pulling meat from carcass.

①{
牛肉……………1 斤
葱………………2 枝
薑………………2 片
辣豆瓣醬………1 小匙
黑豆瓣醬………1 大匙
醬油……………半杯
}

②{
水………………6 杯
味精……………半小匙
花椒……………半小匙
八角……………1 朵
白蘿蔔…………1 條
}

③{
太白粉…………4 大匙
水………………4 大匙
熱飯……………6 人份
}

❶ 牛肉、白蘿蔔洗淨,均切成1寸半之塊狀(圖1、2、3、4)。
❷ 油3大匙燒熱,將①料按照其順序炒香後,放入酒1大匙、②料,連同牛肉移入快鍋,以中火燒煮約
25分鐘,再放入白蘿蔔煮約10分鐘,熟了以③料勾茨,即可淋在熱飯上。

蘿蔔牛肉飯 Spicy Beef-Turnip Stew

材料：6 人份 6 servings

1⅓ lbs. rump roast of beef
①{
2 stalks green onion
2 slices ginger root
1 t. hot bean paste ("la do ban jiang")
1 T. black bean paste ("la do ban jiang")*1
½ C. soy sauce
}

②{
6 C. water
½ t. MSG
½ t. Szechuan peppercorns
1 t. star anise
}
1 medium-sized turnip*2
③{
4 T. cornstarch
4 T. water
}
6 servings hot, precooked rice*3

❶ Rinse turnip; drain. Cut beef rump and turnip into bite-sized pieces. (Fig. 1, 2, 3, 4)
❷ Heat pan and 3T. oil; add ingredients of ① in descending order and stir-fry until fragrant; add 1T. rice wine and ②.
Place mixture and beef pieces in a pressure cooker; cook over medium heat for 25 minutes. (meat should be very tender)*4
Add turnip pieces and cook 10 minutes; add ③ to thicken (sauce). Place rice on serving plates; portion sauce over rice and serve.

*1 You may substitute sweet bean paste ("tien mien jiang").
*2 You may substitute icicle radishes or potato.
*3 See Page 76 step ❶ for directions for cooking rice and quantity.
*4 If you have no pressure cooker, place mixture and beef pieces in a covered casserole and cook 1 hours over low heat.

高湯…………6杯	豆腐…………1½塊	嫩薑絲………3大匙
打結海帶………4兩	① { 鹽…………1½小匙 味精…………半小匙	

❶ 高湯燒開，放入海帶中火燒煮約１０分鐘，隨加豆腐（切小丁），並調①料，待滾，洒上薑絲，即可供食。

■ 高湯做法：將雞骨放入開水內川燙（圖１）撈出（圖２）鍋內備水放入雞骨、葱、薑、酒，水開後改小火慢煮１小時（圖３）。

海帶豆腐湯 Seaweed-Bean Curd Broth

材料：6人份 **6 servings**

6 C. stock
4 oz. seaweed knots*

1½ squares bean curd
① { 1½ t. salt
½ t. MSG

3 T. shredded ginger root

❶ Heat stock until boiling; add seaweed knots; cook 10 minutes over medium heat; add bean curd (cut into cubes) and ①. Bring to a boil and add shredded ginger. Serve.

* This type of seaweed, also called "kombo" in Japanese, is available at any Japanese grocery store. Cut each piece into bite-size pieces and tie each piece into a knot.

■ To prepare stock: Heat boiling water and blanch chicken bones (Fig. 1). Remove chicken and drain (Fig. 2). Refill pan with water; add chicken bones, green onion, ginger and rice wine. Heat water until boiling; turn heat to low and simmer 1 hour (Fig. 3).

①	猪排…………… 1 斤 醬油………… 2 大匙 酒…………… 半大匙 水…………… 4 大匙 太白粉……… 1 大匙	②	洋葱絲………… 3 杯 青豆仁 洋菇片 } 1 杯 紅辣椒(切絲)… 1 條	③	醬油………… 4 大匙 黑醋………… 2 大匙 番茄醬……… 4 大匙 糖…………… 4 大匙 味精………… 1 小匙 水…………… 1 杯	④	太白粉……… 半大匙 水…………… 1 大匙 熱飯………… 6 人份

❶將猪排切六片拍鬆，調入①料醃 1 小時。

❷油 4 大匙燒熱，把醃好的猪排，兩面煎呈金黃色暫時鏟出，餘油炒軟洋葱絲，並放入②料略炒後，再把
③料及煎好之猪排放進燒煮約 4 分鐘，以④料勾芡即可淋在熱飯上。

■洋葱切法：洋葱切去兩端後(圖1)切半除皮(圖2)由中層剝開(圖3)全部切絲(圖4)。

洋葱排骨飯 Chinese Steak over Rice　　　　材料：6 人份　6 servings

① { 1⅓ lbs.(about 6 slices) pork chops
2　T.　soy sauce
½　T.　rice wine
4　T.　water
1　T.　cornstarch

② { 3　C.　onion, shredded
½　C.　green peas
½　C.　mushrooms
1　hot red pepper, shredded

③ { 4　T.　soy sauce
2　T.　worcestershire sauce
4　T.　tomato ketchup
4　T.　sugar
1　t.　MSG
1　C.　water

④ { ½　T.　cornstarch
1　T.　water
6　servings hot, precooked rice*

❶ Using blunt end of cleaver, pound pork chops lightly to tenderize; mix with ① and let soak 1 hour.

❷ Heat pan and 4T. oil; fry pork chops on each side until golden brown; remove. Reheat pan and oil, stir-fry onion and
add ② and ③ ; add fried pork chops and let boil 4 minutes; add ④ to thicken (sauce). Place rice on serving plates;
portion pork chops and sauce over rice and serve.

* For directions on cooking rice and quantity see P. 76 step ❶.

■ To shred onions: (Fig. 1) Cut off ends from onions. (Fig. 2) Cut in half, remove skin. (Fig. 3) Remove inner layers from
each half. (Fig. 4) Shred.

百葉............3 張	絞肉............3 兩	水............6 杯	空心油豆腐...12 個
①{ 小蘇打......1 小匙	醬油......半大匙	③{ 鹽......1½ 小匙	細粉............半包
清水......1 杯	②{ 味精......¼ 小匙	味精......¾ 小匙	小白菜............3 棵
	麻油......⅛ 小匙	麻油......⅛ 小匙	葱花............半大匙
	胡椒......⅛ 小匙	胡椒......⅛ 小匙	
	太白粉......1 小匙		

❶ 將①料備妥（圖1），攪拌待溶化放入百葉（圖2）泡軟後撈出（圖3）用清水洗淨至無鹼味（圖4），瀝乾水份。絞肉拌入②料，每張百葉切半舖滿肉捲成筒狀，切3公分長。油豆腐切塊，細粉以熱水泡軟，小白菜切3公分長段備用。

❷ 將③料燒沸先放入百葉捲燒開後，再加油豆腐、細粉與小白菜煮熟熄火並灑葱花即成。

油豆腐細粉湯 Bean Curd-Rice Noodle Soup   材料：6 人份 6 servings

3 sheets bean curd wrappers	3 oz. chopped pork	6 C. stock or water	12 squares deep-fried bean curd
①{ ¼ t. baking soda	½ T. soy sauce	1½ t. salt	½ package bean threads
1 C. water	¼ t. MSG	③{ ¾ t. MSG	3 stalks white Chinese cabbage*[1]
	②{ ⅛ t. sesame oil	⅛ t. sesame oil	1 t. chopped green onion
	⅛ t. black pepper	⅛ t. black pepper	
	1 t. cornstarch		

❶ Dissolve baking soda in water (Fig. 1), soak bean curd wrappers in this liquid (Fig. 2), remove wrappers when soft*[2] (Fig. 3); lightly rinse until water runs clear (Fig. 4). Mix chopped pork with ② ; cut each bean curd wrapper into half; spread a portion of chopped pork mixture over surface of bean curd skin; roll up jelly-roll-style into a long roll and cut into 1-inch sections. Cut fried bean curd into bite-size pieces. Soak bean threads in warm water until soft (about 5 min.); remove and drain. Cut vegetable into 1-inch long sections.

❷ Bring ③ to a boil; add bean curd roll sections and when liquid comes to a boil, add fried bean curd, bean threads and vegetable sections. Allow liquid to boil once more and then turn off heat; add chopped green onion and serve.

*[1] White Chinese cabbage is the pictured green Chinese vegetable which may be purchased at a Chinese grocery store. If unavailable, substitute spinach.

*[2] Bean curd wrappers should be slightly firm instead of very soft, to prevent tearing while rolling.

紋肉⋯⋯⋯⋯6兩

① 紅葱頭⋯⋯⋯⋯5粒
酒⋯⋯⋯⋯⋯1大匙
醬油⋯⋯⋯⋯半杯
水⋯⋯⋯⋯⋯1½杯
糖⋯⋯⋯⋯⋯1小匙
味精⋯⋯⋯⋯半小匙
五香粉⋯⋯⋯⅛小匙

熱飯⋯⋯⋯⋯6人份

❶紅葱頭切除鬚根(圖1)剝去外皮(圖2)切片(圖3)。

❷豬油4大匙,以中火將紅葱頭炒香呈金黃色(圖4),再放入絞肉略炒,加進①料燒開,改用小火燒煮約1小時即成。

滷肉飯 Spicy Chopped Pork over Rice

材料:6人份 **6 servings**

6 oz. chopped pork

5 shallots
① 1 T. rice wine
½ C. soy sauce
1 C. water
1½ t. sugar
½ t. MSG
⅛ t. five-spice powder

6 servings hot, precooked rice*

❶ Cut off roots (Fig. 1), remove skin from shallots (Fig. 2), mince (Fig. 3).

❷ Heat pan and 4T. oil; saute shallots until golden (Fig. 4) and add chopped pork; briefly stir-fry and add ① Cook covered 1 hour over low heat. Portion meat over rice servings and serve.

* See "Rainbow Rice With Crab" step ❶ for directions on cooking rice and quantity.

■ You may use ① to cook "Spicy Hard Boiled Eggs", "Spicy Chicken", "Fried Bean Curd" etc. Substitute meat, egg etc. and cook as directed for chopped pork.

番茄··············· 1 個		水··············· 6 杯	
豆腐··············· 1 塊	①	鹽··············· 2 小匙	
雞蛋··············· 2 個		味精··········· 1 小匙	
	②	葱花··········· 2 大匙	
		胡椒··········· $\frac{1}{4}$ 小匙	

❶ 番茄(先去皮)豆腐各切小丁，雞蛋打勻備用。

❷ ①料燒開後加入番茄、豆腐中火煮３分鐘，即可將打勻蛋汁徐徐加入待滾，立即熄火，倒入湯碗內上洒②料即成。

■ 番茄處理法：番茄用刀劃十字(圖１)在開水內川燙至皮翻起時撈起(圖２)，去皮(圖３)切丁(圖４)。

番茄蛋花湯 Tomato-Egg Flower Soup

材料：6 人份 6 servings

1	medium tomato		6 C. water
1	square bean curd	①	2 t. salt
2	eggs		1 t. MSG
		②	2 T. chopped green onion
			¼ t. black pepper

❶ Dice tomato and bean curd; lightly beat eggs.

❷ Bring ① to a boil; add tomato and bean curd; simmer over medium heat for 3 minutes.
Slowly add eggs in a thin stream; turn off heat; pour into large soup bowl; add ② and serve.

■ To dice tomato: (Fig. 1) Make 2 light diagonal cuts across top of tomato. (Fig. 2) Blanch tomato in boiling water; remove. (Fig. 3) Peel away skin. (Fig. 4) Dice.

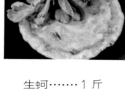

①{	生蚵……1斤 唐好菜……1斤 雞蛋……6個	②{	番薯粉…1½杯 、 酒……1大匙 水……4½杯 、 胡椒…半小匙 鹽……2小匙 、 韭菜……1杯 味精……1小匙 （切0.5公分片）	③{	海山醬…半杯 、 太白粉…1大匙 番茄醬…¼杯 、 水…………1杯 糖……¼杯 、 麻油……1大匙 熱飯………………6人份

❶生蚵洗淨，瀝乾水份，唐好菜洗淨，②料調好，以上各分6等份。

❷油2大匙燒熱將蚵散洒於鍋內（圖1）將1份②料倒入鍋內（圖2），隨即將鍋轉動，使厚薄均一呈圓形俟②料凝固時放入蛋液（圖3）再放唐好菜（圖4）翻面煎熟。

❸將③料燒開淋在蚵煎上，喜食辣者加辣豆瓣醬與飯一起供食。

■生蚵即生蠔。

■如無唐好菜，可用小白菜、空心菜、生菜、芹菜、香菜……等青菜代替。

蚵仔煎燴飯 Fried Oyster Omelet over Rice　　材料：6人份　6 servings

①{	1⅓ lbs. fresh oysters 1½ C. chopped celery 6 eggs	②{	1½ C. potato flour*1 4½ C. water 2 t. salt 1 t. MSG 1 T. rice wine ½ t. black pepper 1 C. Chinese chives or leeks, minced.*2	③{	½ C. "hai shan jiang" (hoisin sauce) ¼ C. tomato ketchup ¼ C. sugar 1 T. cornstarch 1 C. water 1 T. sesame oil 6 servings hot, precooked rice*3

❶ Divide oysters, celery and ② into 6 equal portions.

❷ Heat pan and 2T. oil; add 1 group of oysters (Fig. 1) and 1 group of ② (Fig. 2). Rotate pan so that mixture is distributed evenly and thinly over bottom of pan; When mixture hardens, add 1 beaten egg (Fig. 3) and celery (Fig. 4). Continue rotating pan over fire to prevent omelet from sticking (add more oil if necessary). When egg becomes firm, flip over to uncooked side cook about 3 minutes; remove and place omlet on rice.

*1 If unavailable, substitute cornstarch.

*2 You may substitute green onions.

*3 See Page 76 step ❶ for directions for cooking rice and quantity.

■ Hot bean paste may be added to ③ for extra spiciness.

雞‥‥‥‥‥‥‥‥1 隻 　　味精‥‥‥‥‥‥1 小匙
金針菜‥‥‥‥‥‥半兩 　② 麻油‥‥‥‥‥‥1 小匙
① 酒‥‥‥‥‥‥‥1 大匙 　　葱花‥‥‥‥‥‥1 大匙
　 鹽‥‥‥‥‥‥‥2 小匙
　 清水‥‥‥‥‥‥6 杯

雞剁塊在開水內川燙撈出，金針菜泡軟打結，放入①料內燉約３０分鐘，再加②料即可。
■雞剁塊時：先由胸部剖開成二半(圖１)除下雞翼(圖２)剁半(圖３)分剁小塊(圖４)。

金針燉雞 Chicken and Tiger Lily Broth 材料：6 人份 6 servings

1 whole chicken (about 2⅔lbs.)　　　1 t. MSG
½ C. dried tiger lily buds　　　② 1 t. sesame oil
① 1 T. rice wine　　　　　　　　　　1 T. chopped green onion
　2 t. salt
　6 C. water

Rinse chicken; cut through bone into bite-size pieces. Soak tiger lily buds until soft; discard bitter ends; tie each into a knot. Combine chicken pieces, tiger lily knots and ① in a pan and steam 30 minutes over medium heat; add ② and serve.
■ To cut chicken: (Fig. 1) Cut chicken lengthwise in half from mid-breast. (Fig. 2) Cut off wings. (Fig. 3) Cut each chicken half into two. (Fig. 4) Cut each quarter into bite-size pieces.

小排骨…………1斤

① 豆豉…………3大匙
蒜末…………1大匙
葱末…………1大匙
薑末…………1大匙

② 酒…………半大匙
醬油…………5大匙
糖…………1½小匙
熱飯…………6人份

❶小排骨切約３０塊。豆豉輕洗備用。

❷油4大匙燒熱，放進小排骨爆出油，用鍋鏟，鏟到一邊，以中火將①料炒香，再下②料並把全部材料炒拌均勻，燒煮１分鐘盛起，置中碗蒸約４０分鐘。

■葱末：用刀直劃（圖１）再切碎（圖２）。
■薑末：先切片（圖３）切絲再切碎（圖４）

蒸蛋：將蛋３個、酒１小匙、鹽１小匙、醬油１大匙、味精半小匙、猪油半小匙、蒜頭１個（拍破）芹菜或葱末半大匙、水1¾杯盛碗內調好，以中火蒸約５分鐘熄火，燜１０分鐘，淋於排骨飯上香嫩可口。

豉汁排骨飯 Steamed Spareribs with Black Beans over Rice

材料：6人份 **6 servings**

1⅓ lbs. spareribs

① 3 T. fermented black beans
1 T. chopped garlic
1 T. chopped green onion
1 T. chopped ginger root

② ½ T. rice wine
5 T. soy sauce
1½ t. sugar
6 servings hot, precooked rice*

❶ Cut spareribs into bite-sized pieces (about 30); lightly rinse black fermented beans; drain.
❷ Heat pan and 4T. oil; add spareribs and stir-fry over high heat for about 1 minute; push spareribs to the side of pan and stir-fry ① until fragrant. Add ② and mix together; stir-fry 1 minute and place in bowl in steamer. Steam 40 minutes and portion over rice. Serve.
* See P. 76 step ❶ for directions for cooking rice and quantity.
■ To chop green onion: Holding blade upright, make 2-3 parallel cuts in stalk (Fig. 1). Mince (Fig. 2).
■ To chop ginger: Cut ginger into paper-thin slices (Fig. 3). Shred slices and chop (Fig. 4).

Steamed Egg Pudding

3 eggs
1 t. rice wine
1 t. salt
1 T. soy sauce
½ t. MSG
½ t. lard or sesame oil
1 clove garlic, smashed
½ t. chopped green onion or celery
1¾ C. water

Mix all of the ingredients together and beat lightly. Steam covered 5 minutes; turn off heat and let sit covered in steamer 10 minutes. Serve with spareribs and rice.

豆腐‥‥‥‥‥‥‥ 1 塊　　　　　高湯‥‥‥‥‥‥‥‥ 6 杯　　　　　胡椒‥‥‥‥‥‥ 1/4 小匙

小白菜‥‥‥‥‥ 半斤　　①{ 鹽‥‥‥‥‥‥‥‥ 2 小匙　　②{ 麻油‥‥‥‥‥‥ 1 小匙

　　　　　　　　　　　　　　味精‥‥‥‥‥‥‥ 1 小匙

❶豆腐橫切二片(圖 1)再分切小塊(圖 2)白菜切除根部(圖 3)切成 4 公分長段(圖 4)。

❷①料燒開，將豆腐、白菜放入待滾再加②料即成。

白菜豆腐湯 Bean Curd and Vegetable Soup　　　材料：6 人份 6 servings

1　square bean curd
⅔　lb. white Chinese cabbage*

①{
6　C.　stock or water
2　t.　salt
1　t.　MSG

②{
¼　t.　black pepper
1　t.　sesame oil

❶　Cut bean curd in half (Fig. 1); cut again into bite-size pieces (Fig. 2); remove hard stem of white Chinese cabbage (Fig. 3); cut into 1-inch sections (Fig. 4).

❷　Bring ① to a boil; add bean curd and cabbage; Let liquid boil; add ② and boil a few more minutes. Serve.

*　White Chinese cabbage is the pictured green Chinese vegetable which may be purchased at a Chinese grocery store. If unavailable, substitute spinach.

牛肉………１２兩　　「炸油」‥３杯　　　　酒……１小匙、醋………３大匙　　　太白粉‥‥４大匙
醬油………２大匙　　洋葱……１個　　　　鹽…１½小匙、番茄醬…２大匙　　③水………４大匙
酒………半大匙　　番茄……２個　　②醬油…４大匙、麻油……１小匙　　熱飯……６人份
①小蘇打…半小匙　　荷蘭豆…２兩　　　味精…１小匙、水………４杯
水………３大匙　　　　　　　　　　　　　糖……３大匙
太白粉…１⅓大匙
沙拉油……１大匙

❶牛肉切片調①料拌醃約１小時，洋葱、番茄各切塊，荷蘭豆去硬筋。

❷把牛肉泡熟，撈起留油４大匙，將洋葱炒香，隨加番茄及②料燒開，放入荷蘭豆，並以③料勾汁再放
　入泡熟牛肉攪勻，酌量淋在飯上即可供食。

■牛肉泡油法：「炸油」燒熱(需將鍋燒熱再放油)，暫離火用鍋鏟將油澆勻鍋面，倒入拌好的牛肉(圖１)
　鏟開改大火(圖２)顏色轉白立即撈出(圖３)。

番茄牛肉燴飯 Stir-Fried Beef with Vegetables over Rice

材料：6人份 **6 servings**

	1 lb. flank steak		3 C. oil for frying		1 t. rice wine	4 T. cornstarch,
	2 T. soy sauce		1 medium-sized onion		1½ t. salt	4 T. water
①	½ T. rice wine		2 medium-sized tomatoes		4 T. soy sauce	6 servings hot, precooked rice*
	½ t. baking soda		1 C. snow peas		1 t. MSG	
	3 T. water			②	3 T. sugar	
	1⅓ T. cornstarch				3 T. vinegar	
	1 T. oil				2 T. tomato ketchup	
					1 t. sesame oil	
					4 C. water	

❶ Cut flank steak into paper-thin slices; mix with ① ; let soak 1 hour. Cut onion and tomato into bite-size pieces. Cut off stems and ends from snow peas; pull away any "stringy" veins.

❷ Heat oil until medium hot; add flank steak slices and deep-fry until color changes; remove and drain.　Drain all but 4T. oil from pan; reheat and add onion; stir-fry until fragrant; add tomato and ② . Heat liquid until boiling and add snow peas; add ③ to thicken, then add precooked meat slices and portion over rice. Serve.

*　See P. 76 step ❶ for directions for cooking rice and quantity.

■ To stir-fry beef: Heat pan until very hot; add 4-5T. oil and swirl this around in pan to coat surface; pour out oil. Heat pan again; add 3C. oil and heat until medium hot. Add meat slices (Fig. 1); stir slices to separate and turn heat to high (Fig. ; when meat changes color, remove and drain (Fig. 3).

小排骨‥‥‥‥‥‥半斤
苦瓜‥‥‥‥‥‥１２兩
豆豉‥‥‥‥‥‥１大匙
小魚乾‥‥‥‥‥２大匙

① 酒‥‥‥‥‥‥‥１小匙
　 鹽‥‥‥‥‥‥‥２小匙
　 醬油‥‥‥‥‥‥１小匙
　 清水‥‥‥‥‥‥６杯
　 味精‥‥‥‥‥‥１小匙

　小排骨、苦瓜均切塊，豆豉、小魚乾略洗（圖１），與①料放入燉約３０分鐘，加入味精即成。

■苦瓜切法：苦瓜切除兩端（圖２），用小湯匙將籽挖出（圖３）切１公分厚片（圖４）。

苦瓜燉排骨 Bitter Gourd and Sparerib Soup 材料：６人份 6 servings

⅔ lb. spareribs
1 lb. bitter gourd*[1]
1 T. fermented black beans
2 T. "small dried fish"*[2] ("syau yu gan")

① 1 t. rice wine
　 2 t. salt
　 1 t. soy sauce
　 6 C. water
　 1 t. MSG

Cut spareribs and bitter gourd (seeds already removed) into bite-size pieces. Lightly rinse fermented black beans and dried fish (Fig. 1); drain. Put these ingredients and ① in a bowl and steam 30 minutes over medium heat. Add MSG and serve.

*[1] If unavailable, substitute squash or zucchini.

*[2] Small dried fish are available in packages in any Chinese grocery store.

◀ To cut bitter gourd: (Fig. 2) Cut end tips (discard). (Fig. 3) Use a teaspoon to remove seeds. (Fig. 4) Cut in ½-inch-thick sections.

鴨‥‥‥‥‥‥‥ 1 隻
醬油‥‥‥‥‥‥ 6 大匙
「炸油」‥‥‥‥‥ 6 杯

① {
葱‥‥‥‥‥‥‥ 2 枝
薑‥‥‥‥‥‥‥ 2 片
酒‥‥‥‥‥‥‥ 1 大匙
鹽‥‥‥‥‥‥‥ 1 小匙
糖‥‥‥‥‥‥‥ 2 小匙
八角‥‥‥‥‥‥ 1 朵
花椒粒‥‥‥‥‥ 半小匙
水‥‥‥‥‥‥‥ 2½ 杯
}

② {
太白粉‥‥‥‥‥ 4 大匙
水‥‥‥‥‥‥‥ 4 大匙
}
空心菜‥‥‥‥‥ 1 斤半
熱飯‥‥‥‥‥‥ 6 人份

❶鴨洗淨拭乾水份，以醬油6大匙塗勻鴨身，並入燒熱油鍋以大火炸至金黃色(約5分鐘)撈起，分切爲六塊，置快鍋內，加①料及塗鴨剩餘之醬油燒煮約15分鐘，試其鹹淡。

❷將鴨取起，置飯上，燒鴨餘汁以②料勾成薄糊狀，淋於鴨肉上，並將炒好空心菜放在旁邊，即可供食。

■剁鴨塊時，先剁下頭頸(圖1)由胸部剖開(圖2)成二半(圖3)每半份切三塊(圖4)。

紅鴨燴飯 Red Duckling over Rice

材料：6人份 **6 servings**

1 duckling (about 4lbs.)
6 T. soy sauce
6 C. oil for frying

① {
2 stalks green onion
2 slices ginger root
1 T. rice wine
1 t. salt
2 t. sugar
1 star anise
½ t. Szechuan peppercorns
2½ C. water
}

② {
4 T. cornstarch
4 T. water
}
2 lb. green vegetable*[1]
6 servings hot, precooked rice*[2]

❶ Rinse duckling; drain. Rub outside and inside cavity completely with 6T. soy sauce; drain duckling and retain thi͓ liquid. Heat oil for deep-frying; ease duckling into oil and deep-fry for about 5 minutes over high heat until golde͓ brown; remove and drain. Cut duckling (through bones) into 6 sections; place duckling pieces, ① and retained liqui͓ in pressure cooker and cook 15 minutes over medium heat*[3], season to taste.

❷ Remove duckling pieces and place 1 piece on each portion of rice; heat soup until boiling and add ② to thicken; pou͓ over duckling pieces and rice. Heat pan and 3T. oil until very hot; add vegetable, 1t. salt and ½t. MSG and stir-fry for 1͓ minutes over very high heat (add a little water if vegetable is too dry); remove and place next to duckling on serving plat͓ Serve.

*[1] "Kong syin tsai" is the pictured vegetable and may be purchased at a Chinese grocery store. If unavailable, substitute spinac͓
*[2] See P. 76 step ❶ for directions for cooking rice and quantity.
*[3] If no pressure cooker is available, cook in a covered casserole for 1 hour and 20 minutes over medium heat.

■ To cut duckling: (Fig. 1) Cut off head at neck. (Fig. 2) Beginning at breast, cut lengthwise. (Fig. 3) Continue cuttin͓ down through body into two. (Fig. 4) Cut each half into 6 pieces.

里肌肉‥‥‥‥‥３兩 　　榨菜‥‥‥‥‥１½兩

①{
酒‥‥‥‥‥‥半小匙
鹽‥‥‥‥‥‥¼小匙
太白粉‥‥‥‥１小匙
水‥‥‥‥‥‥１½大匙
}

②{
高湯‥‥‥‥‥‥６杯
鹽‥‥‥‥‥‥‥１小匙
味精‥‥‥‥‥‥⅓小匙
}

③{
胡椒‥‥‥‥‥‥¼小匙
麻油‥‥‥‥‥‥１小匙
}

❶里肌肉切絲調入①料拌勻，榨菜切絲。

❷將②料燒沸，放入里肌肉及榨菜，燒開後放入③料即成。

■肉絲切法：由中間入刀（圖１）將白筋切除（圖２）切片（圖３）切絲（圖４）。

榨菜肉絲湯 Shredded Pork and Pickled Mustard Green Soup

材料：６人份 **6 servings**

①{
3　oz. pork loin
½　t.　rice wine
¼　t.　salt
1　t.　cornstarch
1½ T. water
}

②{
¾　C. Szechuan pickled mustard green*, shredded
6　C. stock
1　t.　salt
⅓　t.　MSG
}

③{
¼　t.　black pepper
1　t.　sesame oil
}

❶ Shredd pork loin; mix with ① .

❷ Heat ② until boiling; add pork loin and stir liquid to separate meat shreds; add pickled vegetable and heat liquid until boiling; add ③ . Serve.

　Available fresh or in cans in a Chinese grocery store.

■ To shred pork loin: (Fig. 1) Make a cut into loin at halfway mark. (Fig. 2) Holding ½ firmly, slide blade of cleaver along white membrane to separate meat and tendon; repeat for other half of loin. (Fig. 3) Slice loin into paper-thin pieces. (Fig. 4) Shred.

里肌肉⋯⋯4兩

① 醬油⋯⋯半大匙　酒⋯⋯半小匙　水⋯⋯1½大匙　太白粉⋯1小匙

② 洋葱⋯⋯1個　冬菇⋯⋯6朵　筍⋯⋯1枝　紅蘿蔔⋯半條

③ 青豆⋯⋯3兩　水⋯⋯3杯　鹽⋯⋯1½小匙　糖⋯⋯1大匙

④ 醬油⋯⋯4大匙　胡椒⋯⋯¼小匙　麻油⋯⋯1小匙　黑醋⋯1½大匙　味精⋯⋯1小匙

⑤ 太白粉⋯⋯3大匙　水⋯⋯3大匙　雞蛋⋯⋯6個　熱飯⋯⋯6人份

❶ 里肌肉切絲調入①料，把②料切絲備用。

❷ 油半杯燒熱，將肉炒開鏟出，留油4大匙先炒洋葱，再入冬菇、筍、紅蘿蔔及③料燒滾，放入青豆，煮約2分鐘，再入肉絲及④料，最後以⑤料勾汁，淋在飯上。

❸ 雞蛋煎至半熟，與飯供食。

■ 筍絲切法：筍修去老皮(圖1、2)先切片(圖3)再切絲(圖4)。

家常燴飯　Everyday Rice

材料：6人份　**6 servings**

4 oz. pork loin

① ½ T. soy sauce / ½ t. rice wine / 1½ T. water / 1 t. cornstarch

② 1 medium onion / 6 Chinese black mushrooms, pre-softened* / 1 bamboo shoot / ½ carrot

③ ⅓ C. green peas / 3 C. water / 1½ t. salt / 1 T. sugar

④ 4 T. soy sauce / ¼ t. black pepper / 1 t. sesame oil / 1½ T. worcestershire sauce / 1 t. MSG

⑤ 3 T. cornstarch / 3 T. water

6 eggs

6 servings hot, precooked rice*

❶ Shred pork loin and mix with ① ; shred ingredients of ② .

❷ Heat pan and ½C. oil until medium hot; stir-fry pork, separating shreds until color changes; remove. Drain all but 4T oil from pan; reheat and add onion, stir-fry until soft; add black mushroom, bamboo shoot and carrot shreds and ③ Let liquid come to a boil and add green peas; cook 2 minutes over medium heat; add pork shreds and ④ Add ⑤ to thicken and portion over rice.

❸ Heat pan and 2T. oil; fry egg and place sunny-side up on serving plates as illustrated in picture. Serve.

* See P. 76 step ❶ for directions for cooking rice and quantity.

■ To shred bamboo shoot: (Fig. 1, 2) Remove any skin or hard end if necessary. (Fig. 3) Cut bamboo shoot into thin slices. (Fig. 4) Shred.

雞肫屯肝‥‥‥‥‥4付
嫩薑絲‥‥‥‥‥1大匙

① 鹽‥‥‥‥‥1½小匙
味精‥‥‥‥‥1小匙
麻油‥‥‥‥‥半小匙
胡椒‥‥‥‥‥¼小匙
酒‥‥‥‥‥1大匙

❶雞肫屯肝切片，用開水川燙撈出。
❷水6杯燒開，放入燙熟雞肫屯肝、嫩薑絲及①料即成。
■肝切法：雞肝除膽(圖1)切半(圖2)在面上劃刀(圖3)，斜切薄片(圖4)。

肫 肝 湯 Chicken Broth with Giblets and Ginger　材料：6人份　6 servings

4　pairs chicken livers
4　pairs chicken giblets
1　T. shredded ginger root

① 1½ t.　salt
1　t.　MSG
½　t.　sesame oil
¼　t.　black pepper
1　T.　rice wine

❶ Cut livers into thin slices; score kidneys lengthwise and crosswise and cut into thin slices. Blanch in boiling water (kidneys will "flower" and livers will change color); remove and drain.
❷ Heat 6C. water until boiling; add kidney and liver slices, ① and ginger shreds. Serve.
■ To cut chicken liver: Take away gall (Fig.1), separate livers (Fig. 2); score lightly (Fig. 3); diagonally cut into thin slices (Fig. 4).

里肌肉‥‥‥‥１２兩
① { 醬油‥‥‥‥１½大匙
太白粉‥‥１½大匙
② { 紅蘿蔔‥‥‥‥‥１枝
馬鈴薯‥‥‥‥‥２個

③ { 油‥‥‥‥‥‥‥‥¾杯
麵粉‥‥‥‥‥‥‥¾杯
洋葱丁‥‥‥‥‥‥１杯
咖哩粉‥‥‥‥‥３大匙
紅椒（去籽切小丁）‥１條

④ { 水‥‥‥‥‥‥‥‥６杯
酒‥‥‥‥‥‥‥１大匙
鹽‥‥‥‥‥‥‥２小匙
味精‥‥‥‥‥‥１小匙
糖‥‥‥‥‥‥‥２小匙
胡椒‥‥‥‥‥半小匙
番茄醬‥‥‥‥‥３大匙
熱飯‥‥‥‥‥‥６人份

❶ 里肌肉切約１公分四方丁，調①料拌勻後炒熟盛盤，②料去皮切丁，入鍋略炒備用。
❷ ③料以小火炒香盛碗即為麵糊。
❸ 油４大匙將洋葱丁、咖哩粉、紅椒炒香後隨入炒好②料及④料燒開，中火煮熟各料並加入肉丁，將麵糊
依個人喜好，勾成適當濃度，淋在飯上即成。
■ 麵糊炒法：鍋燒熱放油（圖１）加麵粉（圖２）小火拌炒（圖３）炒到呈淡金黃色盛起（圖４）。

咖哩肉飯 Curry Meat over Rice   材料：6人份 **6 servings**

① { 1 lb. pork loin
1½ T. soy sauce
1½ T. cornstarch
② { 1 medium-sized carrot
2 medium-sized potatoes } diced

③ { ¾ C. oil
¾ C. flour
1 C. diced onion
3 T. curry powder
1 hot red pepper, diced

④ { 6 C. water
1 T. rice wine
2 t. salt
1 t. MSG
2 t. sugar
½ t. black pepper
3 T. tomato ketchup
6 servings hot, precooked rice*

❶ Dice pork loin; mix with ① ; heat pan and 3T. oil; stir-fry meat until color changes remove and drain. Reheat oil and
stir-fry ② until fragrant; remove.   Reheat oil again and saute ③ until fragrant to make a paste, remove and set a

❷ Heat pan and 4T. oil; stir-fry onion until soft; add curry powder and hot pepper; add ② and ④ . Cook over medium
heat until carrot and potato are tender (about 3 minutes); add pork and ③ to thicken to desired consistency. Portior
over rice and serve.

*   See P. 76 step ❶ for directions for cooking rice and quantity.

■ To stir-fry flour: Reheat pan and ¾C. oil (Fig. 1); add flour (Fig. 2). Stir over low heat (Fig. 3); when flour turns golden
remove (Fig. 4).

①{ 高湯⋯⋯⋯⋯⋯⋯6杯
鹽⋯⋯⋯⋯⋯⋯2小匙
味精⋯⋯⋯⋯⋯1小匙

②{ 菠菜⋯⋯⋯⋯⋯⋯4兩
洋菇⋯⋯⋯⋯⋯1罐

❶將①料燒沸，放入備好的②料，再燒開即成。

■菠菜、洋菇切法：菠菜切除根部（圖1）切成4公分長段（圖2）洋菇去蒂（圖3）大的切半（圖4）。

洋菇菠菜湯 Mushroom and Spinach Broth　　　　材料：6人份　6 servings

①{ 6　C. stock
2　t.　salt
1　t.　MSG

②{ 4　oz. spinach
1　can button mushrooms

❶ Heat ① until boiling; add ingredients in ② ; boil 1 additional minute and serve.
■ To cut spinach: (Fig. 1) Cut off end tip. (Fig. 2) Cut into 1-inch sections.
■ To cut button mushrooms: (Fig. 3) Cut caps from stems. (Fig. 4) Cut large caps into two.

① 雞肉…………１２兩
鹽……………１小匙
酒……………半大匙
蛋白…………１個
水……………３大匙
太白粉……１⅓大匙

② 蒜頭…………５粒
豆豉…………２大匙

③ 小冬菇(泡軟)１２朵
熟紅蘿蔔……半枝
洋菇…………１杯
青椒…………２個
「炸油」………３杯

④ 酒……………１小匙
鹽……………１小匙
醬油…………４大匙
味精…………１小匙
糖……………１小匙
胡椒…………¼小匙
麻油…………１小匙
水……………３杯

⑤ 太白粉………４大匙
水……………４大匙
熱飯…………６人份

❶將雞肉用刀背拍鬆劃刀切塊(圖１、２、３、４)，調①料拌醃。②料剁碎，冬菇、紅蘿蔔、青椒各切片備用。

❷「炸油」燒熱，將雞肉泡熟撈起，留油４大匙將③料略炒盛起，另入油３大匙炒香②料，隨加④料燒開，即可放入泡熟雞肉及炒好③料，以⑤料勾汁，淋在飯上即成。

豆豉雞球燴飯 Chicken in Black Bean Sauce over Rice

材料：６人份　　**6 servings**

① 1 lb. raw chicken meat
1 t. salt
½ T. rice wine
1 egg white
3 T. water
1⅓ T. cornstarch

② 5 cloves garlic
2 T. fermented black beans

③ 12 small Chinese black mushrooms, pre-softened
½ precooked carrot
1 C. button mushrooms
2 green peppers
3 C. oil

④ 1 t. rice wine, 1 t. salt
4 T. soy sauce
1 t. MSG, 1t sugar
¼ t. black pepper
1 t. sesame oil
3 C. water

⑤ 4 T. cornstarch
4 T. water
6 servings hot, precooked rice*

❶ Score chicken meat lengthwise and crosswise; cut into bite-size pieces (Fig. 1, 2, 3, 4); mix with ① ; let soak 20 minutes. Chop ingredients in ② ; cut Chinese mushrooms, carrot and green peppers into bite-size pieces.

❷ Heat oil until medium hot; deep-fry chicken pieces until color changes; remove. Drain all but 4T. oil from pan; reheat and add ③ ; stir-fry until fragrant; remove. Reheat pan and 3T. oil; stir-fry ② until fragrant; add ④ ; let boil and add chicken meat and precooked ③ When liquid boils again, add ⑤ to thicken. Portion over rice and serve.

* See Page 76 step ❶ for directions for cooking rice and quantity.

生蠔⋯⋯⋯⋯⋯半斤
葱（拍扁）⋯⋯⋯2枝
薑（拍扁）⋯⋯⋯2片
① 酒⋯⋯⋯⋯⋯⋯1大匙
太白粉⋯⋯⋯2大匙

水⋯⋯⋯⋯⋯⋯6杯
鹽⋯⋯⋯⋯1½小匙
② 味精⋯⋯⋯⋯1小匙
豆腐⋯⋯⋯⋯1塊
鹹酸菜⋯⋯⋯1兩

薑絲⋯⋯⋯⋯2大匙
③ 胡椒⋯⋯⋯⋯¼小匙
麻油⋯⋯⋯⋯1小匙

❶將生蠔洗淨瀝乾水份，調①料拌醃，豆腐切1公分小丁，鹹酸菜切絲。
❷②料燒開，隨入生蠔待滾，立即熄火，並洒③料即可供食。
　生蠔洗法：用手輕輕漂洗（圖1）撿去売（圖2）換水數次（圖3）瀝乾（圖4）。

生蠔豆腐湯 Bean Curd and Oyster Broth　材料：6人份 6 servings

⅔ lb. fresh oysters
2 stalks green onion, smashed
2 slices ginger root, smashed
1 T. rice wine
2 T. cornstarch

② 6 C. water, 1½t. salt
1 t. MSG, 1 square bean curd
½ C. pickled cabbage, shredded

③ 2 T. shredded ginger root
¼ t. black pepper
1 t. sesame oil

Rinse oysters; drain and mix with ① ; let soak 20 minutes. Cube bean curd.
Heat ② until boiling. Add oysters one by one and let liquid come to a boil; turn off heat and add ③ ; serve.
To prepare oysters: (Fig. 1) Rinse lightly. (Fig. 2) Remove any shells and discard. (Fig. 3) Change water several times.
(Fig. 4) Drain.

① 里肌肉…3兩
醬油…半大匙
酒……半小匙
水……1大匙
太白粉1小匙

② 鴨肫肝……2付
魷魚1條…6兩
蹄筋……3兩

③ 紅蘿蔔(煮熟)…半條
筍(煮熟)……1枝
青江菜………6棵
草菇…………4兩
葱(3公分)…6枝
薑……………6片

④ 酒…1小匙、麻油…1小匙
鹽…1½小匙、水……3杯
醬油…4大匙
味精…1小匙
糖…1小匙
胡椒…¼小匙

⑤ 太白粉…4大匙
水……4大匙
熱飯…6人份

❶里肌肉切片調①料拌醃。

❷鴨肫除筋切花，鴨肝切片，魷魚斜劃花紋後切片加入薑酒1大匙及鹽1小匙，筍、紅蘿蔔各切片，青江菜對剖成2。

❸將醃過之肉，②料、③料順序在油裏炒熟盛起，油3大匙炒香葱薑，隨加④料燒開即可放入全部各料，並以⑤料勾汁酌量的淋在飯上即成。

■肫花切法：由邊剖開(圖1)剝除沙囊膜(圖2)除筋(圖3)先直切後橫切，即成肫花(圖4)。

八珍燴飯 Eight Treasures over Rice

材料：6人份 **6 servings**

① 3 oz. pork loin
½ T. soy sauce
½ t. rice wine
1 T. water
1 t. cornstarch

② 2 pairs duck gizzards
2 pairs duck liver
6 oz. fresh squid meat*[1]
3 oz. pork tendons*[1]

③ ½ precooked carrot
1 precooked bamboo shoot
6 stalks heart of green vegetable
2½ C. straw mushrooms
6 1-inch sections green onion stalk
6 slices ginger root

④ 1 t. rice wine
1½ t. salt
4 T. soy sauce
1 t. MSG
1 t. sugar
¼ t. black pepper
1 t. sesame oil
3 C. water

⑤ 4 T. cornstarch
4 T. water

6 servings hot, precooked rice*[2]

❶ Cut pork loin into paper-thin slices; mix with ① and let soak 20 minutes.
❷ Remove outside white membrane from gizzard; score meat lengthwise and crosswise; cut into bite-size pieces; cut liver into thin slices. Score squid meat lengthwise and crosswise; cut into bite-size pieces; mix gizzard, liver and squid separately with 1T. ginger wine and ½t. salt. Slice carrot and bamboo shoot into thin bite-size pieces; cut vegetable hearts into halves.
❸ Heat pan and 1C. oil; stir-fry pork slices and ② separately until color changes; remove and drain. Reheat oil and stir-fry ③ for 30 seconds; remove and drain. Drain all but 3T. oil from pan; reheat and stir-fry green onion and ginger until fragrant; add ④. Let liquid come to a boil and add above precooked ingredients; add ⑤ to thicken. Portion over rice servings and serve.
*[1] You may substitute another type of meat, fish or omit.
*[2] See Page 76 step ❶ for directions for cooking rice and quantity.
■ To score duckling gizzards: (Fig. 1) Slice gizzards in two from the side (Fig. 2) Remove any white or yellow matter (Fig. 3) Cut away white tendon from each half. (Fig. 4) Score pieces lengthwise and crosswise.

	魚肉片⋯⋯⋯⋯4兩		高湯⋯⋯⋯⋯⋯6杯	
	酒⋯⋯⋯⋯⋯半小匙	②	鹽⋯⋯⋯⋯⋯2小匙	
①	鹽⋯⋯⋯⋯¼小匙		味精⋯⋯⋯⋯1小匙	
	太白粉⋯⋯⋯1小匙	③	胡椒⋯⋯⋯⋯¼小匙	
	西洋菜⋯⋯⋯⋯6兩		麻油⋯⋯⋯⋯1小匙	

❶魚肉片調入①料拌勻，西洋菜切段。

❷將②料燒沸，放入魚肉片、西洋菜，燒開後放進③料即成。

■魚片、西洋菜切法：魚肉先切寬條（圖1），再斜切薄片（圖2）西洋菜切成4公分長段（圖3）。

西洋菜魚片湯 Watercress and Fish Broth 材料：6人份 6 servings

	4 oz. fresh fish meat		6 C. stock	
	½ t. rice wine	②	2 t. salt	
①	¼ t. salt		1 t. MSG	
	1 t. cornstarch	③	¼ t. black pepper	
	6 oz. watercress*		1 t. sesame oil	

❶ Cut fish into paper-thin slices; add ① and let soak 20 minutes. Rinse watercress and cut into 1-inch long sections.

❷ In a saucepan, heat ② until boiling; add fish slices and vegetable sections. When liquid begins to boil, add ③ . Serve.

* Watercress is the pictured Chinese vegetable. If unavailable substitute spinach.

■ To cut fish: Cut fish into wide strips (Fig. 1); diagonally cut sections into paper-thin slices (Fig. 2). Rinse watercress and cut into 1-inch sections. (Fig. 3).

猪前脚 1 隻⋯⋯⋯ 2 斤
醬油⋯⋯⋯ 1½ 大匙
葱⋯⋯⋯⋯ 2 枝
蒜頭⋯⋯⋯ 5 粒

①
酒⋯⋯⋯⋯ 1 大匙
糖⋯⋯⋯⋯ 半大匙
醬油⋯⋯⋯ ¾杯
水⋯⋯⋯⋯ 3杯
八角⋯⋯⋯ 1 朵

味精⋯⋯⋯⋯ 半小匙
熱飯⋯⋯⋯⋯ 6 人份

❶將豬蹄處理乾淨後，剁成１２塊，在開水內川燙撈出，瀝乾水份抹上醬油。葱切３公分長段，蒜頭拍破。
❷油４大匙燒熱，把葱、蒜炒香，放入豬脚炒呈金黃色取出，與①料放進快鍋煮約２０分鐘後，再加味精
即成。
■豬蹄處理法：去毛（圖１）刮除垢穢（圖２）洗淨（圖３）剁塊（圖４）。

猪蹄飯 Red-Cooked Pork Shoulder over Rice
材料：6人份 **6 servings**

2⅔lbs. fresh pork shoulder hock
1½ T. soy sauce
2 stalks green onion
5 cloves garlic

①
1 T. rice wine
½ T. sugar
¾ C. soy sauce
3 C. water
1 star anise

½ t. MSG
6 servings hot, precooked rice*1

❶ Cut pork shoulder nock (through bones) into 12 sections. Heat water until boiling and add shoulder sections; let water boil and cook briefly; drain. Rub outside of each section with 1½T. soy sauce; cut green onion stalks into 1-inch sections; smash garlic cloves.
❷ Heat pan and 4T. oil; stir-fry onion and garlic until fragrant; add pork shoulder sections and fry on all sides until golden brown. Add ① and put this entire mixture into a pressure cooker*2 cook 20 minutes over medium heat (meat should be very soft); add MSG and portion over rice servings. Serve.
*1 See Page 76 step ❶ for directions for cooking rice and quantity.
*2 If no pressure cooker is available, place ingredients in a pan with water to cover and cook covered 1 hour over medium heat. Meat should be very tender and sauce, thick, and greatly reduced in quantity.
■ To prepare pork shoulder: Remove any hair from surface (Fig. 1). Using cleaver edge, lightly scrape away dirt o matter (Fig. 2). Rinse lightly (Fig. 3) and cut shoulder into bite-size pieces (Fig. 4).

蘆筍⋯⋯⋯⋯⋯⋯ 1 罐

① 　鹽⋯⋯⋯⋯⋯⋯ 1 $\frac{1}{2}$ 小匙
　味精⋯⋯⋯⋯⋯⋯ 1 小匙
　胡椒⋯⋯⋯⋯⋯⋯ $\frac{1}{4}$ 小匙
　麻油⋯⋯⋯⋯⋯⋯半小匙
　高湯⋯⋯⋯⋯⋯⋯ 6 杯

❶將蘆筍取出(圖1)切去筍尖(圖2)切半(圖3)，連汁一起倒入①料內燒開即成。

蘆筍清湯 Asparagus Soup　　　　　　　材料：6人份 **6 servings**

1　can white asparagus

①　1½ t.　salt
　　1　t.　MSG
　　¼　t.　black pepper
　　½　t.　sesame oil
　　6　C.　stock

❶ Remove asparagus from can (Fig. 1); cut away tips (Fig. 2); cut each asparagus into half (Fig. 3); add asparagus sections and retained liquid to ① ; bring liquid to a boil and serve.

<table>
<tr><td rowspan="5">①</td><td>蝦仁…………6兩</td><td rowspan="4">②</td><td>蛋……………3個</td><td rowspan="4">③</td><td>冷飯…………9杯</td></tr>
</table>

①
蝦仁…………6兩
鹽…………⅓小匙
酒…………¼小匙
太白粉…1½小匙
開水………3杯

②
蛋……………3個
洋火腿丁（半杯）…2兩
熟青豆仁（半杯）…2兩
葱薑末………1大匙

③
冷飯…………9杯
鹽………2½小匙
味精……1½小匙
胡椒…………半小匙

❶蝦仁洗淨瀝乾水份調①料醃約２０分鐘後放入開水內燙熟撈起。

❷６大匙油燒熱將打勻雞蛋（圖１）中火半煎炒熟（圖２）加②料及蝦仁（圖３、４）再把③料加入同炒均勻，即可盛盤供食。

蝦仁炒飯 Shrimp Fried Rice

材料：6人份 **6 servings**

½ lb. raw, shelled shrimp
① ⅓ t. salt
¼ t. rice wine
1½ t. cornstarch
3 C. boiling water

② 3 eggs
½ C. diced ham
½ C. precooked green peas
½ T. chopped green onion
½ T. chopped ginger root

③ 9 C. cold, precooked rice
2½ t. salt
1½ t. MSG
½ t. black pepper

❶ Rinse and devein shrimp; drain and mix with ① ; let soak 20 minutes. Heat 6C. water until boiling; add shrimp, one at a time; when color changes, remove and drain.

❷ Heat pan and 6T. oil; lightly beat eggs (Fig. 1); pour into pan and scramble over medium heat until firm (Fig. 2); add ② and shrimp (Fig. 3,4). Stir-fry until fragrant; add ③ ; stir-fry until ingredients are mixed and rice is hot. Serve.

里肌肉‥‥‥１２兩
① 醬油‥‥１ ½ 大匙
酒‥‥‥‥１ ½ 小匙
水‥‥‥‥‥５大匙
太白粉‥‥‥１大匙
「炸油」‥‥‥３杯
榨菜‥‥‥‥６兩

葱段（３公分）‥‥５枝
薑‥‥‥‥‥‥‥３片
② 鹽‥‥‥半小匙、胡椒‥‥ ¼ 小匙
醬油‥‥１大匙、麻油‥‥半小匙
味精‥‥半小匙、水‥‥‥‥１杯
糖‥‥‥半小匙、太白粉‥１大匙

③ 葱末‥‥‥‥‥半大匙
鹽‥‥‥‥‥ ¼ 小匙
醬油‥‥‥‥‥２小匙
味精‥‥‥‥‥ ¼ 小匙   每
胡椒‥‥‥‥‥ ¼ 小匙   人
麻油‥‥‥‥‥ ¼ 小匙   份
高湯‥‥‥‥１ ½ 杯

麵‥‥‥‥‥‥１斤
青菜‥‥‥１２兩

❶ 里肌肉切絲，加①料拌勻。榨菜切絲。

❷「炸油」燒熱，將肉絲泡熟撈出，留油３大匙，葱薑炒香，下酒１小匙並入②料燒開，把泡熟之肉絲及榨菜絲放入拌勻盛出。

❸ 每只麵碗內放入③料、高湯、及燙熟的麵、青菜，最後酌量放上炒好的榨菜肉絲即成。

■肉絲泡油法：「炸油」燒熱（需將鍋燒熱再放油）暫離火用鍋鏟將油平均地澆勻鍋面（圖１）倒入拌好的肉絲（圖２）鏟開改大火（圖３）顏色轉白瀝乾油（圖４）。

榨菜肉絲湯麵 Spicy Shredded Pork Noodle Soup

材料：６人份 **6 servings**

① 1   lb. pork loin
1½ T. soy sauce
1½ t. rice wine
5   T. water
1   T. cornstarch
3   C. oil for deep-frying
6   oz. Szechuan pickled mustard green
5   1-inch sections green onion
3   slices ginger root

② ½ t. salt
1   T. soy sauce
½ t. MSG
½ t. sugar
¼ t. black pepper
½ t. sesame oil
1   C. water
1   T. cornstarch

③ ½ T. chopped green onion
¼ t. salt
2   t. soy sauce
¼ t. MSG   Each serving
¼ t. black pepper
¼ t. sesame oil
1½ C. hot stock
1⅓ lbs. precooked noodles
1   lb. green cabbage*

❶ Shred pork loin; mix with ① ; let soak 20 minutes; shred pickled vegetable.
❷ Heat oil; stir-fry pork shreds until color changes; remove and drain. Reheat pan and 3T. oil; stir-fry green onion and ginger until fragrant; add 1t. rice wine and ② ; let boil. Add precooked pork shreds and mustard green; mix together and remove.
❸ Portion ③ into each serving bowl; add hot stock, 1/6 of noodles and 1/6 of pork and vegetable mixture; serve.
* Green cabbage, which is the pictured vegetable, may be purchased at a Chinese grocery store. If unavailable, substitute spinach or another green vegetable.

To stir-fry pork shreds:
Heat pan and 4 to 5T. oil until very hot; remove pan from heat and swirl oil around pan to coat surface (Fig. 1). Add pork shreds (Fig. 2). Using spatula, stir-fry pork shreds to separate over high heat (Fig. 3). Continue to stir-fry until color changes; remove and drain (Fig. 4).

猪肝…………１２兩　　　水…………１２杯
「炸油」………３杯　　　②{麵（預先燙熟）…１斤
洋葱…………３個　　　　　鹽…………１⅓大匙
葱（切３公分）…６枝　　　　味精………半大匙
①{醬油………１大匙
　酒…………１大匙

❶ 猪肝切片（圖１、２），洋葱切絲（圖３、４）。
❷ 「炸油」燒熱，以中火將猪肝泡熟撈出，留油３大匙將葱、洋葱炒香，放入①料，再加水１２杯，俟水
　燒開後，加入②料、猪肝、燒沸分盛６個麵碗內即成。

猪肝湯麵 Liver Noodle Soup　　　　材料：6人份　6 servings

1　lb. beef, pork or chicken liver
3　C. oil for frying
3　medium-sized onions
6　1-inch sections green onion
①{1　T. soy sauce
　{1　T. rice wine

12 C. water
②{1⅓ lbs.precooked noodles
　{1⅓ T. salt
　{½　T. MSG

❶ Slice liver (Fig. 1, 2); shred onion (Fig. 3, 4)
❷ Heat oil for frying; deep-fry liver slices over medium heat until color changes; remove and drain. Reheat pan and 3
　oil; stir-fry green onion and onion until fragrant; add ① and 12C. water. When water boils, add ② and liver slice
　When liquid boils again, portion into 6 bowls; serve.

麵（預先燙熟）1 斤
雞肉‧‧‧‧‧‧‧‧‧4 兩
① 鹽‧‧‧‧‧‧‧‧¼ 小匙
太白粉‧‧‧‧1 小匙
② 猪肝‧‧‧‧‧‧‧3 兩
鴨肫‧‧‧‧‧‧‧3 個
多菇‧‧‧‧‧‧‧6 朶

酒‧‧‧‧‧‧‧‧‧1 大匙
鹽‧‧‧‧‧‧‧‧‧2 小匙
醬油‧‧‧‧‧‧‧2 大匙
③ 味精‧‧‧‧‧‧‧1 小匙
糖‧‧‧‧‧‧‧‧‧1 小匙
胡椒‧‧‧‧‧‧¼ 小匙
麻油‧‧‧‧‧‧‧1 小匙

水‧‧‧‧‧‧‧‧‧9 杯
鵪蛋‧‧‧‧‧‧‧12 個
紅蘿蔔‧‧‧‧‧‧半條
筍‧‧‧‧‧‧‧‧‧1 枝
④ 金針菜‧‧‧‧‧‧半兩
青江菜‧‧‧‧‧‧半斤
葱段（3 公分長）‧‧‧5 枝
薑絲‧‧‧‧‧‧‧2 大匙

❶ 雞肉切片調①料，猪肝切片，鴨肫切花，多菇泡軟切片，鵪蛋煮熟去殼，紅蘿蔔、筍亦切片，金針菜泡軟去硬梗打結，青江菜切半備用。

❷ 油4 大匙燒熱，將雞肉入鍋略炒，隨入②料炒八分熟，再加③料炒勻，使其入味盛盤。

❸ 將水燒開，④料投入煮熟，放入炒好的雞片及②料，再燒滾後，立即將各料撈起，隨將油麵入鍋燒開，即可將麵撈出，分裝在六只麵碗內，上置煮好各料，再淋上適量之湯汁即成。

◀ 紅蘿蔔切成秋葉形：將紅蘿蔔切5 公分長段，對切成兩塊，每塊切口向下，切去兩邊，上邊切弧形成
　 狀（圖1）上、下、兩邊切成鋸齒狀，另一面切去兩角成 （圖2、3）刻好後切片（圖4）。

什錦湯麵 "Many Things" Noodle Soup　　材料：6 人份　6 servings

1⅓ lbs. precooked noodles
4 oz. raw chicken meat
① ¼ t. salt
　 1 t. cornstarch
② 3 oz. pork, beef or chicken liver
　 3 duck gizzards
　 6 Chinese black mushrooms, pre-softened

③ 1 T. rice wine
　 2 t. salt
　 2 T. soy sauce
　 1 t. MSG
　 1 t. sugar
　 1 t. sesame oil
　 ¼ t. black pepper

④ 9 C. water
　 12 quail eggs
　 ½ carrot
　 1 bamboo shoot
　 ⅔ C. tiger lily buds
　 ½ lb. heart of green vegetable
　 6 1-inch sections green onion
　 2 T. shredded ginger root

❶ Cut chicken meat into paper-thin bite-size pieces; mix with ① . Cut liver into thin slices; score gizzards lengthwise and crosswise; cut into bite-size pieces. Cut mushroom caps into half; cook quail eggs until hard-boiled; remove shells. Cut carrot and bamboo shoot into thin slices; let tiger lily buds soak in warm water until soft (20 minutes). Remove bitter ends and tie into knots; cut vegetable hearts into half.

❷ Heat pan and 4T. oil; stir-fry chicken meat until color changes; add ② and cook until gizzard pieces "flower"; add ③ and stir-fry to mix well; remove and drain.

❸ Boil 9C. water; add ④ and cook until carrot and bamboo shoot are tender; add chicken meat and ② . Let boil and remove ingredients except soup (A); add noodles to hot stock. When heated through, remove and portion into 6 servings bowls; add 1/6 of (A) to each bowl and serve.

◀ To cut carrots: cut carrot into 2-inch pieces; cut each piece in half; cut off side of each half so it looks like a triangle (Fig. 1); cut sides of triangle so that they look like the teeth of a saw; cut small stem at base of triangle (Fig. 2, 3); cut into slices (Fig. 4).

叉燒肉…………9兩
芥蘭菜………1斤半
麵……………12兩
葱段(圖1)……6枝
薑(圖2)………6片

① 蠔油…………2大匙
鹽……………半小匙
醬油…………2大匙
味精…………1小匙
糖……………1小匙
胡椒…………¼小匙
麻油…………1小匙
水……………1½杯
太白粉………1½大匙

② 鹽……………¼小匙
醬油…………2小匙
味精…………¼小匙
胡椒…………¼小匙
麻油…………¼小匙
高湯…………1½杯
每人份

❶叉燒肉切片。芥蘭菜取嫩莖(圖3、4),在沸水內燙8分熟,以冷水浸涼撈出。

❷油4大匙燒熱,葱薑炒香,續入芥蘭菜略炒,下酒1小匙及①料燒沸加入叉燒盛出。

❸每個麵碗內放入②料、高湯及燙熟的麵,最後酌量放上煮好的叉燒及湯汁即成。

叉燒湯麵 Roasted Pork Noodle Soup

材料：6人份 **6 servings**

9 oz. roasted pork*
1⅓ lbs. broccoli
1 lb. precooked noodles
6 1-inch sections green onion (Fig. 1)
6 slices ginger root (Fig. 2)

① 2 T. oyster sauce
½ t. salt
2 T. soy sauce
1 t. MSG
1 t. sugar
¼ t. black pepper
1 t. sesame oil
1½ C. water
1½ T. cornstarch

② ¼ t. salt
2 t. soy sauce
¼ t. MSG
¼ t. black pepper
¼ t. sesame oil
1½ C. hot stock
Each serving

❶ Slice pork into thin bite-size pieces. Cut broccoli into 3-inch sections (Fig. 3, 4); precook in boiling water for 2 minutes until slightly tender; remove and plunge into cold water until cool; remove.

❷ Heat pan and 4T. oil; stir-fry green onion and ginger until fragrant; add precooked broccoli and briefly stir-fry; add 1t. rice wine and ① ; let liiquid come to a boil and add roasted pork; remove (A).

❸ Prepare ② and place in each bowl; add 1/6 precooked noodles, hot stock and portion 1/6 of (A) on top each bowl; serve.

* See P. 149 for directions for preparation of roasted pork.

猪排（約1斤）‥‥‥‥‥‥6片		蛋黄‥‥‥‥1個		鹽‥‥‥‥1小匙		葱末‥‥半大匙	
酒‥‥1小匙 、 醋‥‥‥‥1小匙		「炸油」‥‥6杯		醬油‥‥1大匙		鹽‥‥⅟₄小匙	
醬油‥2大匙 、 胡椒‥‥‥半小匙		酸菜‥‥‥‥6兩		味精‥‥半小匙		醬油‥‥2小匙	
鹽‥‥1小匙 、 麻油‥‥‥半小匙		蒜末‥‥1大匙		糖‥‥‥2小匙		味精‥⅟₄小匙	
①味精‥半小匙 、 太白粉‥‥2大匙			②	胡椒‥‥⅟₄小匙	③	胡椒‥⅟₄小匙	每人份
糖‥‥1大匙 、 大蒜（拍碎）‥5粒				麻油‥‥⅟₄小匙		麻油‥⅟₄小匙	
				水‥‥‥‥1杯		高湯‥1⅟₂杯	
				太白粉‥1大匙		麵‥‥‥1斤	

❶猪排拍鬆（圖1），調入①料醃約1小時，炸時塗勻蛋黄（圖2），沾上多量太白粉（圖3、4）。
❷酸菜洗淨，擠乾水分切絲。
❸油4大匙燒熱，將蒜末及酸菜炒香，再入②料拌炒盛出。
❹「炸油」燒熱，以中火將猪排炸熟（約6分鐘）撈出。
❺每個麵碗内放入③料、高湯及燙熟的麵，再酌量放上炒好的酸菜及猪排1片即成。

排骨湯麵 Tasty Pork Chop Noodle Soup　　材料：6人份 6 servings

	6	pork chops (about 1⅓lbs.)		6	oz. pickled cabbage
	1	t. rice wine		1	T. chopped garlic
	2	T. soy sauce		1	t. salt
	1	t. salt		1	t. soy sauce
	½	t. MSG		½	t. MSG
①	1	T. sugar	②	2	t. sugar
	1	t. vinegar		¼	t. black pepper
	½	t. black pepper		¼	t. sesame oil
	½	t. sesame oil		1	C. water
	2	T. cornstarch		1	T. cornstarch
	5	cloves garlic, smashed			
	1	egg yolk			
	6	C. oil for frying			

③	½	T. chopped green onion	Each serving
	¼	t. salt	
	2	t. soy sauce	
	¼	t. MSG	
	¼	t. black pepper	
	¼	t. sesame oil	
	1½	C. hot stock	
	1⅓	lbs.precooked noodles	

❶ Lightly pound pork chops with the blunt end of the cleaver (Fig. 1); mix with ① ; let soak 1 hour. Before deep-frying, dip each pork chop into beaten egg yolk (Fig. 2) and coat with cornstarch (Fig. 3, 4).
❷ Drain pickled vegetable and shred.
❸ Heat pan and 4T. oil; stir-fry garlic and shredded pickled vegetable until fragrant; add ② ; mix well and remove (A).
❹ Heat oil for deep-frying over medium heat, fry pork chops until golden brown (about 6 minutes); remove and drain.
❺ Portion ③ , stock and noodles into each serving bowl; add (A) and fried pork chops. Serve.

① 雞腿（約２斤）６隻
醬油‥‥‥‥２大匙
鹽‥‥‥‥‥１大匙
味精‥‥‥‥半大匙
糖‥‥‥‥‥２小匙
五香粉‥‥‥１小匙
酒‥‥‥‥‥半大匙
太白粉‥‥‥４大匙

蛋黃‥‥‥‥‥２個
「炸油」‥‥‥‥６杯
雪裏紅‥‥‥‥６兩
薑絲（圖１、２）１大匙

② 鹽‥‥‥‥‥‥１小匙
醬油‥‥‥‥‥１大匙
味精‥‥‥‥‥半小匙
糖‥‥‥‥‥‥半小匙
胡椒‥‥‥‥‥¼小匙
麻油‥‥‥‥‥¼小匙
水‥‥‥‥‥‥１杯
太白粉‥‥‥‥１大匙

③ 葱末‥‥‥‥‥半大匙
鹽‥‥‥‥‥‥¼小匙
醬油‥‥‥‥‥２小匙
味精‥‥‥‥‥¼小匙
胡椒‥‥‥‥‥¼小匙
麻油‥‥‥‥‥¼小匙
高湯‥‥‥‥‥１½杯
麵‥‥‥‥‥‥１斤
每人份

❶ 雞腿洗淨，並拭乾水份，調入①料拌勻，醃約１小時，炸時塗勻蛋黃，沾上多量太白粉。
❷ 雪裏紅漂洗淨，擠乾水份（圖３）切碎（圖４）。
❸ 油４大匙燒熱，將薑絲及雪裏紅炒香，再入②料拌炒盛出。
❹ 「炸油」燒熱，以中火將雞腿炸熟（約１０分鐘）撈出。
❺ 每個麵碗內放入③料、高湯及燙好的麵，再酌量放上炒好的雪裏紅及雞腿１隻即成。

雞腿湯麵 Chicken Leg Noodle Soup

材料：６人份 **6 servings**

①
6 chicken legs (about 2⅔ lbs.)
2 T. soy sauce
1 T. salt
½ t. MSG
2 t. sugar
1 t. 5-spice salt
½ T. rice wine
4 T. cornstarch
2 egg yolks
6 C. oil for frying

②
6 oz. salted cabbage*
1 T. shredded ginger root (Fig. 1, 2)
1 t. salt
1 T. soy sauce
½ t. MSG
½ t. sugar
¼ t. black pepper
¼ t. sesame oil
1 C. water
1 T. cornstarch

③
½ T. chopped green onion
¼ t. salt
2 t. soy sauce
¼ t. MSG
¼ t. black pepper
¼ t. sesame oil
1½ C. hot stock
1⅓ lbs. precooked noodles

Each serving

❶ Mix chicken legs with ① ; let soak 1 hour. Before frying, dip each leg in egg yolk and coat with cornstarch.
❷ Drain salted cabbage (Fig. 3) and cut into ¼-inch sections (Fig. 4).
❸ Heat pan and 4T. oil; stir-fry ginger and chopped vegetable. Add ② , let boil and remove (A).
❹ Heat oil for deep-frying. Over medium heat, deep-fry chicken legs until golden brown (about 10 min.). Remove and drain
❺ Portion ③ , hot stock, noodles, (A) and a chicken leg into each serving bowl; serve.
* Salted cabbage ("sye li hong") or "red in snow" is a type of salty preserved vegetable which is available in cans at any Chines grocery store. If unavailable, substitute spinach or watercress.

海參…………１２兩　　　葱(切３公分)…６枝　　　麵(預先浸熟)１斤

①{ 薑…………２片
酒…………１大匙
水…………３杯 }

墨魚(淨肉)…１２兩
蝦…………１８隻

②{ 醬油…………１大匙
鹽…………１⅓大匙
味精…………２小匙
酒…………２大匙 }

③{ 開水…………１２杯
芥蘭菜………１斤半 }

海參切塊，以①料燒煮去腥味，墨魚切片。蝦去鬚及腸泥，芥蘭菜取嫩莖。

油４大匙燒熱，先炒葱段，再將海參、墨魚、蝦炒香放入②料及③料燒開後，將其材料撈出，湯汁留用

煮麵，燒沸，分盛在６個麵碗內，上面並酌量擺上煮好的材料即成。

墨魚切法：墨魚切約４公分寬長條(圖１)斜劃刀紋(圖２)邊斜劃交叉刀紋，邊切塊(圖３)。

三鮮湯麵 Seafood Noodles with Broth

材料：６人份 **6 servings**

{ 1 lb. sea cucumbers*[1] ("beche-de-mer")
2 slices ginger root
1 T. rice wine
3 C. water
1 lb. squid meat }

18 fresh medium-sized
fresh shrimp
(about ⅔lb.)

6 1-inch sections
green onion

②{ 1 T. soy sauce
1⅓ T. salt
2 t. MSG
2 T. rice wine }

③{ 12 C. boiling water
1½ lbs.Chinese broccoli*[2]
1⅓ lbs.precooked noodles }

● Cut sea cucumbers into bite-sized pieces; heat pan and 2T. oil; stir-fry ginger slices until fragrant; add rice wine and water; let liquid come to a boil; add sea cucumbers and boil 4 minutes; remove and drain (discard liquid). Score squid meat lengthwise and crosswise; cut into bite-size pieces, cut off shrimp antennae and appendages; devein. Cut broccoli into bite-size pieces and precook 1 minute in boiling water; remove and plunge into cold water; drain.

● Heat pan and 4T. oil; stir-fry green onion sections until fragrant; add sea cucumbers, squid, shrimp; add and stir-fry ② and ③ briefly. Let boil and remove all ingredients except stock (A). Add noodles to hot stock and when heated, portion into serving bowls; add (A) on top and pour stock into each bowl; serve.

[1] If sea cucumbers are available in dry form in Chinese grocery stores; rinse and place in water to cover. Let water come to a boil and lower heat; simmer 5 minutes. Remove pan from heat, and when water has cooled remove sea cucumbers, rinse and place in fresh water to cover; let soak overnight. Place pan with pre-soaked cucumbres on fire and repeat procedure. Repeat 3 or 4 more times and use as directed in recipe.

[2] If Chinese broccoli is unavailable, use ordinary broccoli and cut as directed; precook 2 additional minutes and use as directed.

● To cut squid: Cut squid into strips 1-inch wide (Fig. 1). Score strips lengthwise, score strips across previous lines (crosswise) (Fig. 2). Cut strips into bite-size pieces (Fig. 3).

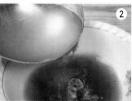

①			②			③			④		
牛肉	……	1斤	辣豆瓣醬	……	1小匙	水	……	6杯	麻油	……	半小匙
葱	……	2枝	黑豆瓣醬	……	1大匙	味精	……	半小匙	胡椒	……	1/4小匙
薑	……	2片	醬油	……	半杯	八角	……	半小匙	醬油	……	1大匙
蒜頭	……	3粒				麵	……	1斤	葱花	……	1大匙
						青菜	……	半斤	高湯	……	6杯

❶牛肉洗淨，切成 1 寸半之塊狀。

❷油 3 大匙燒熱將①料、②料，按照其順序炒香後放入③料，連同牛肉移入快鍋以中火燒煮約３０分鐘，即成紅燒牛肉。

❸將④料備於麵碗（圖１），先加入高湯（圖２），再將煮熟的麵條及青菜，裝入麵碗內（圖３），最後加上牛肉湯及牛肉塊，即可供食（圖４）。

紅燒鴨麵：鴨麵之主要材料爲鴨肉其他配料、調味料及做法參考紅燒牛肉。

紅燒牛肉麵 Red-Cooked Beef Noodles

材料：6人份 **6 servings**

1⅓ lbs. rump roast of beef

① {
2 stalks green onion
2 slices ginger root
3 cloves garlic
}

② {
1 t. hot bean paste ("la do ban jiang")
1 T. black bean paste ("he do ban jiang")
½ C. soy sauce
}

③ {
6 C. water
½ t. MSG
3 sections star anise
}

1⅓ lbs. precooked noodles
⅔ lb. green cabbage*[1]

④ {
½ t. sesame oil
¼ t. black pepper
1 T. soy sauce
1 T. chopped green onion
6 C. hot stock
}

❶ Cut beef rump into bite-size pieces; smash ingredients in ①

❷ Heat pan and 3T. oil; stir-fry ① and ② until fragrant; add ③ and beef pieces. Place this mixture in a pressure cook[er] and cook 30 minutes over medium heat (red-cooked beef)*[2]

❸ Prepare ④ and portion into serving bowls (Fig. 1); add hot stock (Fig. 2), noodles and green cabbage (Fig. 3); portio[n] red-cooked beef and some of its broth on top (Fig. 4), serve.

*[1] Green cabbage, the pictured green vegetable, may be purchased in Chinese grocery stores. If unavailable, substitute spinac[h]

*[2] If no pressure cooker is available, place ingredients in a casserole and simmer covered for 1 hour (meat should b[e] very tender).

Red-Cooked Duckling Noodles :

Follow recipe for Red-Cooked Beef Noodles, and substitute duckling for beef.

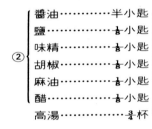

台式油麵……12兩		酒…………1大匙		醬油…………半小匙		香菜…………少許	
韮菜…………6兩		醬油…………半杯		鹽……⅛小匙		蒜末…………1大匙	
豆芽菜………6兩		水……………2杯		味精……⅛小匙		熟蝦…………6隻	
紅葱頭………5粒	①	糖…………1小匙	②	胡椒……⅛小匙	每人份		
冬菇…………2朵		五香粉……⅛小匙		麻油……⅛小匙			
絞肉…………6兩		味精…………半小匙		醋……⅛小匙			
				高湯…………¾杯			

❶韮菜切約3公分長段，豆芽菜洗淨，紅葱頭切薄片，冬菇泡軟切小丁。

❷油4大匙以中火將紅葱頭炸香（呈金黃色），隨入冬菇及絞肉略炒，即可加①料燒開改小火燜煮約1小時成魯肉備用。

❸將水燒開，每隻竹漏杓裝約2兩油麵（圖1）上置韮菜、豆芽菜（圖2）燙熟（圖3、4），倒入麵碗內，加②料、魯肉及高湯，洒上香菜數葉，並加蒜末半小匙及蝦1隻即成。

台南担仔麵 Tainan "Dandz" Noodles

材料：6人份 **6 servings**

lb. precooked noodles		1 T. rice wine		½ t. soy sauce ⅛ t. black pepper	
oz. Chinese chives*		½ C. soy sauce		⅛ t. salt ⅛ t. sesame oil	Each serving
oz. bean sprouts	①	2 C. water	②	⅛ t. MSG ⅛ t. vinegar	
shallots		1 t. sugar		¾ C. hot stock	
Chinese black mushrooms		⅛ t. 5-spice powder		1 sprig coriander or parsley	
oz. chopped pork		½ t. MSG		1 T. chopped garlic	
				6 precooked medium-size shrimp, shelled and deveined.	

Cut chives into 1-inch sections; rinse bean sprouts; mince shallots; Pre-softened Chinese black mushroom caps chopped.

Heat pan and 4T. oil; saute shallots until golden brown; add chopped mushrooms and pork; stir-fry to separate pork shreds. When color of meat has changed, add ① ; let boil and lower fire. Simmer 1 hour over low heat. (A)

Boil water; place 1/6 of noodles (1 serving) in strainer (Fig. 1), with 1 oz. (1/6) of chives and bean sprouts (Fig. 2) Place in boiling water and when noodles become heated through (about 1 minute later) (Fig. 3, 4), remove and place in serving bowls (vegetables on bottom); add ② , (A) and stock. Add coriander, chopped garlic and 1 shrimp per bowl. Serve.

If Chinese chives are unavailable, substitute green vegetable of choice.

113

里肌肉⋯⋯⋯⋯6 兩　　金針菜(圖1)⋯1 兩

① 醬油⋯⋯⋯⋯1 大匙　　木耳⋯⋯⋯⋯1 兩
　太白粉⋯⋯⋯1 大匙　　筍(或青江白菜)1 斤
　麻油⋯⋯⋯⋯1 小匙

② 高湯⋯⋯⋯⋯9 杯　　　④ 蒜末⋯⋯⋯⋯2 大匙
　鹽⋯⋯⋯⋯⋯1 大匙　　　　醬油⋯⋯⋯⋯半杯
　味精⋯⋯⋯⋯半大匙　　　　麻油⋯⋯⋯⋯1 大匙

③ 太白粉⋯⋯⋯8 大匙　　　　胡椒⋯⋯⋯⋯半小匙
　水⋯⋯⋯⋯⋯8 大匙　　　　麵⋯⋯⋯⋯⋯1 斤
　雞蛋⋯⋯⋯⋯3 個

❶里肌肉切薄片，拌上①料。

❷金針泡水，去硬梗打結，木耳泡軟切半，筍去皮煮熟，水裏泡冷撈出切片，雞蛋打散備用。

❸油4大匙燒熱，將肉片炒熟，隨即加入金針、木耳、筍同炒數下，即傾入②料待滾，以③料調成薄糊狀，再把碗裏的蛋徐徐倒入立即熄火，加上④料，並澆上豬油1大匙。

❹水半鍋燒開，將麵條下鍋煮熟，撈起(圖2、3、4)分別盛在麵碗，並將做好的滷汁澆在麵上即可供食
■如愛食辣味者可加豆瓣醬少許，另加些醋，味道更佳。

大魯麵 Assorted Vegetable Noodles

材料：6人份　**6 servings**

① ½ lb. pork loin
1 T. soy sauce
1 T. cornstarch
1 t. sesame oil
1 oz. dried tiger lily buds (Fig. 1)
1 oz. dried wood ears
1⅓ lbs.bamboo shoot or green vegetable

② 9 C. stock
1 T. salt
½ T. MSG

③ 8 T. cornstarch
8 T. water

3 eggs

④ 2 T. chopped garlic
½ C. soy sauce
1 T. sesame oil
½ t. black pepper
1⅓ lbs.noodles

❶ Slice pork into thin, bite-sized pieces; mix with ①
❷ Soak tiger lily buds in warm water until soft; remove bitter ends and tie into knots. Soak wood ears in warm water unt
soft; cut each into 2 pieces. Precook bamboo shoot until tender; plunge into cold water until cool; drain and cut
paper-thin bite-size pieces; beat eggs lightly.
❸ Heat pan and 4T. oil; stir-fry pork until color changes; add tiger lily knots, wood ears and bamboo shoot. Stir-fry 10 second
add ② and bring liquid to a boil; add ③ to thicken and slowly add eggs in a thin stream. Turn off fire immediate
and add ④ and 1T. oil (sauce).
❹ Place noodles in ½ pan boiling water and cook until soft; remove, drain (Fig. 2, 3, 4) and place in serving bowls; portio
sauce over noodles and serve.
■ Hot bean paste ("la jiau jiang") or vinegar may be added to ④ for extra seasoning.

① 蝦仁…………半斤
酒 1 大匙、麻油、鹽各 1 小匙
味精、糖各半小匙
胡椒…¼小匙、蛋白……3 個
水 3 大匙、葱、薑末各 1 大匙

② 熟筍……1 枝(切小片)
洋菇……半杯(切小片)
高湯………………3 杯
鹽 1 小匙、味精半小匙
太白粉………3½大匙

③ 高湯………9 杯
鹽………2 小匙
味精……1 小匙
醬油……半大匙
麵………1 斤

❶蝦仁洗淨剁碎，拌入①料成蝦茸。

❷將②料燒沸，並放入蝦茸。

❸每個麵碗內，放入燒沸的③料及燙熟的麵，最後酌量放上煮好的蝦茸即成。

■蝦的處理法：去頭(圖1)除殼(圖2)去尾殼(圖3)抽出腸泥(圖4)。

雞茸窩麵：將蝦仁改用雞肉即成。

蝦茸窩麵 Shrimp Bits over Noodles

材料：6 人份 **6 servings**

① ⅔ lb. raw shelled shrimp
1 T. rice wine
1 t. salt, ½ t. MSG
½ t. sugar, ¼ t. black pepper, 1 t. sesame oil
3 egg whites
3 T. water
1 T. chopped green onion
1 T. chopped ginger root

② 1 precooked bamboo shoot
½ C. button mushrooms
3 C. stock
1 t. salt
½ t. MSG
3½ T. cornstarch

③ 9 C. stock
2 t. salt
1 t. MSG
½ T. soy sauce
1⅓ lbs. precooked egg noodles

❶ Clean and devein shrimp; chop finely and mix with ① ; let soak 20 minutes. Dice bamboo shoot and button mushrooms.
❷ Heat ② until boiling; add shrimp mixture. Stir to separate shrimp bits and turn off heat (A).
❸ Portion noodles and boiling ③ into each serving bowl; add (A) on top. Serve.
■ To shell whole shrimp: Remove head (Fig. 1). Peel away shell (Fig. 2). Remove tail tip (Fig. 3). Devein and rinse; drain (Fig. 4).

Chicken Bits over Noodles : Follow the same procedure as "Shrimp Bits over Noodles" and substitute chicken for shrimp.

虱目魚1條12兩
① ｛ 薑酒………1大匙
　 ｜ 塩…………半小匙
　太白粉…1½大匙
　魚漿………6兩

② ｛ 高湯………7½杯
　 ｜ 塩…………2½小匙
　 ｜ 味精、糖各1小匙
③ ｛ 太白粉……6大匙
　 ｜ 水…………6大匙

薑絲………6大匙
麵…………1斤

❶ 虱目魚取肉，切約3公分×2公分魚片，調入①料醃約20分鐘，拌上太白粉及魚漿備用。
❷ ②料燒開，將備好魚肉一片片投入待滾，以③料勾成濃稠汁，熄火加入薑絲，即成虱目魚粳。
❸ 水燒開，將麵條下鍋煮熟撈出，分盛在麵碗內，淋上做好虱目魚粳即成。
■ 虱目魚切片法：虱目魚(圖1)由背部剖開去骨(圖2)除皮(圖3)切片(圖4)。

虱目魚粳麵 Fish Slices over Noodles with Broth 材料：6人份　6 servings

⅔ lb. fish meat
① ｛ 1　T. ginger wine
　 ｜ ½　t. salt
　1½ T. cornstarch
　½　lb. fish paste*

② ｛ 7½ C. stock
　 ｜ 2½ t. salt
　 ｜ 1　t. MSG
　 ｜ 1　t. sugar

③ ｛ 6　T. cornstarch
　 ｜ 6　T. water

6　T. shredded ginger root
1⅓ lbs. precooked noodles

❶ Cut fish meat into paper-thin bite-size pieces; mix with ① ; let soak 20 minutes. Mix with cornstarch and fish paste.
❷ Heat ② until boiling; add fish meat, piece by piece, making sure that each is thoroughly coated with fish paste mixture. When liquid comes to a boil, add ③ to thicken; turn off heat and add shredded ginger root (A).
❸ Portion noodles into serving bowls; pour boiling (A) mixture over noodles and serve.
* See Page 152 ''Fish Balls'' step ❶ for directions for making fish paste.
■ To cut fish: Place fish flat on counter (Fig. 1), make 2 cuts lengthwise along bone; separate meat from bone (Fig. 2), remove skin (Fig. 3). Cut fish meat into thin slices (Fig. 4).

紅葱頭⋯⋯⋯5粒
水⋯⋯⋯⋯7½杯
① 鹽⋯⋯⋯⋯2½小匙
味精、糖各1小匙

乾木耳(泡水)⋯⋯⋯⋯半兩
冬菇(泡水)⋯⋯⋯⋯4朵 ⌉切
大白菜半斤、炸豆腐包2片 ⌡絲
② 紅蘿蔔、筍⋯⋯⋯各半枝
金針(泡水除梗)⋯⋯⋯半兩
洋菇片⋯⋯⋯⋯⋯半杯

③ 太白粉、水⋯⋯⋯各6大匙
醬油、黑醋⋯⋯各2大匙
④ 胡椒半小匙、麻油1小匙
蒜末、辣椒絲⋯各1大匙
麵⋯⋯⋯⋯⋯⋯1斤
香菜⋯⋯⋯⋯⋯⋯半杯

❶ 溫油4大匙把紅葱頭(切片)炒香，下醬油1大匙及①料待滾再放入②料，以③料勾成糊狀，熄火加入④料即成素菜粳。

❷ 將做好的素菜粳適量淋在煮好麵上，並洒些香菜即可。

■ 筍的處理法：外皮劃一刀(圖1)剝皮(圖2)削去硬的部份(圖3、4)。

素菜粳麵 Vegetarian Noodles

①
5 shallots, minced
7½ C. water
2½ t. salt
1 t. MSG
1 t. sugar

②
2 C. wood ears, pre-softened
4 Chinese black mushrooms, pre-softened
⅔ lb. Chinese cabbage
½ carrot
½ bamboo shoot shredded
12 fried gluten balls ("mien jin pau")
1 C. tiger lily buds, presoftened
½ C. button mushrooms

③
6 T. cornstarch
6 T. water

④
2 T. soy sauce, ½ t. black pepper
2 T. worcestershire sauce
1 t. sesame oil, 1T. chopped garlic
1 hot red pepper, shredded
1⅓ lbs. precooked noodles
½ C. coriander

❶ Remove bitter ends from tiger lily buds; tie softened buds into knots; slice button mushrooms very thinly.

❷ Heat pan and 4T. oil; saute shallots until golden brown; add 1T. soy sauce and ① . Let liquid come to a boil and add ② cook 2 minutes over medium heat and add ③ to thicken. Turn off heat and add ④ . (A)

❸ Portion noodles into serving bowls; add boiling (A) mixture and top with a sprig of coriander; serve.

■ To prepare bamboo shoot: Cut a slit on bamboo shoot (Fig. 1), skin (Fig. 2), cut off hard pat (Fig. 3, 4).

麵‥‥‥‥‥‥‥‥‥ 1 斤　　　　葱段‥‥‥‥‥‥ 6 枝　　　　　水‥ 4 杯、醬油‥‥ 3 大匙
蝦仁、雞絲‥‥‥‥各 6 兩　　薑片‥‥‥‥‥‥ 6 片　　④　鹽 1 ½ 小匙、味精 1 小匙
① 鹽 ¼ 小匙、酒‥‥‥半小匙　③ 冬菇（泡軟）‥ 6 朵　　　　　糖‥ ¾ 小匙、胡椒 ¼ 小匙
　蛋白半個、太白粉半大匙　　　筍‥‥‥‥‥‥ 1 枝　　⑤　太白粉‥‥‥‥‥‥ 3 大匙
② 鹽、酒‥‥‥‥各 ⅓ 小匙　　　紅蘿蔔‥‥‥‥半條　　　　水‥‥‥‥‥‥‥ 3 大匙
　蛋白半個、太白粉半大匙　　　油菜（煮熟）1 2 棵

❶ 蝦仁拭乾水份調①料，雞絲調②料，並將③料切絲備用。
❷ 麵條以開水煮九分熟撈起，加油 1 大匙拌勻，分成 2 份。
❸ 油 4 大匙燒熱將 1 份麵入鍋（圖 1 、 2 ），如見麵條黏鍋，可加少許油，且搖動鍋子，使麵在鍋裏轉動，煎至兩
　面呈金黃（圖 3 、 4 ）盛盤。（依此法全部煎好各盛盤）
❹ 油 8 大匙燒熱，分別將蝦及雞絲炒熟盛起，餘油把葱薑炒香，隨入③料略炒，再加④料燒開後即可將油菜（預
　先煮熟）蝦仁、雞絲入鍋，並以⑤料勾汁，加油 1 大匙，分別淋在麵條上即可。

雞絲蝦仁燴麵　Chicken and Shrimp Noodle Platter　材料：6 人份　6 servings

1⅓ lbs. dry Chinese egg noodles
1　C. raw, shelled shrimp
1　C. raw, chicken meat, shredded
① ¼　t. salt, ½ t. wine
　½　egg white, ½ T. cornstarch
② ⅓　t. salt. ⅓ t. wine
　½　egg white, ½ T. cornstarch

6　1-inch sections green onion
6　slices ginger root
③ 6　pre-softened Chinese black mushrooms
1　bamboo shoot, ½ carrot
12　stalks precooked spinach or green vegetable

④ 4　C. water, 3 T. soy sauce.
　1½ t. salt, 1 t. MSG
　¾　t. sugar, ¼ t. pepper
⑤ 3　T. cornstarch
　3　T. water

❶ Rinse and devein shrimp; drain and mix with ① . Mix ② with shredded chicken meat; shred ingredients in ③ .
❷ Cook noodles in boiling water until soft; remove and drain. Add 1T. oil and mix; divide noodles into 2 portions.
❸ Heat pan and 4T. oil; add one group of noodles (Fig. 1, 2), portioning thinly and evenly over bottom of pan, move pan continuously in a circular motion over heat to prevent noodles from sticking (add more oil if necessary); cook until golden brown. Flip noodles over uncooked side down and repeat (Fig. 3, 4). Place noodles on serving plate. Repeat procedure for other group.
❹ Heat pan and 8T. oil; stir-fry shrimp and chicken shreds separately until change color; remove and drain. Reheat pan and oil; stir-fry ginger and onion until fragrant; add ③ and mix together; add ④ and bring to a boil. Add green vegetable, shrimp and chicken shreds; add ⑤ to thicken and 1T. oil. Portion equally over noodles and serve.
■ You may substitute any brand of egg noodles.

麵‥‥‥‥‥‥‥ 1 2 兩

① { 花椒粉、味精‥‥各 1 小匙
醬油 4 大匙、糖‥2 小匙
麻油、黑醋各‥‥‥‥ 1 大匙
辣油、葱薑末各‥‥ 1 大匙 }

② { 蝦仁‥‥‥‥‥‥ 6 兩
小黃瓜 3 枝、筍‥1 枝
蛋 3 個(煎成蛋皮切絲)
紅辣椒‥‥‥‥‥‥ 1 枝 }

❶ 麵在滾水內煮熟撈出,加入油 1 大匙拌勻。

❷ 把②料中蝦仁拌入太白粉 1 大匙,燙熟撈出,小黃瓜、筍(先煮熟)切絲,雞蛋打散用中火煎成蛋皮切絲,紅辣
椒切絲。

❸ 將麵及②料分別盛入 6 個盤內,把①料拌好,適量淋在麵上,食時拌勻即成。

■蛋皮煎法:鍋燒熱,塗少許油,倒入打勻蛋液(圖 1)將鍋轉動成圓形(圖 2)以小火烙至蛋皮邊乾且翻起時,(
圖 3)翻面略烙隨即取出(圖 4)。

棒棒汁:芝麻醬、醬油、辣油各 4 大匙、味精 1 小匙、 糖、麻油、黑醋、葱、薑、蒜末各 1 大匙。

薑醋汁:黑醋、麻油各 1 大匙、醬油 4 大匙、味精 1 小匙、糖 2 小匙、薑末 2 大匙。

紅油汁:辣油、醬油各 4 大匙、味精 1 小匙、糖 2 小匙、麻油、黑醋、葱、薑末各 1 大匙。

■以上調味汁及主配料(熟雞胸肉、洋火腿、冬菇、豆芽菜、荷蘭豆或各種蔬菜等)可依各人喜愛任選調拌。

椒麻汁拌麵 Spicy Szechuan Tossed Noodles I　材料:6 人份　6 servings

1　lb. dry Chinese noodles

① { 1　t. Szechuan peppercorn powder
4　T. soy sauce, 1 t. MSG
2　t. sugar, 1 T. sesame oil
1　T. worcestershire sauce
1　T. hot pepper oil ("la you")
1　T. chopped green onion
1　T. chopped ginger root }

② { ½　lb. raw, shelled shrimp
1½ C. shredded cucumber
1　C. shredded bamboo shoot
3　eggs (make an egg skin)
1　hot red pepper }

❶ Cook noodles in boiling water until soft; remove and drain. Add 1T. oil and mix; set aside to cool.

❷ Add 1T. cornstarch to shrimp; mix thoroughly and precook in boiling water until color changes; remove and drain. Shred hot red pepper and egg skin.

❸ Place a serving of cool noodles into each serving bowl; portion ① ingredients equally on top of noodles and add sauce to season; toss lightly and serve.

■ To prepare egg skin: Heat pan and rub surface lightly with an oil-soaked cloth; add beaten eggs (Fig. 1). Tilt pan to distribute egg evenly in pan (Fig. 2). Cook over low heat until firm (Fig. 3). Flip over egg sheet and cook briefly; remove (Fig. 4).

"Spicy Szechuan" Sauce: 4 T. sesame paste, 4 T. soy sauce, 1 t. MSG, 1T. sugar, 1 T. sesame oil, 1 T. worcestershire sauce, 4 T. hot pepper oil ("la you"), 1 T. chopped green onion, 1 T. chopped ginger root, 1 T. chopped garlic.

"Gingery" Sauce: 1 T. worcestershire sauce, 4 T. soy sauce, 1 t. MSG, 2 t. sugar, 1 T. sesame oil, 2 T. chopped ginger root.

"Red Hot" Sauce: 4 T. hot pepper oil ("la you"), 4 T. soy sauce, 1 t. MSG, 2 t. sugar, 1 T. sesame oil, 1 T. worcestershire sauce 1 T. chopped green onion, 1 T. chopped ginger root.

■ For several variations you may substitute precooked chicken, bean sprouts, pea pods, mushrooms, ham and every kind of vegetable.

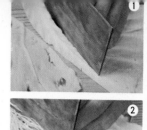

麵·············1 斤	①	醬油·············1 大匙	②	酒·············1 大匙	紅蘿蔔·············1 條
洋葱(大)·······1 個		酒·············1 小匙		醬油·············5 大匙	小黃瓜·············6 條
豆腐乾(大)·····1 塊		水·············3 大匙		糖·············1 大匙	包心菜(高麗菜)···6 兩
里肌肉·········半斤		太白粉·········2 小匙		味精·············1 小匙	蒜頭(拍破)·······5 粒
		甜麵醬·········4 兩			

❶洋葱、豆腐乾、里肌肉各切小丁，將肉丁調①料拌醃，甜麵醬調②料攪勻，紅蘿蔔、小黃瓜、包心菜均切絲盛盤備用。

❷油1杯燒熱，將肉丁及豆腐乾略炒盛起，餘油炒香洋葱丁，隨入攪勻甜麵醬燒開，即可加入豆腐乾、肉丁及蒜頭炒拌均勻備用。

❸麵入鍋煮熟盛碗，上淋煮好肉醬並加青菜絲即可供食。

■包心菜切法：家庭用每片洗淨去除中間硬梗(圖1)數片重疊切絲(圖2)餐廳用量多，橫切半(圖3)洗淨，再切絲(圖4)。

炸醬麵 Saucy Noodles ("Ja Jiang Mien") 材料：6人份 6 servings

1⅓ lbs. precooked noodles
1 large onion
1 square dried or pressed bean curd
⅔ lb. pork loin

①
1 T. soy sauce
1 t. rice wine
3 T. water
2 t. cornstarch
4 oz. sweet bean paste ("tien mien jiang")

②
1 T. rice wine
5 T. soy sauce
1 T. sugar
1 t. MSG
2 C. shredded carrot
2 C. shredded cucumber
2 C. shredded cabbage
5 cloves garlic, smashed

❶ Dice onion, bean curd and pork loin. Mix ① with pork; let soak 20 minutes; mix ② and sweet bean paste together until smooth.

❷ Heat pan and 1C. oil; stir-fry pork loin until color changes; remove and drain; add bean curd and stir-fry for 30 seconds, remove and drain. Drain all but 6T. oil from pan; reheat and saute diced onion until soft; add ② . When liquid comes to a boil, add bean curd, precooked pork and smashed garlic; stir-fry to mix together and remove.

❸ Cook noodles in boiling water until soft; remove and drain. Portion noodles into individual serving bowls; add saucy mixture and shredded vegetables on top; toss lightly and serve.

■ To cut cabbage: (Family method) Rinse leaves and cut away hard stalk (Fig. 1). Stack pieces together and shred (Fig. 2). (Restaurant method) Cut cabbage in two from the side (Fig. 3). Wash and shred (Fig. 4).

台式油麵(圖1) ······ 1斤半	炸香葱頭片··· 1 小匙	
韭菜············ 6 兩	醬油·········· 1 小匙	
豆芽菜········· 6 兩	鹽··········· ¼ 小匙	每
熟腿肉········· 3 兩　①	味精········· ¼ 小匙	人
	胡椒········· ¼ 小匙	份
	麻油········· ¼ 小匙	
	高湯········· 1 ½杯	

❶韭菜切為約3公分長段，豆芽菜洗淨。

❷鍋燒滾水，每隻竹漏杓裝4兩麵，上放韭菜、豆芽菜燙熟，倒入麵碗內(圖2)，加①料及高湯(圖3)
　上擺熟肉片(圖4)即成。

切 阿 麵 Taiwanese-Style Noodles　　材料：6人份 **6 servings**

1⅓ lbs.precooked noodles (Fig. 1)
½ lb. Chinese chives*
½ lb. (2C.) bean sprouts
½ lb. 18 slices precooked pork shank (¾lb.)

①
1　t.　minced, sauteed shallots	
1　t.　soy sauce	
¼　t.　salt	
¼　t.　MSG	Each serving
¼　t.　black pepper	
¼　t.　sesame oil	
1½ C. hot stock	

Cut chives into 1-inch long sections; rinse bean sprouts.

Boil water; place 1/6 of noodles (1 serving) in strainer with 1 serving each of chives sections and bean sprouts. Place in boiling water and when noodles become heated through (about 2 minutes later), remove and place in serving bowls (vegetables on bottom)(Fig. 2); add ① and hot stock (Fig. 3); arrange pork slices on top (Fig. 4) and sprinkle sauteed shallots; serve. If unavailable, substitute green onions.

白粗麵········2斤		里肌肉········6兩	醬油······3大匙		太白粉·····1大匙	
蝦仁········6兩	②	醬油······半大匙	高湯······2杯	④	水··········1大匙	
① 鹽········¼小匙		太白粉·····半大匙	鹽········半小匙			
太白粉····2小匙		洋葱········2個	③ 味精······半小匙			
		「炸油」······3杯	胡椒······¼小匙			
			番茄醬····1大匙			
			糖········1大匙			
			麻油······1小匙			

❶ 白粗麵在開水內燙洗撈出，蝦仁調入①料，里肌肉切絲調入②料，洋葱切絲。

❷「炸油」燒熱，把蝦仁、里肌肉分別泡熟撈出，留油4大匙，把洋葱炒至軟（香），再放入③料燒沸，隨即放入麵，以中火煮至汁快乾時，再加蝦仁及里肌肉，並以④料勾汁即成。

■ 蝦仁洗法：蝦仁入鹽少許（圖1）拌勻（圖2）以清水多洗數次（圖3）瀝乾水分（圖4）。

蝦仁洋葱炒麵 Saucy Shrimp Noodles

材料：6人份　**6 servings**

2⅔ lbs. thick noodles		½ lb. pork loin	3 T. soy sauce		④ 1 T. cornstarch	
½ lb raw, shelled shrimp	②	½ T. soy sauce	2 C. stock		1 T. water	
① ¼ t. salt		½ T. cornstarch	½ t. salt			
2 t. cornstarch		2 medium-sized onions	③ ½ t. MSG			
		3 C. oil	¼ t. black pepper			
			1 T. tomato ketchup			
			1 T. sugar			
			1 t. sesame oil			

❶ Precook noodles in boiling water until soft; remove and drain. Mix cleaned shrimp with ① ; shred pork loin and mix with ② ; let mixtures soak 20 minutes; shred onions.

❷ Heat pan and oil; separately stir-fry shrimp and pork until each changes color; remove and drain. Remove all but 4T. oil from pan; saute onion shreds until soft; add ③ and let boil; add noodles and mix together. When mixture comes to a boil, cook 3 minutes over medium heat; add precooked pork, shrimp and ④ to thicken. Remove and serve.

■ To clean shrimp: Add salt to shrimp (Fig. 1); lightly toss (Fig. 2); rinse lightly with cold water several times (Fig. drain. (Fig. 4)

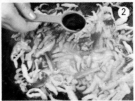

台式油麵……… 2 斤	韭菜…………… 6 兩		高湯………… 2 杯	
五花肉……… 6 兩	豆芽菜……… 6 兩		鹽…………… 半小匙	
① 冬菇………… 3 朵	醬油………… 2 大匙	②	味精………… 半小匙	
蝦米………… 2 大匙			胡椒………… $\frac{1}{4}$ 小匙	
			辣豆瓣醬…… 1 小匙	
			黑醋………… 1 大匙	

❶ 油麵在開水內燙洗撈出，五花肉切絲，冬菇泡軟切絲，蝦米略洗，韭菜切3公分長段，豆芽菜洗淨。

❷ 油4大匙燒熱，先將韭菜白色部份及①料炒香（圖1），再加醬油（圖2）及②料燒沸（圖3），隨即入油麵
、韭菜及豆芽菜炒拌均勻（圖4）即可。

台式炒麵 Taiwanese-Style Fried Noodles

材料：6人份 **6 servings**

1⅓ lb. precooked noodles	½ lb. Chinese chives*	2 C. stock
① ½ lb. fresh bacon	½ lb. (2C.) bean sprouts	½ t. salt, ½ t. MSG
3 pre-softened Chinese black mushrooms	2 T. soy sauce,	② ¼ t. black pepper,
2 T. dried shrimp		1 t. hot bean paste ("la do ban jiang")
		1 T. worcestershire sauce

Shred pork loin and Chinese black mushrooms; wash dried shrimp and cut Chinese chives into 1-inch sections; separate green and white sections, rinse bean sprouts.

❸ Heat pan and 4T. oil; stir-fry the white sections of Chinese chives and ① until fragrant (Fig. 1); add soy sauce and ② let liquid come to a boil (Fig. 3). Add precooked noodles, green chive sections and bean sprouts; stir-fry together and serve (Fig. 4).

If unavailable, substitute green onions.

①			②			③		
麵‧‧‧‧‧‧‧‧‧‧‧‧‧‧ 1 斤			鹽‧‧‧‧‧‧‧‧‧‧‧‧‧ ¼小匙			沸水‧‧‧‧‧‧‧‧‧‧ 1 杯		
海參‧‧‧‧‧‧‧‧‧‧‧‧ 1 斤			酒‧‧‧‧‧‧‧‧‧‧‧‧‧ 半小匙			醬油‧‧‧‧‧‧‧‧‧‧ 3 大匙		
薑‧‧‧‧‧‧‧‧‧‧‧‧‧‧ 2 片			太白粉‧‧‧‧‧‧‧‧ 2 小匙			鹽‧‧‧‧‧‧‧‧‧‧ 1½小匙		
酒‧‧‧‧‧‧‧‧‧‧‧‧‧ 1 大匙			芥蘭菜‧‧‧‧‧‧‧ 1 2 棵			味精‧‧‧‧‧‧‧‧‧‧ 1 小匙		
水‧‧‧‧‧‧‧‧‧‧‧‧‧‧ 3 杯			葱(3公分)‧‧‧‧‧6枝			糖‧‧‧‧‧‧‧‧‧‧‧ ¾小匙		
墨魚(淨肉)‧‧‧‧‧ 1 斤			薑‧‧‧‧‧‧‧‧‧‧‧‧‧‧‧ 6 片			胡椒‧‧‧‧‧‧‧‧‧ ¼小匙		
蝦‧‧‧‧‧‧‧‧‧‧‧‧ 1 8 隻								

❶ 麵條在開水內煮熟撈起，加油 1 大匙拌勻。

❷ 海參切塊，以①料燒沸去腥味，墨魚劃刀切片，蝦去殼留尾以②料拌醃，分別過油或炒熟，芥蘭菜取嫩
  莖洗淨煮熟備用。

❸ 油4大匙燒熱，將葱薑炒香放入③料燒沸後加入煮好的麵、海參、墨魚、蝦、芥蘭菜拌勻即可。

■ 海參處理法：除去腸臟（圖1）洗淨（圖2）直切（圖3）斜切二半（圖4）。

三鮮炒麵 Sea Food-Trio Fried Noodles

材料：6人份 **6 servings**

1⅓ lbs. dry egg noodles
1⅓ lbs. sea cucumbers*[1]

① 2 slices ginger root
   1 T. rice wine
   3 C. water

1⅓ lbs. squid meat
18 medium-sized raw shrimp (with shell)

② ¼ t. salt
   ½ t. rice wine
   2 t. cornstarch

12 5-inch sections Chinese broccoli (1 lb.)*[2]
6 1-inch sections green onion
6 slices ginger root

③ 1 C. boiling water
   3 T. soy sauce
   1½ t. salt
   1 t. MSG
   ¾ t. sugar
   ¼ t. black pepper

❶ Precook noodles in boiling water until soft; remove and drain; add 1T. oil and toss lightly.

❷ Cut sea cucumbers into bite-sized pieces; heat pan and 2T. oil; stir-fry ginger slices until fragrant; add rice wine and water let liquid come to a boil; add sea cucumbers and boil 4 minutes; remove and drain (discard liquid). Score squid mea lengthwise and crosswise; cut into bite-size pieces; mix shrimp and ② ; let soak 20 minutes. Heat pan and 1C. oil and sti fry shrimp and squid meat separately until each changes color; remove and drain. Precook broccoli until near-tende (about 1 minute).

❸ Heat pan and 4T. oil; stir-fry green onion sections and ginger until fragrant; add ③ and let liquid come to a boil. Ad noodles, precooked sea cucumbers, squid, shrimp and broccoli. Mix together and serve.

*[1] See note on P. 111 concerning sea cucumbers.
*[2] If Chinese broccoli is unavailable, use ordinary broccoli and cut as directed; precook an additional two minutes and u as directed.

■ To clean pre-softened sea cucumber: Remove entrails from inside sea cucumber (Fig. 1). Rinse lightly (Fig. 2). Cut length in half (Fig. 3). Cut aslantwise in half (Fig. 4).

台式油麵……2斤	「炸油」……3杯	醬油……2大匙
嫩牛肉……半斤	葱末……1大匙	高湯……2杯
醬油……1大匙	薑末……1大匙	鹽……半小匙
糖……⅓小匙	蒜末……1小匙	味精……半小匙
酒……1小匙	沙茶醬……1大匙	胡椒……¼小匙
太白粉……1½大匙		空心菜……1斤
沙拉油……1大匙		
水……4大匙		

①（左） ②（中） ③（右）

❶空心菜取嫩葉(圖1)洗淨(圖2)瀝乾(圖3)。

❷牛肉切絲調①料醃約1小時,以温油泡熟撈起,空心菜略炒盛出。

❸油4大匙燒熱,先將②料炒香,隨加醬油及③料燒開,即可放入空心菜,油麵牛肉絲炒拌均勻盛盤即成。

沙茶牛肉炒麵 "Sha Cha" Beef-Fried Noodles 材料:6人份 6 servings

1⅓ lbs. Precooked noodles	3 C. oil	2 T. soy sauce
⅔ lb. flank steak	1 T. chopped green onion	2 C. stock
1 T. soy sauce	1 T. chopped ginger root	½ t. salt
⅓ t. sugar	1 t. chopped garlic	½ t. MSG
1 t. rice wine	1 T. "sha cha jiang"*[1]	¼ t. black pepper
1½ T. cornstarch		1 lb. green vegetable*[2]
1 T. oil		
4 T. water		

① (left)   ② (middle)   ③ (right)

● Cut green vegetable into 1-inch long sections (Fig. 1), wash vegetable (Fig. 2); drain (Fig. 3).

● Shred flank steak; mix with ① and let soak 1hr. Heat oil until medium hot; stir-fry beef until color changes; remove and drain. Heat pan and 4T. oil; stir-fry vegetable briefly and remove; drain.

● Heat pan and 4T. oil; stir-fry ② until fragrant; add soy sauce and ③. Let liquid come to a boil and add green vegetables, noodles and beef shreds; mix together and serve.

[1] See P. 171 for note on "sha cha jiang". If unavailable substitute hoisin sauce.

[2] "Kong syin tsai" is the pictured Chinese vegetable which may be purchased at a Chinese grocery store. If unavailable, substitute spinach.

①		②	
麵（預先燙熟）⋯⋯１２兩		水⋯⋯⋯⋯⋯⋯⋯１２杯	
牛肉⋯⋯⋯⋯⋯⋯１２兩		鹽⋯⋯⋯⋯⋯⋯⋯１大匙	
豆腐⋯⋯⋯⋯⋯⋯２塊		醬油⋯⋯⋯⋯⋯２大匙	
草菇⋯⋯⋯⋯⋯⋯６兩		味精⋯⋯⋯⋯１½小匙	
魚丸⋯⋯⋯⋯⋯⋯４兩		糖⋯⋯⋯⋯⋯⋯⋯１小匙	
唐好菜⋯⋯⋯⋯⋯半斤		胡椒⋯⋯⋯⋯⋯¼小匙	
葱段（３公分長）６枝		麻油⋯⋯⋯⋯⋯⋯半大匙	
番茄⋯⋯⋯⋯⋯⋯２個			

❶牛肉切薄片，豆腐、番茄均切塊。唐好菜（圖１）摘除老葉（圖２），並修去根部（圖３），洗淨（圖４）。
❷水燒沸，將豆腐、草菇分別川燙撈出。
❸油４大匙將葱、番茄炒香，加②料移入砂鍋燒沸，放入麵及①料並加入唐好菜後，蓋鍋燒沸即可食。

牛肉鍋燒麵 Beef Hot Pot with Noodles　　材料：6人份 **6 servings**

①
1 lb. precooked noodles
1 lb. flank steak
2 squares bean curd
2 C. straw mushrooms
4 oz. fish balls*[1]
⅔ lb. green vegetable*[2]
5 1-inch sections green onion
2 medium-sized tomatoes

②
12 C. water
1 T. salt
2 T. soy sauce
1½ t. MSG
1 t. sugar
¼ t. black pepper
½ T. sesame oil

❶ Slice beef into paper-thin bite-size pieces; cut bean curd and tomatoes into bite-size pieces. Remove old leaves fr vegetable (Fig. 1, 2); trim hard edges (Fig. 3), drain (Fig. 4).
❷ Boil 6 cups water; Precook bean curd and straw mushrooms for 3 minutes; remove and drain.
❸ Heat pan and 4T. oil; stir-fry green onion sections and tomatoes until fragrant; add ② and move this entire mixt to casserole. Heat liquid until boiling; add noodles, ① and vegetable; cover and let liquid boil again; remove and ser
*[1] See P. 152 for directions for making fish balls or omit.
*[2] "Tang hau tsai" is the pictured vegetable which may be purchased at a Chinese grocery store. If unavailable, substit spinach, watercress or another variety of fresh green vegetable.

麵（預先燙熟）12兩　　蒜苗…………2枝　　　②｛鹽…………1大匙

大明蝦………6條　　　水…………12杯　　　　　醬油………2大匙

魷魚…………1條　　　　　　　　　　　　　　　味精………1½小匙

鮮干貝………4兩　　　　　　　　　　　　　　　糖…………1小匙

海參、生蠔各…6兩　　　　　　　　　　　　　　胡椒………¼小匙

大白菜………1斤　　　　　　　　　　　　　　　麻油………半大匙

● 大明蝦剪除鬚足（圖1、2），抽出腸泥（圖3）用剪刀將蝦背剪開（圖4），魷魚劃花切片，鮮干貝切片，海參、大白菜各切塊。蒜苗切斜薄片，分蒜白及蒜葉備用。

● 水12杯燒沸，將①料分別燙熟撈出，湯汁留用。

● 油4大匙燒熱，將蒜白炒香，放入大白菜炒軟，移入砂鍋，倒入湯汁燒沸，再放入麵、②料及①料後，蓋鍋燒沸，起鍋時洒上蒜葉即可。

海鮮鍋燒麵 Seafood Hot Pot with Noodles　　材料：6人份　6 servings

1 lb. precooked noodles	2 stalks green garlic or leeks	1 T. salt
6 prawns (¾ lb.)	12 C. water	2 T. soy sauce
1 squid (½ lb.)		1½ t. MSG
⅓ lb. fresh scallops		1 t. sugar
½ lb. sea cucumbers		¼ t. black pepper
½ lb. fresh shelled oysters		½ T. sesame oil
1⅓ lb. cabbage		

Cut legs from prawns (Fig. 1, 2); devein (Fig. 3). Use scissors to cut shell along back (Fig. 4). Score squid lengthwise and crosswise; cut to bite-size pieces. Slice scallops into paper-thin bite-size pieces; cut sea cucumbers into bite-size pieces. Cut cabbage into bite-size sections; slice garlic stalk diagonally into very thin sections; separate white part of stalk from green part.

● Bring 12C. of water to a boil; cook each ingredient of ① separately in this water until color changes; remove and retain stock.

● Heat pan and 4T. oil; stir-fry white garlic sections until fragrant; add cabbage sections and stir-fry over high heat until cabbage is limp and fragrant, place in bottom of casserole and add retained liquid. Heat liquid until boiling and add precooked noodles, ② and ① . Cover and let boil again. Sprinkle green garlic sections to top and serve.
See note on P. 111 concerning sea cucumbers.

里肌肉‥‥‥‥‥半斤	葱末‥‥‥‥‥2大匙	米粉‥‥‥‥‥‥半斤
① 醬油‥‥‥‥‥半大匙 水‥‥‥‥‥‥3大匙 太白粉‥‥‥‥2小匙 蝦皮‥‥‥‥‥1兩	冬菇‥‥‥‥‥3朶 筍‥‥‥‥‥‥1枝 白菜‥‥‥‥‥1斤 水‥‥‥‥‥12杯	② 鹽‥‥‥‥‥1⅓大匙 味精‥‥‥‥2小匙 胡椒‥‥‥‥¼小匙

❶里肌肉切絲，拌入①料，蝦皮略洗備用。冬菇(泡軟)、筍與白菜全部切絲。

❷油8大匙燒熱，先將肉絲炒開鏟出，餘油將蝦皮及葱末炒香，再入冬菇、筍、白菜炒至軟了，加水燒開，並入米粉、②料及肉絲燒沸即成。

■蝦皮可用魚乾代替，以魚乾燒湯味鮮美，其他主配料任意調配。

■白菜切絲：根部略切(圖1)，將白菜剝開洗淨(圖2)，切5公分長段(圖3)直切細絲(圖4)。

蝦皮米粉湯 Dried Shrimp and Rice Noodles with Broth

材料：6人份 **6 servings**

⅔ lb. pork loin	2 T. chopped green onion	⅔ lb. rice noodles
①{ ½ T. soy sauce 3 T. water 2 t. cornstarch 1 oz. dried shrimp	3 pre-softened Chinese black mushrooms 1 bamboo shoot 1⅓ lbs.cabbage 12 C. water	②{ 1⅓ t. salt 2 t. MSG ¼ t. black pepper

❶ Shred pork loin, mix with ① ; let soak 20 minutes. Rinse dried shrimp and shred Chinese black mushrooms, bamboo shoot and cabbage.

❷ Heat 8T. oil; stir-fry pork loin until color changes; remove and drain. Reheat oil and stir-fry dried shrimp, chopped green onion and Chinese black mushroom shreds until fragrant; add bamboo shoot and cabbage shreds. Cook untill soft over medium heat; add water and let liquid come to a boil; add rice noodles, ② and pork shreds. When liquid come to a boil, remove and serve.

■ To cut cabbage: Cut away hard stalk (Fig. 1); separate leaves and rinse (Fig. 2); cut into 2-inch pieces (Fig. 3); stack pieces together and shred (Fig. 4).

<table>
<tr><td>①</td><td>虱目魚‧‧‧‧‧‧‧‧1 斤半
鹽‧‧‧‧‧‧‧‧‧‧‧1 小匙
薑酒‧‧‧‧‧‧‧‧‧1 大匙
米粉（圖1）‧‧‧‧‧半斤
水‧‧‧‧‧‧‧‧‧‧‧1 2 杯</td><td>②</td><td>酒‧‧‧‧‧‧‧‧‧‧‧半大匙
鹽‧‧‧‧‧‧‧‧‧‧‧1 大匙
味精‧‧‧‧‧‧‧‧‧1 小匙
胡椒‧‧‧‧‧‧‧‧‧¼小匙
麻油‧‧‧‧‧‧‧‧‧¼小匙
薑絲‧‧‧‧‧‧‧‧‧2 大匙</td></tr>
</table>

❶ 將魚切塊，拌入①料，醃約３０分鐘。米粉加溫水（圖２）泡軟（圖３）瀝乾（圖４）。

❷ 水燒開，放入米粉再燒開，放進魚塊及②料燒沸，魚熟了，把米粉分盛６碗，酌量加入魚塊及湯在米粉上即可。

虱目魚米粉湯 Fish Slices over Rice Noodles with Broth   材料：6人份 **6 servings**

<table>
<tr><td>①</td><td>2 lbs.fish meat (red snaper, bluefish or mackerel).
1 t. salt
1 T. ginger wine
⅔ lb. rice noodles (Fig. 1)
12 C. water</td><td>②</td><td>½ T. rice wine
1 T. salt
1 t. MSG
¼ t. black pepper
¼ t. sesame oil
2 T. shredded ginger root</td></tr>
</table>

Cut fish into sections ½-inch thick; mix with ① ; let soak 30 minutes. Add warm water to rice noodles (Fig. 2); let soak until soft (Fig. 3); drain (Fig. 4).

❷ Bring water to a boil; add rice noodles and when water begins to boil again, and fish slices and ② . Let boil again and cook 2 minutes (fish should be tender); portion into serving bowls and serve.

<table>
<tr><td>

① {
熟鱔魚１２兩
「炸油」…３杯
韮菜黃…半斤
豆芽菜…半斤
</td><td>

② {
醬油…２大匙
鹽……１小匙
味精…１小匙
糖……１大匙
胡椒…半小匙
麻油…１小匙
</td><td>

蒜末…………２大匙
米粉…………１２兩
葱段（３公分長）５枝
</td><td>

③ {
醬油…２大匙
鹽……半小匙
味精…半小匙
胡椒…¼小匙
高湯…２杯
</td></tr>
</table>

❶鱔魚切７公分長段（圖１），韮菜黃略修（圖２）切成４公分長段（圖３），「炸油」燒熱，將鱔魚泡熟撈起。

❷油４大匙燒熱，把①料炒約８分熟，隨即放入鱔魚、蒜末及②料炒拌均勻盛起。

❸油６大匙燒熱，將葱段爆香，隨下③料燒開，即可放入洗好的米粉，慢慢炒勻後，把炒好的鱔魚等倒入½拌勻盛盤。

❹將剩餘½鱔魚等材料，洒在炒好的米粉上即成。

鱔魚炒米粉 Eel with Stir-Fried Rice Noodles　材料：6人份 6 servings

① { 1 lb. precooked eel*1 3 C. oil ⅔ lb. Chinese chives*2 4 C. bean sprouts	③ { 2 T. soy sauce 1 t. salt 1 t. MSG 1 T. sugar ½ t. black pepper 1 t. sesame oil	2 T. chopped garlic 1 lb. rice noodles 5 1-inch green onion sections	③ { 2 T. soy sauce ½ t. salt ½ t. MSG ¼ t. black pepper 2 C. hot stock

❶ Cut eels into 2-inch long sections (Fig. 1); cut Chinese chives into 2-inch section (Fig. 2, 3); rinse rice noodles lightly in hot water; drain. Heat oil until medium hot; deep-fry eel sections for 30 seconds; remove and drain.

❷ Heat pan and 4T. oil; add ① and stir-fry briefly about 30 seconds; add eel sections garlic and ② ; stir-fry together and remove. (A)

❸ Heat pan and 6T. oil, stir-fry green onion sections until fragrant; add ③ and let liquid come to a boil; add rice noodles and ½ (A); stir-fry to mix well; portion this mixture onto serving plate.

❹ Portion remaining half of (A) on top on stir-fried noodles; serve.

*1 To precook eels: boil 2 quarts water; cook eels until color changes; remove and debone; use as directed.

*2 If unavailable, substitute green onions.

猪脚⋯⋯⋯⋯⋯2斤　　　　味精⋯⋯⋯⋯⋯1小匙

水⋯⋯⋯⋯⋯⋯12杯　　　麵線⋯⋯⋯⋯⋯12兩

鹽⋯⋯⋯⋯⋯⋯2小匙　　　薑絲⋯⋯⋯⋯⋯3大匙

① 酒⋯⋯⋯⋯⋯⋯1大匙

葱⋯⋯⋯⋯⋯⋯2條

薑⋯⋯⋯⋯⋯⋯2片

❶ 猪脚去毛，刮除垢穢洗淨，剁成12塊（圖1），水燒開放入猪脚（圖2）川燙待滾（圖3）撈出（圖4）。

❷ 燙好猪脚置快鍋加入①料以中火燉煮20分鐘後加味精1小匙。

❸ 麵線入開水內煮熟撈起，分別盛在6個中型碗裏，上置猪脚，並加猪脚湯及薑絲少許趁熱供食。

猪脚麵線 Savory Pork and Noodles

材料：6人份　6 servings

2⅔ lbs. pork picnic shoulder

① 12 C. water
2 t. salt
1 T. rice wine
2 stalks green onion
2 slices ginger root

1 t. MSG
1 lb. "mien sien"*
3 T. shredded ginger root

❶ Remove any hair from skin; rinse lightly and cut into 12 pieces (Fig. 1); heat water until boiling and add shoulder (Fig. 2); let water boil and cook briefly (Fig. 3); remove and drain (Fig. 4).

❷ Put pork sections into pressure cooker with ① ; cook 20 minutes over medium heat*; add 1t. MSG.

❸ Heat 12 cups water until boiling; drop noodles into boiling water and cook until tender; remove, drain and portion into serving bowls. Add cooked pork sections and broth; sprinkle servings with shredded ginger root and serve.

* "Mien sien" is a type of thin noodle. If unavailable, substitute ordinary thin noodles or softened rice noodles.

■ If no pressure cooker is available, increase water in ① to 15C.; cook covered over medium heat for one hour; pork should be very tender.

131

鴨…………1隻3斤　　　米酒…………3大匙

①
葱…………2枝　　　　麵線…………12兩
薑…………2片　　　　薑絲…………2大匙
酒…………1杯
當歸…………2錢
水…………10杯

❶將鴨加①料放入燉盅內，燉約1小時後，倒進米酒3大匙，並取出鴨待冷分切成6塊。

❷麵線在開水內燙熟後，與薑絲分成6份盛在碗內，淋入熱鴨湯及鴨肉一塊即成。

■家庭做法，可將鴨先剁塊放入①料內燉煮，較爲方便。

■麵線(圖1) 如太長宜揪成兩半(圖2)燒煮前撥散(圖3)。

當歸鴨麵線 Dang Kuei Duck Noodles 　　材料：6人份 6 servings

①
1　duckling (about 4lbs.)
2　stalks green onion
2　slices ginger root
1　C. rice wine
¼　C. "dang kuei" *[1]
10　C. water

3　T. rice wine
1　lb. "mien sien" *[2]
2　T. shredded ginger root

❶ Mix duckling with ① ; place in pan and steam 1 hour over medium heat (duckling should be tender); add 3T. rice wine to liquid. Remove duckling; drain and allow to cool; cut into 6 sections (retain duckling liquid). Boil 2 quarts water; add "mien sien" and cook until tender; remove and drain.

❷ Portion cooked noodles into 6 bowls; place a piece of duckling meat over noodles. Add hot, retained liquid and sprinkle each serving with shredded ginger root; serve.

*[1] "Dang kuei" is a type of dry, pungent herb used for flavoring. It is very beneficial nutritionally to the body and is available at any Chinese drug store.

*[2] See note on P. 131 concerning "mien sien".

■ For informal, family cooking, duckling may first be cut into 6 sections, then steamed.

■ To cook "mien sien": "mien sien" (Fig. 1), if noodles are long, cut into half or thirds (Fig. 2). Before adding noodles to water, separate (Fig. 3).

雞‥‥‥‥‥‥‥‥‥‥‥ 1 隻
鮑魚‥‥‥‥‥‥‥‥‥‥ 半罐

① {
清水‥‥‥‥‥‥‥‥‥ 6 杯
酒‥‥‥‥‥‥‥‥‥‥ 1 大匙
鹽‥‥‥‥‥‥‥‥‥‥ 2 小匙
葱‥‥‥‥‥‥‥‥‥‥ 2 枝
薑‥‥‥‥‥‥‥‥‥‥ 2 片
}
麵線‥‥‥‥‥‥‥‥‥ 1 2 兩

❶ 雞剁塊，入開水內川燙撈起，鮑魚切片備用。

❷ 將燙好雞塊與①料放入燉盅內燉約３０分鐘後，加入鮑魚片及味精１小匙。

❸ 麵線在開水內煮熟撈起，分別盛在６個中型麵碗裏，上置雞塊及鮑魚片，並加上湯趁熱供食。

■ 雞塊川燙法：先將水燒開放入雞塊(圖１)再燒開時撈出(圖２、３)。

鮑魚雞麵線 Abalone and Chicken with Noodles

材料：6 人份 6 servings

1 whole roasting chicken (about 3lbs.)
½ lb. can abalone

① {
6 C. water
1 T. rice wine
2 t. salt
2 stalks green onion
2 slices ginger root
1 lb. "mien sien"*
}

❶ Cut chicken into bite-size pieces; cut abalone into paper-thin slices; blanch chicken in boiling water.

❷ Mix chicken pieces with ① ; steam 30 minutes over medium heat; add abalone slices and 1t. MSG.

❸ Boil 6 cups water; cook "mien sien" until tender; remove and drain; portion into serving bowls. Add abalone slices, chicken pieces and broth; serve.

* See note for "mien sien" on p. 131.

■ To clean chicken: Heat boiling water and add chicken (Fig. 1). Let water boil again. Remove chicken pieces and drain. (Fig. 2, 3).

雞 1 隻 ·············· 2 斤　　　黑麻油 ··········· 4 大匙　　　　　　　水 ·············· 7 杯
　　　　　　　　　　　　　　老薑 ·········· 1 〇 片　　　① 糖 ············· 1 大匙
　　　　　　　　　　　　　　酒 ················ 2 杯　　　　　鹽 ············· 1 小匙
　　　　　　　　　　　　　　　　　　　　　　　　　　　　麵線 ··········· 1 2 兩

❶ 將雞剁塊備用 。

❷ 麻油燒熱，薑片下鍋炒香（圖 1），即將雞塊倒入爆炒約 1 分鐘（圖 2），加酒 2 杯待滾（圖 3），隨入①料（圖 4）燒開，改用小火煮約 2 〇 分鐘 。

❸ 麵線在開水內煮熟撈出，分別盛在六個中型碗內，上置雞塊，並加麻油湯少許即成 。

麻油雞麵線 Sesame Chicken with Noodles　　材料：6人份　6 servings

1	whole chicken (about 2⅔ lbs.)		4	T. sesame oil		7	C. water
			10	slices ginger root	①	1	T. sugar
			2	C. rice wine		1	t. salt
						1	lb. "mien sien"

❶ Cut chicken (through bones) into bite-size pieces.

❷ Heat pan and sesame oil; stir-fry ginger slices until fragrant (Fig. 1); add chicken and stir-fry 1 minute over high heat until pieces are lightly golden (Fig. 2); add 2 cups rice wine and let boil (Fig. 3); add ① (Fig. 4) and let boil again; reduce heat to low, cover and cook 20 minutes (chicken should be tender).

❸ Boil 10 cups water; cook "mien sien" until tender; remove and drain; equally portion noodles into serving bolws; add chicken pieces, broth and serve.

麵線‥‥‥‥‥‥１２兩　　黑麻油‥‥‥‥‥‥６大匙　　⎧鹽‥‥‥‥‥‥１½小匙
豬腰（大）‥‥‥‥３隻　　老薑‥‥‥‥‥‥６片　　①⎨味精‥‥‥‥‥‥１小匙
豆苗‥‥‥‥‥‥３兩　　酒‥‥‥‥‥‥‥１½杯　　⎪糖‥‥‥‥‥‥‥半小匙
　　　　　　　　　　　　　　　　　　　　　　⎩高湯‥‥‥‥‥‥‥９杯

❶豬腰對剖（圖１）去白筋（圖２），在面上直劃數刀（圖３）再橫劃刀邊切塊（圖４），豆苗取嫩葉分別在開水
　內川燙一下，剛熟即撈出。
❷麵線在開水內煮熟，分盛在碗內。
❸將麻油燒熱，放進薑片炒香，先入酒燒沸，再入①料燒開時，把燙好的腰花及豆苗放入湯內後，酌量分
　別澆在麵線上即成。

猪腰麵線 Pork Kidney with Noodles

材料：６人份　**6 servings**

1　lb. "mien sien"*
3　pork kidneys (1½lb.)
3　oz. green vegetable

6　T. sesame oil
6　slices ginger root
1½ C. rice wine

① ⎧1½ t.　salt
⎨1　t.　MSG
⎪½　t.　sugar
⎩9　C.　stock

❶ Cut kidneys into half (Fig. 1); remove white membrane from kidneys (Fig. 2); score lengthwise (Fig. 3); crosswise and cut into bite-size pieces (Fig. 4). Cut green vegetable into 1-inch sections; heat 2 quarts water until boiling; cook kidney pieces until color changes and kidneys "flower"; remove and drain; blanch green vegetable; remove and drain.
❷ Boil 10 cups water until boiling; cook "mien sien" until tender; remove and drain; portion equally into serving bowls.
❸ Heat pan and sesame oil; stir-fry ginger slices until fragrant; add rice wine and let liquid come to a boil; add ① and let boil again; add precooked kidney and green vegetable; let boil and portion onto noodles; serve.
*　See note concerning "mien sien" on P. 131.

生蚵(生蠔)１斤　　蒜頭(拍破)‥‥‥‥‥‥５粒
薑　酒‥１大匙　　水‥‥‥‥‥‥‥‥１２杯
太白粉‥６大匙　　麵線‥‥‥‥‥‥１２兩

①{ 味精‥‥‥‥‥‥‥‥‥‥‥２小匙
    九層塔(切３公分長段)１２兩

❶薑拍破加酒１大匙擠出汁謂薑酒(圖１、２)。
❷生蚵洗淨，漏乾水加薑酒１大匙(圖３)拌入太白粉備用(圖４)。
❸油４大匙，將蒜頭炒香，隨入水１２杯待滾，即下麵線及生蚵燒開再加①料即可供食。
■可將肉絲、筍絲，任意調配，也可以太白粉水，勾芡成濃稠狀。

蚵仔麵線 Oyster Noodles

材料：６人份　**6 servings**

1⅓ lbs.fresh, shelled oysters
1　T. rice wine
2　slices ginger root
6　T. cornstarch

5　cloves garlic, smashed
12　C. water
1　lb. "mien sien"*[1]

①{ 2　t.　MSG
    1　lb. "gau chen ta"*[2]

❶ Smash ginger root; add wine and squeeze juice from ginger (Fig. 1, 2).
❷ Rinse oysters; drain; add ginger wine (Fig. 3) and cornstarch (Fig. 4). Let soak 20 minutes. Cut vegetable into 1-inch sections.
❸ Heat pan and 4T. oil; stir-fry smashed garlic until fragrant; add 12C. water and let boil. Add "mien sien" and oysters; let liquid come to a boil and add ① . When liquid boils again, serve.
*[1] See P. 131 for note on "mien sien".
*[2] "Gau chen ta" is the pictured vegetable which has a refreshing mint taste; if unavailable substitute spinach.
■ You may substitute pork shreds and bamboo shoot for oysters and add a mixture of cornstarch and water as a thickener.

猪腸…………1斤半

① 鹽……1½大匙
　醋……1½大匙

② 水………6杯
　酒………1大匙
　鹽………1大匙
　葱………2枝
　薑………2片

紅葱頭(切薄片)3粒
高湯(或水)…12杯
蒸麵線…………9兩

③ 薑絲……………半杯
　味精………2小匙
　醬油………4大匙
　香菜(切段)……半杯
　辣豆瓣醬………適量

❶ 猪腸加①料搓去黏液，用清水洗過，反覆數次後，以清水漂洗多次，入快鍋加②料煮約10分鐘，待冷取出切約3公分長段。

❷ 油4大匙將紅葱頭炒香，隨入水12杯待滾，即下麵線、猪腸燒開，立即熄火，再加③料，即可供食。

■ 猪腸處理法：用1枝筷子從猪腸1端1公分處插入(圖1)至另1端拉出成反面(圖2)，加入①料(圖3)搓去黏液(圖4)。

猪腸麵線 Pig's Intestines with Noodles

材料：6人份　**6 servings**

2 lbs.pig's intestines
① 1½ T. salt
　1½ T. vinegar
② 6 C. water
　1 T. rice wine
　1 T. salt
　2 stalks green onion
　2 slices ginger root

3 shallots, minced
12 C. stock (or water)
⅔ lb. "mien sien"*¹

③ ½ C. shredded ginger root
　2 t. MSG
　4 T. soy sauce
　½ C. Chinese coriander or parsley
　1½ t. hot bean paste ("la do ban jiang")

❶ Rub inside and outside of pig's intestines with ① ; rinse with water. Repeat this process 3 or 4 times until the intestines are rid of any sticky coating; place in a pressure cooker with ② and cook 10 minutes over medium heat*². Remove pig's intestines and cut into 1-inch long sections; discard liquid.

❷ Heat pan and 4T. oil; saute shallots until golden brown; add 12C. water, and let liquid come to a boil; add"mien sien" intestine sections and let boil. Turn off fire and portion into serving bowls; serve with ③ .

*¹ See P. 131 for note on "mien sien".
*² If no pressure cooker is available, place in a covered pot or casserole and cook 45 minutes over medium heat.

■ To prepare pig's intestines:
Using a chopstick, pierce the pig's intestines 1/3-inch from end (Fig. 1). Gather intestines on chopstick and turn inside out (Fig. 2). Rub intestines with ① (Fig. 3), rinse with water and drain (Fig. 4).

雞肉‥‥‥‥‥１２兩	葱(切段)‥‥‥‥２枝		沙河粉(２斤半)６片	
酒‥‥‥‥‥‥１小匙	薑(切絲)‥‥‥‥２片		豆芽菜‥‥‥‥‥‥６兩	
① 鹽‥‥‥‥‥‥１小匙	醬油‥‥‥‥‥３大匙		韮菜黃‥‥‥‥‥‥６兩	
蛋白‥‥‥‥‥‥１個	鹽‥‥‥‥‥‥１小匙			
太白粉‥‥‥‥１大匙	② 味精‥‥‥‥‥半小匙			
「炸油」‥‥‥‥３杯	胡椒‥‥‥‥‥¼小匙			
	高湯‥‥‥‥‥‥３杯			

❶ 雞肉切絲，調①料醃約２０分鐘，沙河粉(圖１)切１公分寬(圖２)，在開水內川燙用筷子攪開並撈出（圖３、４），韮菜黃切３公分長段備用。

❷ 「炸油」略燒熱，將雞絲泡熟撈起，留油４大匙炒香葱薑，隨下②料，沙河粉及豆芽菜炒勻，最後加入韮菜黃及雞絲略炒即成。

雞絲炒沙河粉 Stir-Fried Chicken and Vermicelli Shreds

材料：6人份 **6 servings**

	1 lb. raw chicken meat		6 1-inch green onion sections	6 vermicelli sheet ("sha he fen") *[1]
	1 t. rice wine		2 T. shredded ginger root	3 C. bean sprouts
①	1 t. salt		3 T. soy sauce	½ lb. Chinese chives *[2]
	1 egg white	②	1 t. salt	
	1 T. cornstarch		½ t. MSG	
	3 C. oil		¼ t. black pepper	
			3 C. stock	

❶ Shred chicken meat; mix with ① and let soak 20 minutes. Cut vermicelli sheets (Fig. 1) into ½-inch strips (Fig. 2), add to boiling water; stir lightly with chopsticks and remove (Fig. 3, 4); drain. Cut Chinese chives into 1-inch sections

❷ Heat pan and oil until medium hot; stir-fry chicken shreds until color changes; remove and drain.   Remove all but 4T. oil from pan; reheat and stir-fry green onion sections and ginger root until fragrant; add ② and let liquid come to a boil. Add vermicelli strips, bean sprouts and mix together; at last add Chinese chives sections, chicken shreds and stir-fry together. Serve.

*[1] Vermicelli sheets may be purchased at any Chinese grocery store.

*[2] You may substitute green onions.

①		②		
大蝦仁…………9兩		鹽…………¾小匙		
酒…………半小匙		醬油…………1小匙		
鹽…………半小匙		味精…………¼小匙	每人份	
蛋白…………半個		胡椒…………¼小匙		
太白粉…………2小匙		麻油…………¼小匙		
豆苗…………半斤		炸香紅葱頭片1小匙		
沙河粉（2斤半）6片		高湯…………9杯		

❶蝦仁洗淨，在蝦背直劃一刀（圖1、2、3）調①料醃約２０分鐘，豆苗取嫩莖（圖4）洗淨，沙河粉切約１公分寬、備中型麵碗6個，各入②料。

❷１０杯水燒開，將沙河粉及豆苗分別燙熟撈起，分盛在備好②料的碗內。

❸高湯燒開，將醃好蝦仁放入煮熟，即刻連湯分盛在碗內。

蝦球沙河粉湯 Shrimp Balls with Shredded Vermicelli Sheets and Broth

材料：6人份　6 servings

①		②		
¾ lb. raw, shelled shrimp		¾ t. salt		
½ t. rice wine		1 t. soy sauce		
½ t. salt		¼ t. MSG		
½ egg white		¼ t. black pepper	Each serving	
2 t. cornstarch		¼ t. sesame oil		
⅔ lb. dou miau (any green vegetable)		1 t. minced, sauteed shallots		
6 vermicelli sheets ("sha he fen")		9 C. stock		

❶ Rinse shrimp; devein and make a shallow cut along the backside of each one, running parallel to vein line (Fig. 1, 2, 3); mix with ① and let soak 20 minutes. Rinse spinach and cut into 1-inch sections (Fig. 4); cut vermicelli sheets into ½-inch strips; prepare ② and place in serving bowls.

❷ Boil 10C. water; precook vermicelli sheets and spinach separately until water boils again; remove and portion into serving bowls.

❸ Heat stock until boiling; add shrimp and when color changes and shrimp form "ball" shapes, portion equally into serving bowls with broth; serve.

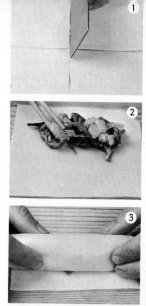

| ① | 里肌肉……4兩
醬油……半大匙
酒………半小匙
水………1大匙
太白粉…1小匙 | 蝦仁………2兩
太白粉…半小匙 | ② | 冬菇………2朶
熟筍………1枝 | | ④ | 酒……半大匙、胡椒……¼小匙
鹽……1小匙、麻油……¼小匙
醬油……半大匙、水………⅓杯
味精……半小匙、太白粉…半大匙
糖……半小匙 |
| | | | ③ | 豆芽菜……2兩
韭菜黃……2兩
薑絲………1大匙 | | | |

沙河粉……………………………3張
芝麻……………………………1½大匙

❶肉切絲調①料，蝦仁加太白粉拌匀，冬菇泡軟，切絲，熟筍亦切絲，韭菜黃切約3公分長段。

❷油8大匙燒熱，分別把肉、蝦仁炒熟盛起，另燒油4大匙將②料炒香，隨加③料同炒，即可放入炒熟肉絲、蝦仁及④料炒匀成餡，待冷。

❸沙河粉切爲10公分四方(圖1)，將餡分成18份，取1份置沙河粉中(圖2)捲成長條狀(圖3)水開蒸5分鐘取出。

❹芝麻炒香，洒在上面即可供食(圖4)。

三絲粉捲 3-Shred Rice Rolls

材料：18個 **Makes 18**

① ⅓ lb. pork loin
½ T. soy sauce
½ t. rice wine
1 T. water
1 t. cornstarch

2 oz. raw, shelled shrimp
½ t. cornstarch

② 2 pre-softened Chinese black mushrooms
1 precooked medium-sized bamboo shoot

③ 2 oz. bean sprouts
2 oz. Chinese chives*
1 T. shredded ginger root

④ ½ T. rice wine , ¼ t. black pepper
1 t. salt , ¼ t. sesame oil
½ T. soy sauce , ⅓ C. water
½ t. MSG , ½ T. cornstarch
½ t. sugar

3 vermicelli sheets ("sha he fen")
1½ T. sesame seeds

❶ Shred pork loin; mix with ① and let soak 20 minutes. Rinse shrimp and devein; add ½t. cornstarch. Shred Chinese black mushrooms and bamboo shoot; cut Chinese chives into 1-inch sections.

❷ Heat pan and 8T. oil; stir-fry separately pork shreds and shrimp until color changes; remove and drain. Remove all but 4T. oil from pan; reheat and stir-fry ② until fragrant and add ③ . Briefly stir-fry and add pork shreds, shrimp and ④ ; heat liquid until boiling and remove (filling). Let cool.

❸ Cut vermicelli sheets into 4-inch squares (Fig. 1); divide filling into 18 equal portions and spoon onto vermicelli sheets (Fig. 2). Roll up sheets to form rolls, 1½-inches wide (Fig. 3); place in steamer with "seam-side down".

❹ Stir-fry sesame seeds until golden brown; remove and set aside. Steam filled rolls for 5 minutes over medium heat; sprinkle sesame seeds over hot rolls and serve (Fig. 4). You may dip rolls in soy sauce before eating for extra flavor.

* If unavailable, substitute green onions.

<table>
<tbody>
<tr><td rowspan="2">①</td><td>蒜頭‥‥‥‥‥‥‥3 粒</td></tr>
<tr><td>蝦米‥‥‥‥‥‥‥1 兩</td></tr>
</tbody>
</table>

①
- 蒜頭‥‥‥‥‥‥‥3 粒
- 蝦米‥‥‥‥‥‥‥1 兩

②
- 肉‥‥‥‥‥‥‥‥半斤
- 芋頭‥‥‥‥‥‥1 2 兩
- 紅蘿蔔‥‥‥‥‥1 條
- 米‥‥‥‥‥‥‥‥3 杯
- 水‥‥‥‥‥‥‥1 5 杯

- 毛豆‥‥‥‥‥‥‥2 兩
- 荸薺‥‥‥‥‥‥‥2 兩

③
- 鹽‥‥‥‥‥‥‥4 小匙
- 味精‥‥‥‥‥‥2 小匙
- 胡椒‥‥‥‥‥‥半小匙

❶蒜頭拍破，蝦米洗淨，②料及荸薺切 1 公分四方小丁，米洗淨備用。

❷油 4 大匙燒熱，把①料炒香，即將②料及米加入略炒，隨加水 1 5 杯燒開，以小火煮到米熟了，即可加入毛豆及荸薺待滾，調入③料即可供食。

■台式粥做法簡單，其材料可因各人喜愛變換，例如主料以雞肉、牛肉、絞肉、生蠔，配料以筍、芹菜、絲瓜等等。

■芋頭切法：去皮（圖 1）切片後切條（圖 2、3）再切丁（圖 4）。

台式芋頭粥 Rainbow Taro Congee

材料：6 人份 **6 servings**

①
- 3 cloves garlic
- ¼ C. dried shrimp

②
- ⅔ lb. pork loin
- 1 taro or sweet potato (about 1lb.)
- 1 carrot
- 3 C. rice
- 15 C. water

- ½ C. green peas
- ½ C. water chestnuts

③
- 4 t. salt
- 2 t. MSG
- ½ t. black pepper

❶ Smash garlic; rinse shrimp; drain. Dice ingredients in ② and water chestnuts. Rinse rice until water runs clear.

❷ Heat pan and 4T. oil; stir-fry ① until fragrant; add ② and rice; stir-fry to mix together and add water; heat liquid until boiling and turn fire to small; cook until rice is done (about 20 minutes). After rice is cooked, add peas, water chestnuts and let boil; add ③ and serve.

■ Variations of this congee may be made by substituting chicken meat, chopped pork, oysters, bamboo shoot, celery or zucchini.

■ To dice taro root: Peel skin (Fig. 1). Cut into thick slices, then cut into strips (Fig. 2,3). Dice strips (Fig. 4).

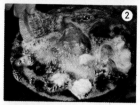

扁魚乾⋯⋯⋯半兩
「炸油」⋯⋯⋯1杯
① 白米⋯⋯⋯⋯2杯
高湯⋯⋯⋯⋯24杯
牛肉⋯⋯⋯12兩

② 醬油1½大匙、糖1小匙
酒半大匙、太白粉2大匙
水⋯⋯⋯⋯⋯6大匙

③ 鹽1⅓大匙、味精2小匙
豬油⋯⋯⋯⋯2大匙

④ 雞蛋⋯⋯⋯⋯⋯6個
葱絲⋯⋯⋯⋯5大匙
薑絲⋯⋯⋯⋯5大匙
油條（切2公分長）2條
香菜葉⋯⋯⋯2大匙

❶ 扁魚乾，炸呈金黃色，取出剁碎。
❷ 將炸好扁魚乾放入①料內，大火燒開後，改用小火燒煮1小時。
❸ 牛肉切片，拌入②料與③料放入粥內，輕拌勻至肉轉白熄火，分盛6碗加1個雞蛋在上面，與④料趁熱拌食。
■ 炸扁魚乾：油鍋內放入2、3粒蒜頭（圖1）隨入扁魚乾（圖2）用小火炸至蒜頭呈金黃色時，扁魚乾也好了（圖3）。

滑蛋牛肉粥 Sliced Beef With Scrambled Egg Congee

材料：6人份 **6 servings**

① ½ oz. dried brill fish
1 C. oil for frying
2 C. white rice
24 C. stock
1 lb. flank steak

② 1½ T. soy sauce
1 t. sugar
½ T. rice wine
2 T. cornstarch
6 T. water

③ 1⅓ T. salt
2 t. MSG
2 T. lard

④ 6 eggs
5 T. shredded green onion
5 T. shredded ginger root
2 "you tiau", cut into ½-inch sections
2 T. coriander

❶ Heat pan and oil until medium hot; deep-fry brill fish over low heat until golden brown; remove, drain and chop finely.
❷ Add chopped brill fish to ① . Heat ① until boiling; reduce heat to low and cook 1 hour, partially overed (congee).
❸ Cut beef into thin slices; add ② and mix; let soak 20 minutes. Add beef slices and ③ to congee; stir until meat pieces change color and turn off heat. Portion congee into serving bowls; add 1 egg on top of each serving and sprinkle ④ over all.
■ How to fry brill fish:
Heat oil and add 2 to 3 cloves garlic. (Fig. 1)
Add dried brill fish. (Fig. 2)
Fry brill fish over low heat until garlic is golden; remove. (Fig. 3)

142

①	扁魚乾…半兩 「炸油」…１杯 白米……２杯 高湯…２４杯	②	田雞…１２隻 鹽……１小匙 薑酒…１大匙	③	鹽…１⅓大匙 味精…２小匙 豬油…２大匙	④	葱絲…………５大匙 薑絲…………５大匙 油條(切２公分長)２枝 香菜葉………２大匙

❶ 扁魚乾，慢火炸呈金黃色取出剁碎。

❷ 將炸好扁魚乾放入①料內，大火燒開後，改用小火燒煮約１小時。

❸ 每隻田雞切為四塊，調入②料醃約２０分鐘。

❹ 臨起鍋時，將醃好田雞及③料放進粥內，燒沸分盛６碗，上淋麻油半小匙及④料即成。

■田雞切法：每隻田雞切為４塊(圖１)由小腿一端，將粗骨輕輕敲斷(圖２)將骨推擠出來(圖３)並用刀將小腿部份粗骨取出(圖４)。

■可用其他不同的材料取代田雞煮成不同的粥。例如：雞球、牛丸、魚片、鮑魚雞絲、蝦球等粥。

田雞粥 Frog's Legs Congee

材料：６人份 **6 servings**

½ oz. dried brill fish ("bien yu gan")*[1]
1 C. oil
12 frog's legs
① { 2 C. rice
24 C. stock
② { 1 t. salt
1 T. ginger wine
③ { 1⅓ T. salt,
2 t. MSG,
2 T. lard
④ { 5 T. shredded green onion
5 T. shredded ginger root
2 "you tiau", cut to ½ inch sections*[2]
2 T. coriander

❶ Heat pan and oil until medium hot; deep-fry brill fish over low heat until golden brown; remove, drain and chop finely.

❷ Add chopped brill fish to ① ; bring to a boil over high heat; reduce heat to low and cook for one hour, partially covered (congee).

❸ Cut each pair of frog's legs to half; mix with ② ; let soak 20 minutes.

❹ Add frog's legs and ③ to precooked congee; let boil and portion into serving bowls; add ½t. sesame oil and ④ to each portion and serve.

*[1] Dried brill fish may be purchased at a Chinese grocery store.

*[2] See P. 145 for directions for "you tiau".

■ To debone frog's legs: (Fig. 1) Cut frog legs into 4 sections. (Fig. 2) Make a vertical cut in each leg to expose bone; lightly cut through bone at joint. (Fig. 3) Fold over leg to expose tip of bone. (Fig. 4) Using tip of cleaver to secure bone, pull away leg from bone.

■ You may substitute other ingredients for the frog's legs and make a variety of congees: Follow steps ❶❷❹ as in Frog's Legs Congee and substitute the following ingredients: chicken congee, meatball congee, congee with fish slices, abalone, abalone and shrimp congee, abalone and chicken congee.

麵粉‥‥‥‥‥‥6杯	油酥‥‥‥‥‥‥¾杯	白芝麻‥‥‥‥‥‥¼杯
① 滾水‥‥‥‥‥1½杯	鹽‥‥‥‥‥半大匙	
冷水‥‥‥‥‥½杯	麵粉‥‥‥‥‥1大匙	

❶ 把麵粉放在盆裏，將①料依次倒入，攪拌均勻，揉至光滑成麵糰。

❷ 將麵糰放在擦上油的案板上，用趕麵桿趕壓成４５公分×４５公分四方麵片，然後把油酥均勻塗在麵片，並洒上鹽，再洒麵粉後，從麵片的一邊捲起，捲到盡頭成圓柱形，分成２０個小麵塊（切口處兩端捏緊，以免油酥流出）。

❸ 把小麵塊橫著，抓處兩端在左右（圖１），從⅔處往前趕約１０公分長（圖２）向前折二次翻面直放，從中間壓扁（圖３）向前折一次（圖４）於½處壓一下又折一次（圖５）在光滑面沾上白芝麻（圖６），中央輕壓一下（圖７），然後放直芝麻面朝下趕成１５公分×８公分之長方形麵餅（圖８）。

❹ 將長方形麵餅（芝麻面朝下），放進烤箱，烤約５分鐘後，翻面再烤５分鐘呈金黃色，即成「燒餅」。

■ 油酥做法：油１½杯燒滾，徐徐倒入３杯麵粉內(宜邊攪邊倒)，置爐上用小火熬１０分鐘，有香味呈淡咖啡色時，待冷即成油酥。

燒　餅　Flaky Sesame Flat Breads ("Shau Bing") 　　材料：２０個 Makes 20

6　C. flour	¾　C. roux mixture*	¼　C. sesame seeds
① 1½ C. boiling water	½　T. salt	
½ C. cold water	1　T. flour	

❶ Place flour in a mixing bowl; add boiling water; mix and add cold water; mix again; knead into a smooth, elastic dough (about 5-8 minutes).

❷ Lightly oil surface of counter; using a rolling pin, roll dough into a square 1½-feet long and 1½-foot wide; spread surface evenly with roux mixture and sprinkle with salt and flour. Starting from nearest horizontal edge, roll up jelly-roll style; cut into 20 pieces and pinch ends of each piece so that filling doesn't spill out edges.
Pinched edges on sides of one piece (Fig. 1). Place rolling pin at about two-third's mark from furthest edge; roll out (away from you) about 4-inches (Fig. 2). Fold piece into thirds; turn piece to vertical. Place rolling pin at half-way mark and flatten (Fig. 3); fold piece into half (Fig 4). Place rolling pin at half-way mark and flatten; fold into half again (Fig. 5). With seam-side down dip into sesame seeds (Fig. 6); Place rolling pin at half-way mark to flatten (Fig. 7) sesame side down and roll into a 6 x 3 inch rectangle (Fig. 8). Place in an ungreased pan, sesame side down and repeat procedure for all other pieces.

❸ Preheat oven to 400° and bake 5 minutes; turn over breads and bake another 5 minutes until both sides are crispy and golden brown; remove and serve.

* To make roux mixture: heat 1½C. vegetable oil until hot; add 3C. flour and mix together; place pan over low heat and continue to mix until golden brown (about 10 minutes); remove and use as directed.

■ These breads may be served stuffed with hot "you tiau" accompanied by "Do Jiang" for a traditional Chinese breakfast or stuffed with meat, vegetables, etc. for snacks or a light meal.

燒餅 Flaky Sesame Flat Breads ("Shau Bing")

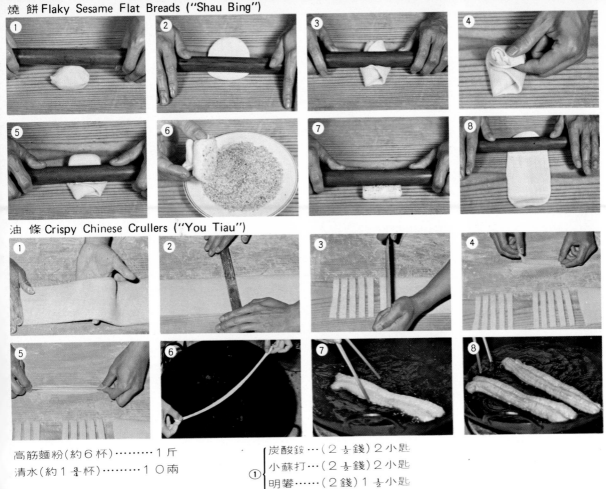

油條 Crispy Chinese Crullers ("You Tiau")

高筋麵粉(約6杯)‥‥‥‥1斤
清水(約1¾杯)‥‥‥‥10兩

① ┌ 炭酸銨‥‥(2½錢)2小匙
  │ 小蘇打‥‥(2½錢)2小匙
  │ 明礬‥‥‥(2錢)1½小匙
  └ 鹽‥‥‥‥(2錢)1½小匙

❶將①料放在盆裡加入清水，略攪拌使完全溶解後，加入麵粉調勻，擱置15～20分鐘，將麵自四週圍拉起向中央揉和，使之滑潤，再待15～20分鐘，重拉一次，如此三或四次，即已非常滑潤，把整塊麵糰翻面，再抹少許油，以防乾皮，放置一小時後，用塑膠布或玻璃紙包成長條，擱置約4小時即可使用。(若做大量時，可將麵糰分為一斤之麵塊，再一一包好)。

❷將麵解開放在案板上慢慢拉長(圖1)，並趕成約7公分寬，0.3公分厚之長條(圖2)，再切成約一公分寬小條(圖3)，每2小條上下重疊(圖4)，用細棒順長條中央壓一下(圖5)，用手指捏着兩端拉長，放在滾熱油鍋裏(圖6)不停翻撥(圖7)，待定型為止，炸至金黃色取出即成(圖8)。

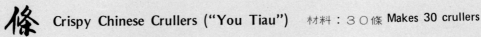

油 條 Crispy Chinese Crullers ("You Tiau")　材料：30條 Makes 30 crullers

6　C. high-rising flour
1¾ C. water

① ┌ 2　t.　ammonium bicarbonate
  │ 2　t.　baking soda
  │ 1½ t.　alum　(food grade)
  └ 1½ t.　salt.

❶ Place ingredients of ① in mixing bowl; add water and stir until ingredients have dissolved, than add flour and mix well, stirring in a circular upward direction until dough is smooth; let stand 15-20 minutes. Using hands, pick up a portion of dough surrounding edge and drop into center of dough; continue procedure around the entire edge; let rest 15-20 minutes. Repeat this entire procedure 3-4 more times until the dough is elastic and smooth. Using index finger and thumb of each hand, pick up each end of dough piece and turn over, right side down. Lightly coat surface with oil so that dough will stay moist; let rest 1 hour in refrigerator. Remove dough carefully from bowl and place on a piece of cellophane paper; wrap up tightly and let sit 4 hrs. in refrigerator. (If you make more than one times the recipe, cut the dough to sections, wrap in cellophane and refrigerate).

❷ Lightly flour rolling board; unwrap dough from cellophane and place dough piece horizontally across board, using hands, lightly stretch piece to a long (Fig.1), strip 2 inches wide and 1/8-inch thick; lightly flatten strip with rolling pin (Fig. 2). Using a cleaver or knife, cut the dough piece into smaller strips ½-inch wide (Fig. 3), pick up a strip, turn it around, and place it directly on top of next strip so that opposite ends are together (Fig. 4) taking a thin rod, press directly in middle of double strips to attach them more securely to each other; (Fig. 5) repeat process for other strips. Heat oil for deep-frying; picking up a strip at the ends, stretch lightly so that piece is about 15 inches long, then drop into hot oil (Fig. 6) and flip over continuously with chopsticks (Fig. 7) until cruller expands and turns golden brown; remove and drain (Fig. 8). Repeat for other strips; place hot crullers in split "Flaky Sesame Flat Breads" ("Shau Bing") and serve with "Salty or Sweet Soy Bean Milk".

黃豆…………半斤　　　　　糖…………２杯

❶ 黃豆洗淨用清水浸泡（圖１）（需淹蓋黃豆面３倍以上，夏天約６～８小時，冬天約１２～１４小時）至黃豆膨脹２～２.５倍（圖２）。

❷ 浸好之黃豆瀝乾水份，加７杯水分幾次放入果汁機內攪碎。

❸ 將打碎黃豆裝入清潔之白布袋內（紗布亦可）（圖３）再加水８杯擠出汁除去豆渣，即爲「生豆漿」（圖４）。

❹ 將生豆漿以中火燒滾後改小火繼續燒煮１０分鐘（以去豆腥味）加糖即成。

鹹豆漿： 備中型湯碗一個，放入適量之油條、蝦米、榨菜、葱、香菜、肉鬆及黑醋、辣油、醬油、味精、麻油、塩，沖入滾豆漿即成。

甜豆漿 Sweet Soybean Milk ("Do Jiang")　　　材料：６人份 **6 servings**

⅔ lb. soybeans　　　2 C. sugar

❶ Rinse soybeans in water (Fig. 1); drain and let soak in water 3 times the amount of soybeans. (In summer, soak beans 6 to 8 hours; in winter, soak beans 12 to 14 hours). Soak until soybeans are 2 to 2½ times original size (Fig. 2).

❷ Drain soybeans; add 7 C. water and blend (using 3 C. to 4 C. at one time) until mixture is fine (about 10 minutes).

❸ Place mixture in a cheesecloth bag (Fig. 3) and pour 8 C. water into blended soybean paste and squeeze into retained soybean liquid (Fig. 4). Throw away dry sediment left in chessecloth bag and pour strained liquid into a saucepan (bean milk).

❹ Heat bean milk over medium heat until liquid reaches a boil; cook 10 min. add sugar and mix well; serve plain or with "Syau Bing" and "You Tiau".

■ For extra nutrition, add 1 raw egg to individual serving bowl; beat lightly and add boiling soybean milk; stir and serve.

Salty Bean Milk:

Put proper portion of "you tiau", chopped dried shrimp, chopped Szechuan pickled mustard green, chopped green onion, chopped coriander, dried shredded pork ("rou soong"), worcestershire sauce, hot pepper oil ("la you"), soy sauce, MSG sesame oil, ,salt.

猪肉（夾心、後腿各半）……5斤
腸衣………………………20尺

① 鹽、味精各…………2½大匙
糖………¾杯、硝……1小匙
高粱酒…半杯、五香粉1小匙
（依個人喜愛酌量加入玉桂粉
或蒜粉等香料）

❶將肉去皮，並分切肥肉、瘦肉兩部份，肥的切約半公分四方，瘦的切約1公分四方，加①料拌勻並多次
的甩打幾下醃一天備用。

❷腸衣以溫水泡軟，握乾水份，將腸衣一端以繩子綁住，另端套上漏斗，把腸衣全部推上（圖1），將醃好的
肉灌入（圖2），如此將整條的腸衣都灌滿了肉，以針在腸的四週打洞（圖3）使其透氣，即可在每隔10
公分處，用繩子紮住（圖4），用溫水洗淨後吊在通風處晾約3天即成。

❸將香腸入鍋以慢火煎、烤或炸熟即可供食。

■做香腸應在天氣晴朗時，以免發霉。

香　腸　Tasty Chinese Sausage

材料：60小段　**Makes 60**

6½ lbs. fresh ham
20 feet sausage casing

① 2½ T. salt
2½ T. MSG
¾ C. sugar
1 t. niter or saltpeter*
½ C. scotch
1 t. 5-spice powder (if preferable, add a dash of garlic powder or cinnamon)

❶ Remove skin from pork; separate fat and lean meat. Cut fat into 1/8-inch thick slices and cut lean meat into 1/3-inch-thick
slices; add ① and mix vigorously for 3-4 minutes; let soak 24 hours.

❷ Soak sausage casing in warm water until soft; remove and drain. Tie off one end of sausage. Attach a funnel to the other end
and gather sausage casing on funnel tube (Fig. 1); stuff marinated meat into casing (Fig. 2); squeeze to distribute filling evenly
throughout the casing. Using a needle, prick generously all sides of sausage to allow air out of sausage (Fig. 3); tie sausages
every 4 inches (Fig. 4); rinse in warm water and drain; hang outside to dry or in a well-circulated area for 3 days.

❸ Sausage may be steamed, deep-fried or baked, all over low heat for about 8 minutes; slice into paper-thin pieces and serve with
fresh garlic slivers.

* Niter aids in preservation, however, if may be omitted.

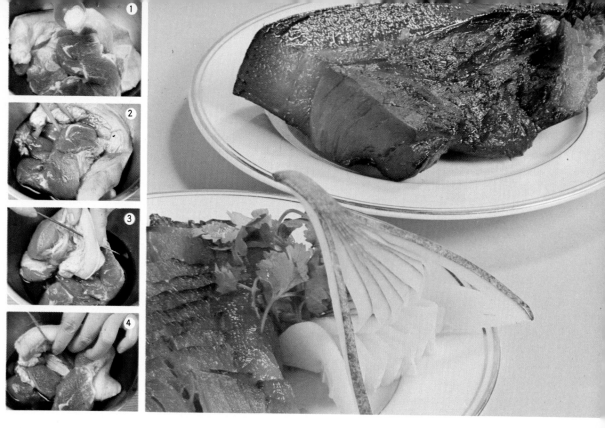

前腿肉⋯⋯⋯⋯ 1 斤

①{
鹽⋯⋯⋯⋯⋯ 1 大匙
糖⋯⋯⋯⋯ 1½ 大匙
酒⋯⋯⋯⋯ 1½ 大匙
醬油⋯⋯⋯ 1½ 大匙
硝⋯⋯⋯⋯⋯ ⅛ 小匙
}

❶肉加①料拌勻（圖 1、2），隔半小時翻拌一次，使其入味，醃約 1 〇小時，將肉一端穿一個小洞（圖 3）以繩子穿上繫好（圖 4），溫水輕輕洗滌一次，用長竹竿穿上，放在烈日下晒 1～2 日後，改在蔭涼處輕吹乾（約 2～3 日），即可蒸熟切片供食。

■酒最好用高粱酒醃。

臘　肉　Spicy Dried Pork

1⅓ lbs. fresh bacon

①{
1　T.　salt
1½ T.　sugar
1½ T.　rice wine *1
1½ T.　soy sauce
⅛　t.　niter or saltpeter *2
}

❶ Cut bacon into 1-inch wide sections; mix with ① (Fig. 1, 2) and let soak 10 hours mixing marinade and meat every 30 minutes. Puncture a hole in each pie (Fig. 3) and pull string through hole (Fig. 4). Lightly rinse in warm water and hang up to dry in the sunshine for 1-2 days; move to a breezy place for 2-3 additional days. Steam 8 minutes over high heat; cut into paper-thin slices and serve.

*1 This dish is much tastier if made with a strong wine or scotch.
*2 Niter aids in preservation, however, it may be omitted.

瘦前腿肉⋯⋯⋯ 1 斤

①
酒⋯⋯⋯⋯⋯ 1 大匙
糖⋯⋯⋯⋯⋯ 2 大匙
鹽⋯⋯⋯⋯⋯ 半大匙
醬油⋯⋯⋯⋯ 1 大匙
海山醬⋯⋯⋯ 1 大匙

將肉切長條(圖1、2)，調①料拌勻(圖3、4)，醃約1小時後，即可用烤箱500°烤約20分鐘即成。

叉燒肉 Chinese Roasted Pork

1⅓ lbs. pork picnic shoulder

①
1 T. rice wine
2 T. sugar
½ T. salt
1 T. soy sauce
1 T. "hai shan jiang" (hoisin sauce)

Cut meat into 2-inch wide sections (Fig. 1, 2); add ① and mix (Fig. 3, 4); let soak 1 hour. Preheat over to 500°; bake 20 minutes remove, slice and serve or use as directed in "Roasted Pork Buns" on P. 4 .

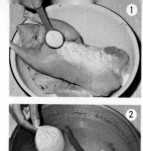

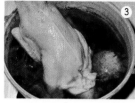

鴨‥‥‥‥‥‥‥‥‥３斤
鹽‥‥‥‥‥‥‥‥‥４大匙

① ｜丁香、八角｜
｜花椒、陳皮｜
｜草菓、小茴｜ 50g
｜三乃、甘草｜
｜肉桂｜

② ｜水（水要滿過鴨身）１５杯
｜鹽‥‥‥‥‥‥‥‥‥半杯
｜葱‥‥‥‥‥‥‥‥‥６條
｜薑‥‥‥‥‥‥‥‥‥６片
｜辣椒‥‥‥‥‥‥‥‥２枝

❶鴨去內臟洗淨，用鹽將鴨全身內外抹勻，醃２小時後洗淨（圖１）。

❷①料放入②料內燒煮約半小時，煮出味（圖２），即成滷汁。

❸把鴨放入滷汁內（圖３）小火燒煮２０分鐘，將鴨身翻轉再煮２０分鐘至鴨熟續浸３０分鐘取起待冷，即
可剁塊，排列在菜盤上，澆上滷汁即成。

■煮鴨鹽水可以保存不壞，繼續使用。

■香料在中藥店購買。如要簡化，可僅用丁香、八角、花椒、陳皮。

塩水鴨 Spicy Water Duckling

1 duckling (about 4 lbs.)
4 T. salt

① cloves ("丁香")
star anise ("八角")
Szechuan peppercorns ("花椒")
dried orange peel ("陳皮")
fennel ("草菓")
cumin ("小茴")
"san ny" ("三乃")
licorice ("甘草")
cinnamon stick ("肉桂")

Combined ②
ingredients
equal ¾C.
or 2 oz.*

15 C. water (water must cover duckling
½ C. salt
6 stalks green onion
6 slices ginger root
2 hot red peppers

❶ Clean duckling thoroughly; drain and rub interior with 4 T. salt; let sit 2 hours (Fig. 1); clean and drain.

❷ Place ① and ② together in a pan and cook covered over medium heat for 30 minutes (Fig. 2) (braising sauce).

❸ Place duckling in the braising sauce (Fig. 3), cook covered over low heat for 20 minutes, turn other side and cook another 20
minutes (duckling should be tender). Turn off the fire, let sit covered for 30 minutes, remove and drain. After the duckling is
cool, cut duckling into bite-size pieces, arrange on serving plate and pour a little braising sauce over pieces. Serve.

* These spices are available at any Chinese herbal drug store or substitute 5-spice salt with cinnamon and fennel added.

■ Braising sauce will keep for a long time if stored in refrigerator. It may be used for stewing chicken liver, meat, hard-boiled
eggs, etc.

150

鴨肫肝‥‥‥‥‥‥6付

將鴨肫肝洗淨，放入鹽水鴨滷汁內，參照鹽水鴨，蓋鍋燒開，即熄火燜至汁冷時，取出切片。

■鴨肫處理法：去薄膜(圖1)從中間剖開(圖2)，除去沙囊膜(圖3)用鹽洗淨(圖4)。

■鹽水鴨滷汁做法：請參照第150頁鹽水鴨。

鹽水肫肝 Salty Water Liver and Kidney

6 pairs duckling liver
6 pairs duckling gizzard

❶ Rinse livers and gizzards; place in pan with ① from "Spicy Water Duckling"; cover and bring liquid to a boil; turn off heat and let sit covered until soup has cooled to room temperature; remove gizzards and livers and slice into paper-thin pieces; serve.

■ To clean gizzards: Remove any membrane (Fig. 1). Make a cut in gizzards at half-way mark (Fig. 2). Remove any white tendons or yellow matter (Fig. 3). Rub gizzards with salt and rinse with water (Fig. 4).

新鮮後腿瘦肉⋯半斤
或　　牛肉
　　魚淨肉
　墨魚淨肉
　　蝦仁

① ┌ 肥肉(剁爛)⋯⋯⋯半兩
　│ 薑酒⋯⋯⋯⋯ 1 小匙
　│ 味精⋯⋯⋯⋯ $\frac{1}{4}$ 小匙
　│ 胡椒⋯⋯⋯⋯ $\frac{1}{4}$ 小匙
　│ 糖⋯⋯⋯⋯⋯ $\frac{1}{4}$ 小匙
　│ 麻油⋯⋯⋯⋯ $\frac{1}{4}$ 小匙
　│ 蛋白⋯⋯⋯⋯ 1 個
　└ 太白粉⋯⋯⋯ 1 大匙

❶將肉洒上鹽 1 小匙(圖 1)，搗成泥(圖 2)，調入①料用力攪至有黏性，成肉茸(圖 3)。
❷將肉茸用手抓住，擠成一個個的丸子(圖 4)放入鍋內，以中火煮至丸子熟了浮出水面，即可撈起盛盤。
■水煮外也可用蒸、炸或紅燒。

貢　丸 Pork Balls

⅔ lb. fresh ham
　　or
⅔ lb. rump roast of beef
　　or
⅔ lb. firm, white fish meat
　　or
⅔ lb. squid meat
　　or
⅔ lb. raw, shelled shrimp

① ┌ ½ oz. pork fat, chopped finely
　│ 1 t. ginger wine
　│ ¼ t. MSG
　│ ¼ t. black pepper
　│ ¼ t. sugar
　│ ¼ t. sesame oil
　│ 1 egg white
　└ 1 T. cornstarch

❶ Sprinkle meat or fish of choice with 1t. salt (Fig. 1) and chop finely(Fig. 2); add ① and mix 3-4 minutes; lightly throwing mixture against inside of mixing bowl to thoroughly combine ingredients (paste) (Fig. 3).
❷ Add 10 C. cold water to a pan; grab a handful of fish paste and squeeze paste into balls(Fig. 4). Add to cold water, one by one, and cook over medium heat. When balls rise to surface and are tender, remove and drain; serve.
■ Balls may also be steamed, fried or stewed in sauce as directed for "Spicy Pork over Rice" on P. 84.

瘦肉⋯⋯⋯⋯⋯ 1 斤　　①{ 醬油⋯ 1 大匙、味精 1 小匙　　油⋯⋯⋯⋯⋯ 2 大匙
　　　　　　　　　　　鹽⋯⋯ 2 小匙、糖 4 大匙

❶將肉去除白筋分割成數塊加水３杯，　水開改小火燒煮３０分鐘（湯汁留用），肉塊搗鬆（圖１）再撕成細
　　絲狀（圖２），即可移入炒鍋（圖２），連同煮肉湯汁並加①料（圖３）小火翻炒至乾即成肉脯。

❷將肉脯加油２大匙以小火繼續炒鬆即成肉鬆。

魚　鬆：

❶將魚肉１斤切大片加蔥２枝薑２片酒１大匙蒸約１０分鐘，趁熱移入炒鍋用鍋鏟將蒸熟魚片壓細，並加
　　①料用小火炒乾，再加油２大匙繼續以小火炒鬆即成魚鬆。

肉　鬆　Meat Flakes (Soft and Crispy)

1⅓ lbs. pork picnic shoulder

①{ 1　T.　soy sauce
　　2　t.　salt
　　1　t.　MSG
　　4　T.　sugar

2 T.　lard or vegetable oil

❶ If pork contains different grain sections, cut to separate; cook with 3C. water; when water boiling turn to medium heat cook 30 minutes until soft.* Using the bottom of a bottle, mash to flat pieces (Fig. 1); place mashed meat and liquid in pan (Fig. 2); add meat liquid and ① (Fig. 3) continue to mix over low heat until very dry. (Soft meat flakes) Serve.

❷ To make "Crispy Meat Flakes" add 2T. lard or oil to soft meat flakes and continue to stir-fry over low heat until dry and golden brown; remove and serve.

* If no pressure cooker is available, place meat in a covered casserole and cook 1 hour over low heat until meat is very tender.

Fish Flakes：

Cut 1⅓ lb. fish into ½-inch thick slices; steam with 2 stalks green onion, 2 slices ginger root, 1T. rice wrine over medium heat for 10 minutes. Place fish and steamed liquid and in pan and mash finely over low heat; add ① ; continue to stir-fry until mixture is dry; and 1½T. lard (this stir-frying process should take about one hour). Continue to mix and fry over low heat until mixture becomes flaky and golden brown. Remove and serve.

後腿豬瘦肉……2斤

| ① | 鹽………1½小匙、醬油………2大匙
糖………4大匙、米酒………1大匙
玉桂粉……⅛小匙、紅粉………⅛小匙
五香粉……⅛小匙、味精………1小匙
甘草粉……⅛小匙 |

❶順肉紋切成薄片（圖１），調①料醃泡一天後（圖２），將肉片密接平舖在直徑７０公分之竹篩上（圖３），晒（風）乾或烤乾（約七成乾）。

❷乾燥後之肉片自竹篩整片取出，並分割爲十二片，然後以燒紅木炭火，中火將每片肉乾慢慢烤至熟即成。

■每一竹篩可舖二斤肉片，如無竹篩可用鋁盤代替，但晒（風）乾時，需將肉翻面晒乾。

猪肉乾 Tasty Dried Meat Squares

2⅔ lbs. fresh ham or pork lion

| ① | 1½ t. salt
4 T. sugar
⅛ t. cinnamon
⅛ t. 5-spice powder
⅛ t. licorice powder *1
2 T. soy sauce
1 T. rice wine
⅛ t. red food coloring
1 t. MSG |

❶ Partially freeze meat to facilitate cutting; cut along grain into paper-thin slices (Fig.1); add ① and mix; let soak 24 hours (Fig. 2). Press soaked meat slices side by side in a lightly oiled bamboo basket*2 2-1/3 feet in diameter (as a patchwork quilt) (Fig. 3); place basket outside, and let dry 24 hours (pieces should be 70% dry and slightly moist).

❷ Remove meat "piece" (Pieces should have dried together to make one big square) and cut into 12 squares. Grill each square over a barbecue 1½ minutes on each side, until lightly browned or bake at 400° on a grill until brown.

*1 If unavailable, omit.

*2 A 2-1/3 foot-round bamboo basket will hold 2-2/3 lb. meat; if bamboo basket is unavailable, use a serving tray of this size and turn over meat piece after 12 hours to dry thoroughly.

①	牛肉（後腿肉）……1 斤		②	醬油………1 大匙
	清水……………3 杯			鹽…………2 小匙
	薑………………2 片			糖…………3 大匙
	葱………………2 枝			味精………1 小匙
	大茴（八角）	香料半兩或僅用八角3朵		酒…………1 大匙
	小茴（芫茜子）	（在中藥店購買）		
	三奈、陳皮、草菓			

❶牛肉整塊加入①料，以快鍋燒煮約２５分鐘或用普通鍋煮至熟取出待冷，汁留用。

❷牛肉切片(順紋路厚薄自定)（圖１），加入牛肉汁及②料（圖２）用小火炒至汁乾（圖３）放入烤盤內（圖４）
，以 ３５０ 度烤２０分鐘即成。

■辣牛肉乾：②料內另加辣椒粉１大匙。■咖喱牛肉乾：②料內另加咖喱粉１大匙。

五香牛肉乾 Tasty Dried 5-Spice Meat Squares

1⅓ lbs. lean, boneless chuck steak

①	3 C. water
	3 slices ginger root
	2 stalks green onion
	star of anise ("大茴")
	coriander seeds ("小茴")
	"san ny" ("三奈")
	dried orange peel ("陳皮")
	fennel ("草菓")

Combined ingredients equal ½ oz. or substitute 3 star anise

②	1 T. soy sauce
	2 t. salt
	3 T. sugar
	1 t. MSG
	1 T. rice wine

❶ Mix ① with beef; place in a pressure cooker and cook 25 minutes or place in a covered pot and cook 1½ hours over medium heat until meat is tender; let cool and drain (retain liquid).

❷ Cut beef along grain into paper-thin slice (Fig. 1), place in a pan with retained liquid and ② (Fig. 2); stir over low heat until mixtures is dry (Fig. 3); remove and spread pieces flat on a cookie sheet (Fig. 4); preheat oven to 350°; bake 20 minutes; remove and serve.

◀ Variations:

"Spicy Hot Beef Squares": Follow directions for "Tasty Dried 5-Spice Meat Squares" and add 1T. hot pepper powder ("la jiau fen") to ② .

"Curry Beef Squares: Follow directions for "Tasty Dried 5-Spice Meat Squares" and when stir-frying add 2t. curry powder.

黃豆⋯⋯⋯⋯⋯⋯1斤　　①{燒石膏⋯(１５公克)１大匙　　水⋯⋯⋯⋯⋯⋯３０杯
　　　　　　　　　　　　温開水⋯⋯⋯⋯⋯⋯１杯

❶黃豆洗淨，加３～５倍水浸泡夏天約６～８小時，冬天約１２～１４小時，至黃豆膨脹２～2.5倍。

❷浸好之黃豆瀝乾水份，加水１５杯，分數次放入果汁機內攪碎。裝入白布袋內(紗布亦可)(圖１)，再
　加水１５杯擠出汁(圖２)，濾去豆渣，即爲「生豆漿」。

❸將「生豆漿」中火煮開後，改小火繼續燒煮１０分鐘，以去豆腥味，煮時須不停攪動，以免黏鍋。

❹豆漿趁熱(８０度以上)攪拌，慢慢加入調勻①料(圖３)，至全部加完，立即停止攪拌，靜置１０分鐘(
　圖４)，即爲「豆腐腦」。

❺豆腐模型先舖入８０公分方形白布(圖５)，再倒入「豆腐腦」(圖６)輕輕搗碎，再將白布覆好(圖７)，
　蓋上木板模(圖８)上加重壓(約１５公斤重)，使水份濾出(約１５分鐘)除去模型白布，即爲「豆腐」。

■豆腐之老嫩視重壓物之輕重及時間長短而定。　■煮豆漿時火不可太大，以免產生泡沫溢出鍋外。

豆腐 Bean Curd

1⅓ lbs. soybeans　　①{1 T. gypsum　　　30 C. water
　　　　　　　　　　　　1 C. water

❶ Rinse soybeans in water; drain and let soak in water 3 times the amount of soybeans (In summer, soak beans 6 to 8 hours; in winter, soak beans 12 to 14 hours). Soak until soybeans are 2 to 2½ times original size.

❷ Drain soybeans; add 15 C. water and blend (using 3 C. to 4 C. at one time) until mixture is fine (about 10 minutes).
Pour blended mixture into a cheesecloth bag (Fig. 1) and add 15 C. water through strainer. Discard remaining sediment in cheesecloth bag and retain strained liquid (bean curd milk) (Fig. 2).

❹ Add bean curd milk to a saucepan and heat until boiling; turn heat to low and cook 10 minutes, stirring constantly so mixture won't burn.

❺ Remove bean curd milk from heat and slowly add ① mixture, stirring constantly (Fig. 3); let sit 10 minutes (bean curd jelly) (Fig. 4).

❻ Line bean curd mold with 31½ inches square cloth (Fig. 5). Add bean curd jelly (Fig. 6) and lightly cut bean curd jelly to break up into pieces; fold material to cover top of bean curd (Fig. 7); place wooden cover of bean curd mold on top (Fig. 8) Place weights (equal to 33 lbs.) on top and let rest 15 minutes; remove wooden cover and cloth; remove bean curd and use a desired.

■ Bean curd may be made soft or hard according to your preference. Varying the resting period (long or short) and the weight of weights (heavy or light) will influence the texture of bean curd; vary either according to your own taste.
If heat is too high while cooking bean curd milk, the liquid will overflow.

黄豆……………… 1 斤

① ⎧ 燒石膏…（８公克）½大匙
　 ⎨ 太白粉(玉米粉)…６大匙
　 ⎩ 溫開水……………… 1 杯

❶ 參照豆腐做法❶❷❸❹。

❷ 豆漿保持８０度以上，邊攪拌慢慢加入調勻①料至全部加完，立即停止攪拌，靜置１０分鐘即爲「豆腐腦」。

❸ 食用時可加入適量糖水，依個人 喜好加入薑汁或煮爛之花生湯。

■ 做豆腐腦①料內加太白粉則滑嫩，效果較好。

豆腐腦 Bean Curd Jelly

1⅓　lbs. soybeans

① ⎧ ½　T. gypsum
　 ⎨ 6　T. cornstarch
　 ⎩ 1　C. warm water

❶ Follow steps ❶ , ❷ , ❸ , ❹ , as directed in the recipe above.
❷ Remove bean curd milk from heat and add ① ; let stand 10 minutes (bean curd jelly).
❸ Serve bean curd jelly with hot sweet soup (sugar and water), hot sweetened ginger water and cooked peanuts, if desired.

花生⋯⋯⋯⋯⋯⋯⋯ 1 杯　　　柴魚片⋯⋯⋯⋯⋯⋯適量
洋菜⋯⋯⋯⋯⋯⋯⋯½兩　　①{葱、薑末／醬油露}⋯⋯⋯適量
水⋯⋯⋯⋯⋯⋯⋯ 1 〇杯

❶花生用温水4杯泡約3〇分鐘，去皮另加水1杯，以果汁機攪細後倒入白布袋（或紗布），擠出汁備用。
❷洋菜洗淨，泡約3〇分鐘（圖1）撈出放入水1〇杯內（圖2）後燒開，改小火續煮至洋菜完全溶化時（圖3），加入花生汁，再燒滾隨即熄火，倒於鋁盤中（36公分×26公分×2公分），或小便當盒內（圖4），待涼即爲「冷凍豆腐」。
❸每塊冷凍豆腐上置柴魚片（約半杯）及①料適量即成。
■可將煮好洋菜花生汁，分裝小便當盒內取食較便。

冷凍豆腐 Jelled Bean Curd

1　C. peanuts.
½ oz. agar-agar*
10 C. water

①{ stock fish / chopped ginger root / chopped green onion / soy sauce } amount to your preference

❶ Soak peanuts for 30 minutes in 4C. warm water; remove skin from peanuts and add 1 C. water; blend at high speed in electric blender, strain mixture through cheesecloth.
❷ Wash agar-agar; soak for 30 minutes (Fig. 1); remove and add 10 C. water (Fig. 2); bring to a boil; lower heat and cook until dissolved (Fig. 3); add peanut sauce, bring to a boil and then turn off heat; pour mixture into 1"x 8" x 12" pan or small, individual square pans (Fig. 4). Let cool; cut into slices.
❸ Arrange on top of each slice about ½ C. (stock fish) and as much of ① as desired. Serve.
*　If unavailable, use gelatin and follow instructions on package.

中筋或高筋麵粉‧‧‧‧‧‧‧‧‧‧‧‧6杯
鹽‧‧‧‧‧‧1½小匙、清水‧‧‧‧‧3杯

❶鹽放入清水內待溶化，加入篩過麵粉拌勻，並以清水¼杯濕潤表面，以免乾燥，置半小時(俗稱醒麵)至
　表面起泡。
❷用手將麵逐次自四週拉起向中央揉和反覆數次至麵生筋。
❸以中火將平底鍋均勻燒熱，擦淨，並以油布將欲做春捲皮之大小周圍擦出一道圓形。
❹用手抓起一糰麵(圖1)迅速自鐵鍋中央向外均勻地擦一圓形(圖2)隨將多餘之麵糰抓起(圖3)並將留在
　麵皮上的小麵粒按平(圖4)把麵皮略烙熟，皮邊稍有翻起現象時，即成春捲皮。
■做春捲皮有專用之鐵板，如無可用大同鍋或厚的大平底鍋來試做。
■若鍋過熱時，擦出之春捲皮會粘着手中之麵糰時，應以乾淨濕布擦擦鐵板，使熱度降低。

春捲皮 Spring Roll Skins　　　　　　材料：３５張 **35 skins**

6 C. flour　　　　　　3 C. water
1½ t. salt

❶ Sift flour and salt together in a bowl; gradually add water, mixing thoroughly after each addition . Continue stirring until
dough is smooth; pour ¼C. water on top to keep dough from drying; let stand ½ hour (bubbles should appear around edge in
bowl).
❷ Using hands, pick up a portion of dough surrounding edge of bowl and drop into center of dough; continue procedure around
the entire edge and repeat until dough is smooth and elastic. Sprinkle a little water on top of dough to keep it moist.
❸ Place flat, heavy grill over medium heat and let heat evenly. Clean grill with scraper and with an oil-soaked cloth, outline a 6-
inch circle on grill. Grab a fistful of dough (Fig. 1) and lightly ''wipe'' grill with dough in a circular motion to create a 6-inch
paper-thin pancake (Fig. 2, 3). Lightly dab holes (Fig. 4), if any, with dough. When edges of circle begin to curl up, peel skin
off grill and place on serving plate , Repeat for other skins.
■ If grill is too hot, pancakes will stick; lightly wipe grill with a moist cloth to lower temperature; then outline size again with oil
soaked cloth.

159

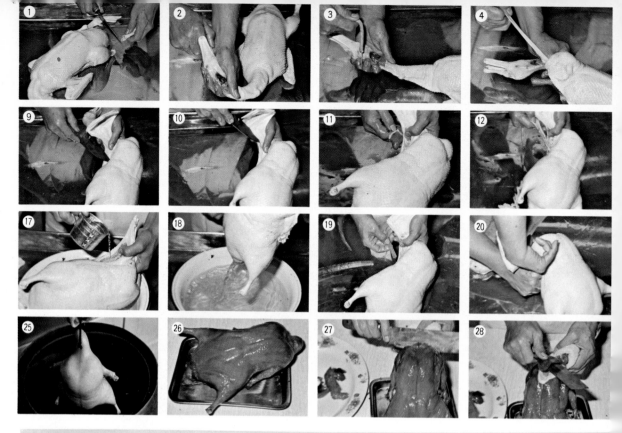

北平烤鴨

鴨(4～5斤)………1隻	荷葉餅……………12張	沾料：	麻油……2大匙
麥芽糖(或蜂蜜)…3大匙	葱(5公分長)……24枝		甜麵醬…4大匙
		①	糖………4大匙
			水…………半杯

■荷葉餅做法：參照本書荷葉餅(第19頁)。

■沾料做法：麻油2大匙燒熱，加入攪勻之①料，中火燒煮2分鐘，至濃稠狀即可。

■烤鴨做法：圖1～圖32　(張鳳山先生示範)

❶切除鴨掌。

❷用手指勾出鴨舌。

❸由頸部拉出氣管。

❹將頸部之食道拉鬆。

❺抓住鴨腿上部向前扭鬆關節。

❻用口或打氣筒由頸部吹氣至鴨皮與肉分開，
　至全身充氣為止。

❼食指伸入肛門，將食指繞腸頭一圈，鈎住腸頭。

❽掏出腸頭。

❾由腋下劃刀。

❿至翅膀6公分長。

⓫食指由切口處伸入先掏出鴨心。

⓬拉出食道。

⓭將食道捲住左手食指拉緊。

⓮取出肫肝。

⓯取出腸等。

⓰最後取出鴨肺。

⓱由切口處灌水。

⓲將鴨身內外洗淨。

⓳取7公分長竹片，由開口處伸入。

⓴竹片一端頂住鴨胸之三叉骨，另一端頂住脊
　椎骨、撐高胸部。

㉑切除鴨翅膀。

㉒用掛勾勾住鴨頸。

㉓以滾水將鴨全身燙勻，最後淋上糖汁(麥芽
　糖或蜂蜜3大匙、水6杯預先煮開)。

㉔掛於通風處風乾。

㉕烤爐(或烤箱)燒至350～400度，放入
　鴨子，先烤背部20分鐘後，翻轉再烤胸部

㉖前後40～50分鐘，呈金黃色取出。

㉗先從頸部兩邊用刀片皮。

㉘再由三叉骨處片皮。

㉙將刀由下端往上片皮及肉。

㉚掀開三叉骨。

㉛胸脯正中切1刀再片皮及肉。

㉜荷葉餅包上1片鴨皮(或肉)、葱段、甜麵醬
　包好食之。

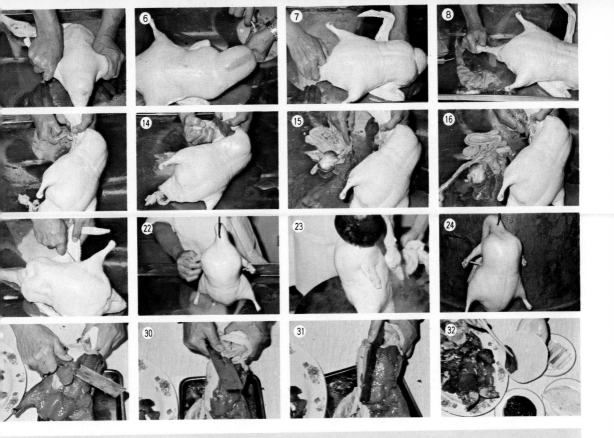

Peking Duckling

whole duckling (5 to 6 lbs.)
T. honey or maltose

12 Pieces Mandarin Pancakes
24 2-inch green onion sections

Dipping Sauce:
2 T. sesame oil

pre-mix {
4 T. sweet bean paste ("tien mien jiang")
4 T. sugar
½ C. water

To prepare Mandarin Pancakes: Follow recipe P. 28 as directed in "Lotus Pad" Mandarin Pancakes.
To prepare dipping sauce: Heat pan and sesame oil; add premixed ingredients and stir-fry over high heat until sauce has thickened (about 2 minutes).

Preparation : Fig. 1—Fig. 32 offered by Mr. Chang Phone-san

ig. 1: Cut off duck feet and discard
ig. 2: Grab tongue firmly
ig. 3: Grab windpipe
ig. 4: Remove esophagus
ig. 5: Push legs back to loosen joints
ig. 6: Using a pump or mouth, blow into air pipe so that meat and skin separate and duckling inflates
ig. 7: Using index finger, probe inside of duckling, the tip of intestine around index finger.
ig. 8: Pull intestines and remove
ig. 9: Lift wing to expose breast
ig. 10: Make a 2-inch cut in the breast
ig. 11: Using index finger, remove heart
ig. 12: Remove any remaining loose inner organs in breast
ig. 13: Wrap esophagus around index finger of left hand
ig. 14: Remove duckling gizzard and liver from breast hole
ig. 15: Remove stomach
ig. 16: Remove lungs
ig. 17: Rinse interior of breast hole
ig. 18: Wash interior and exterior of duckling
ig. 19: Force a 2½-inch bamboo stick or skewer into breast hole
ig. 20: Wedge stick horizontally in duckling breast
ig. 21: Cut wing tips

Fig. 22: Hook neck of duckling
Fig. 23: Holding duckling by hook in one hand, ladle boiling water over evenly, then ladle the mixture (3T. honey and 6C. water boiled)
Fig. 24: Hang duckling in a sunny, windy place and let dry 4 hours.
Fig. 25: Preheat oven to 350° to 400°F. Roast back for 20 minutes, then turn over roast breast.
Fig. 26: Place duckling on a roasting rack over a broiler pan and bake 40 to 50 minutes (turning duckling over once) until outside skin is golden brown and crisp; remove.
Fig. 27: Place duckling on cutting board, breast side up
Fig. 28: Cut thin slices of skin from half side of breast and place on serving plate
Fig. 29: Cut thin slices of skin and meat from mentioned half side of breast and continue along topside body
Fig. 30: The same procedure on the other half side
Fig. 31: Remove wishbone and cut away remaining breast meat
Fig. 32: Serve; each person places 1 piece of duck skin or meat, 1 section green onion and sauce in a pancake; wrap and eat.

鴨蛋(雞蛋)⋯⋯１０個

① 鹽⋯⋯⋯⋯⋯⋯⋯⋯⋯１杯
酒⋯⋯⋯⋯⋯⋯⋯⋯⋯３大匙
花椒粒⋯⋯⋯⋯⋯⋯１大匙
温開水⋯⋯⋯⋯⋯⋯⋯６杯

❶鴨蛋洗淨（圖１），①料備好在容器内（圖２）攪拌至鹽完全溶化後待涼（圖３），放入洗淨之鴨蛋（圖４），
醃約３０天即成「生鹹蛋」。

鹹　蛋 Salty Eggs

10 duck eggs (or chicken eggs)

①
1 C. salt
3 T. rice wine
1 T. Szechuan peppercorns
6 C. warm water

❶ Wash eggs (Fig. 1); put ① in a large container (Fig. 2); mix until salt is completely dissolved; let cool (Fig. 3); add eggs (Fig. 4); pickle for about 30 days.

雞蛋‥‥‥‥‥２０個		鹽‥‥‥‥‥１½大匙
水‥‥‥‥‥１０杯		茶葉（半兩）‥‥‥‥半杯
	①	八角‥‥‥‥‥３朵
		桂皮‥‥‥‥‥１大匙
		水‥‥‥‥‥１０杯

■備鍋放入水及雞蛋（圖１）待滾後改小火續煮１０分鐘至熟撈出，輕輕敲裂蛋殼備用（圖２），以便燒煮時容易入味。

■將①料燒開（圖３）加入煮熟雞蛋，以小火煮（圖４），約１小時即成「茶葉蛋」。

■味道太淡時可沾鹽食之。

茶葉蛋 Tea Eggs

20	eggs		1½ T. salt
10 C. water			½ C. tea leaves
		①	3 star anise
			1 T. cinnamon
			10 C. water

❶ Place eggs and water in large pot (Fig. 1); heat until water comes to a full boil; lower heat and simmer for 10 minutes; remove eggs; lightly tap eggs so that shells are cracked (Fig. 2) (when eggs are boiled again the flavor will seep through cracks).

❷ Bring ① to a boil (Fig. 3); add the hard-boiled eggs (with shell) (Fig. 4) and simmer over low heat for 1 hour; remove and serve.

■ If flavor is not strong enough, add salt when ready to eat.

蝦仁⋯⋯⋯⋯2兩	太白粉⋯⋯⋯半大匙	麵粉⋯⋯⋯⋯半杯
肥肉⋯⋯⋯⋯半兩	②{香蕉(１０兩)⋯2條	水⋯⋯⋯⋯6大匙

① 鹽⋯⋯⋯⋯⅓小匙
味精⋯⋯⋯⋯¼小匙
麻油⋯⋯⋯半小匙
酒⋯⋯⋯⋯１小匙
胡椒⋯⋯⋯⅛小匙

② 太白粉⋯⋯⋯２大匙

③ 鹽⋯⋯⋯⋯¼小匙
發粉⋯⋯⋯半小匙
花生油⋯⋯１大匙
「炸油」⋯⋯⋯6杯

❶ 蝦仁、肥肉剁碎調①料攪勻後加太白粉，攪拌備用。

❷ 香蕉去皮去頭尾，每條香蕉切成３段(圖１)，每段切爲４片(圖２)，每片沾上乾太白粉(圖３)，每二片夾上蝦絨(圖４)，可做爲１２個蝦夾。

❸ 將③料麵糊調好備用。

❹ 將每個蝦夾在麵糊裏沾滾一下，隨即投入油鍋內，以中火炸至呈淺黃色約３分鐘左右撈起即可供食。

■ ③料麵糊稱爲酥炸粉，可用做炸蝦或魚。

香蕉蝦夾 Stuffed Bananas

材料：１２個 **Makes 12**

⅛ lb. raw, shelled shrimp
½ oz. pork fat

① ⅓ t. salt
¼ t. MSG
½ t. sesame oil
1 t. rice wine
⅛ t. black pepper

½ T. cornstarch
② 2 medium-sized bananas (not too ripe)
2 T. cornstarch

③ ½ C. flour
6 T. water
¼ t. salt
½ t. baking powder
1 T. peanut oil
6 C. oil for frying

❶ Chop shrimp and pork fat until fine; mix with ① and cornstarch; stir mixture by lightly throwing against inside of bowl for 3-4 minutes so that ingredients are thoroughly combined (filling).

❷ Peel bananas, cut each into 3 sections (Fig. 1); cut each section into 4 pieces (Fig. 2); coat the cut surface of banana sections with cornstarch (Fig. 3); spread filling on 12 sections and top section with corresponding plain sections to make 12 sandwiches (Fig. 4).

❸ Mix ③ thoroughly for using.

❹ Coat each banana sandwich with ③ ; heat oil for deep-frying. Drop banana sandwiches into oil and deep-fry for 3 minutes over medium heat until golden; remove and drain; serve.

■ You may use ③ as a batter to deep-fry fish slices, shrimp, chicken, meat, etc.

香蕉……………… 3 條　　　蛋糊 { 雞蛋……………… 1 個　　　糖……………… ½杯
麵粉……………… 3 大匙
太白粉…………… 3 大匙
清水……………… 1 大匙

❶ 備碗 1 只將蛋糊用料在碗內調成糊狀。

❷ 香蕉去皮，切成塊，倒入蛋糊內使每塊香蕉沾裏均勻，以中火炸１５秒鐘撈起，再將油燒開，炸好香蕉再入鍋炸至呈金黃色時撈出。

❸ 油２大匙燒熱，中火將糖下鍋炒(圖１)，邊炒邊攪至糖溶化成淡黃色透明糖汁離火(圖２、３)，隨即倒入已炸熟香蕉翻拌(圖４)，即可盛入已抹油之盤內。(也可以洒些熟芝麻)。

■ 上桌時附上冷開水 1 小碗，吃時沾上冷開水香脆可口。

■ 可依個人喜歡之材料如番薯、芋頭、洋芋、山藥等任意選用，但炸時間改爲３分鐘至熟，再與糖漿翻拌。

拔絲香蕉 Candied Banana Fritters　　　材料：6 人份 **6 servings**

3　medium-sized bananas (not too ripe)　　　egg batter { 1　egg　　　½　C. sugar
3　T. flour
3　T. cornstarch
1　T. water

1. Lightly beat egg; add flour, cornstarch and water; mix thoroughly.
2. Peel bananas; cross-cut into pieces; dip in egg batter. Heat oil for deep-frying; deep-fry 15 seconds and remove; drain. Reheat oil, deep-fry bananas sections, a second time until golden; remove.
3. In another pan, heat 2T. oil, add sugar (Fig. 1) and stir over moderate heat until sugar melts. When melted sugar turns golden (Fig. 2, 3) add fried bananas, mix lightly to coat bananas (Fig. 4) and place on a greased serving plate.
   When served, you may dip it in cold water, for a crisp and more delicious taste.
   For several variations you may substitute sweet potato, taro root, potato, etc. as desired, but change the deep-frying time to 3 minutes.

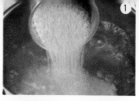

西谷米…………半杯		糖……………1 杯
水……………4 杯	②	奶水…………¼ 杯
① { 洋菜…………半兩		芒菓（2個）…1 杯
水……………6 杯		（切1公分四方小片）

❶鍋燒水待滾，西谷米倒入（圖1）用筷子攪動，以免黏聚在一起（圖2），中火煮約5～6分鐘撈起，用冷水泡洗，瀝乾水份備用（圖3）。

❷將①料燒滾，洋菜溶化後加②料按照其順序放入燒開，最後放進西谷米，即可倒入約20公分寬30公分長之四方盤待冷，入氷箱氷涼，吃時切塊端出。

■洋菜需事先泡水半小時，水菓種類依個人之喜愛選擇。

西米芒菓凍糕 Mango-Tapioca Pudding　　材料：6人份 6 servings

½ C. tapioca		1 C. sugar
4 C. water	② {	¼ C. evaporated milk
① { ½ oz. agar-agar *1		1 C. mangoes *2 (about 2), cut into paper-thin slices ½-inch long.
6 C. water		

❶ Soak agar-agar in water to cover for ½ hour; drain. Heat 4 cups water until boiling, slowly add tapioca (Fig. 1) while stirring constantly to prevent sticking (Fig. 2); cook 5-6 minutes over moderate heat. Drain tapioca and place in cold water to cool drain again (Fig. 3).

❷ Bring ① to a boil and cook until agar-agar is completely dissolved; remove from heat and add ② in descending order; mix until sugar is totally dissolved. Add tapioca and pour into a 8 x 12-inch pan. Let cool and refrigerate until firm. Cut into slices and serve.

*1 If unavailable, substitute gelatin; and follow instructions on package.

*2 You may also substitute fruit of your choice.

土司麵包⋯⋯⋯ 1 節
糖⋯⋯⋯⋯⋯⋯ 半杯

① {
蛋⋯⋯⋯⋯⋯⋯ 3 個
鮮乳⋯⋯⋯⋯⋯ 1 杯
豬油⋯⋯⋯⋯⋯ 3 大匙
香草片(壓碎)⋯ 1 片
}

② {
水⋯⋯⋯⋯⋯ 1½ 杯
糖⋯⋯⋯⋯⋯ 4 大匙
鮮乳⋯⋯⋯⋯ ¼ 杯
}

③ {
太白粉⋯⋯⋯ 1 大匙
水⋯⋯⋯⋯⋯ 1½ 大匙
}

❶ 土司去四週硬皮(圖 1),用清水浸約 5 分鐘,取出擠乾水份(圖 2),先加糖(圖 3)用手搓勻(圖 4)然後 再把①料放入,全部攪勻,倒入已抹油之模型內,大火蒸 40 分鐘。

❷ 蒸熟布丁,反扣在盤上,將②料燒開,以③料勾汁淋在布丁上即成。

■ 此甜點可依個人之喜愛加葡萄乾或蘋菓丁。土司加①料時需照順序,每加一種用料攪勻後,再加第二種 ,以此類推。

布 丁 Steamed Bread Pudding

材料: 1 2 人份 **12 servings**

5   slices white bread
½ C. sugar

① {
3   eggs
1   C. milk
3   T. melted lard or margarine
1   t. vanilla extract (crushed)
}

② {
1½ C. water
4   T. sugar
¼ C. milk
}

③ {
1   T. cornstarch
1½ T. water
}

❶ Trim crust from bread (Fig. 1) and soak in warm water 5 minutes; remove and squeeze to remove all water (Fig. 2); place mixture in a bowl and add sugar (Fig. 3); mix well to combine thoroughly (Fig. 4); add ① and beat lightly. Grease a mold 3-inches high and 7-inches in diameter; add pudding mixture and place in steamer; steam 40 minutes over high heat; remove and invert onto serving plate.

❷ Bring ② to a boil; add ③ to thicken; pour over pudding and serve.

◄ Raisins or apples may be added to ① for extra flavor.

蒸熟芋頭‥‥‥‥‥‥半斤　　　　　豆沙‥‥‥‥‥2兩

①{
白糖‥‥‥‥‥‥‥‥半斤
猪油‥‥‥‥‥‥‥‥¼杯
冬瓜糖(切碎)(圖1)‥2兩
桔子餅(切碎)(圖2)‥2兩
炸香紅葱頭‥‥‥‥2大匙
}

②{
水‥‥‥‥‥‥‥1杯
糖‥‥‥‥‥‥3大匙
}

③{
太白粉‥‥‥‥2小匙
水‥‥‥‥‥‥2小匙
}
玻璃紙‥‥‥‥‥1張

❶蒸熟芋頭趁熱壓成泥狀，加入①料攪拌均勻備用(圖3)

❷中碗內置一張玻璃紙，再把攪勻的芋泥⅔放入成凹形，中間放豆沙，剩餘⅓芋泥舖滿(圖4)入鍋蒸約
　20分鐘，即可反扣在盤內，拿掉玻璃紙。

❸將②料燒開，俟溶化後，以③料勾成糊狀，澆在芋屯上即成。

■豆沙做法：參照本書豆沙包(第3頁)。

芋　屯　Steamed Taro Pudding　　　　材料：6人份 6 servings

⅔ lb. precooked taro*¹ (cover to keep hot)

① {
½ C. sugar
¼ C. lard or margarine
¼ C. chopped candied winter melon (Fig. 1)
¼ C. chopped candied orange peel (Fig. 2)
2 T. minced, sauteed shallots
}

2 oz. (½C.) red bean paste*²

② {
1 C. water
3 T. sugar
}

③ {
2 t. cornstarch
2 t. water
}

1 10-inch round cellophane

❶ Mash taro while still hot; add ① and mix so that ingredients are thoroughly combined (Fig. 3).

❷ Line a 7-inch bowl with cellophane; place 2/3 of ① mixture in bowl; pack down firmly so that mixture is higher on sides and there is an indentation in the middle; place red bean paste in indentation and pack down; add other third of taro mixture to bowl and pack firmly to cover red bean paste (Fig. 4). Place over boiling water, cover and steam 20 minutes over medium heat; remove and invert onto serving plate; peel away cellophane.

❸ Place ② in a pan and bring to a boil; cook until sugar has dissolved and add ③ to thicken; pour over steamed pudding; serve.

*¹ See P. 40 "Skin" step ❶ for directions for precooking taro; if unavailable, substitute sweet potato.

*² See P. 3 "Sweet Buns with Red Bean Paste" for directions for making red bean paste.

小排骨…１２兩

①
甜麵醬…２大匙、糖………１小匙
辣豆瓣醬半大匙、麻油……１大匙
醬油……２大匙、清水……３大匙
味精……１小匙、、酒………１大匙

蒸肉粉………３包
番薯…………半斤

②
鹽…………半小匙
蒸肉粉·($\frac{1}{4}$杯)１包

❶小排骨剁２４塊，拌入①料醃約３０分鐘，再拌上蒸肉粉(圖１、２)。

❷番薯去皮切滾刀塊，拌入②料備用。

❸將番薯擺在小蒸籠底，小排骨置其上(圖３)，水開蒸３０分鐘即可。

■蕃薯可以用豌豆仁、花生、南瓜等代替，做法相同。

粉蒸排骨 Steamed Spareribs with Sweet Potato 材料：６人份 **6 servings**

1 lb. small spareribs

①
2 T. sweet soybean paste ("tien mien jiang")
½ T. hot bean paste ("la do ban jiang")
2 T. soy sauce
1 t. MSG
1 t. sugar
1 T. sesame oil
3 T. water
1 T. rice wine

3 pkg. (¾C.) "jen rou fen"*[1]
⅔ lb. sweet potato*[2]

②
½ t. salt
1 pkg. (¼C.) "jen rou fen"*[1]

❶ Cut spareribs into 24 sections; add ① and let soak 30 minutes; add "jen rou fen" and mix well (Fig. 1, 2).

❷ Peel sweet potato; cut into bite-size pieces and mix with ②

❸ In a steamer, place sweet potato mixture on one layer and portion spare ribs on top (Fig. 3); steam 30 minutes over medium heat; serve.

*[1] "Jen rou fen" is a special type of prepared meat-flavored rice powder available in packages at a Chinese grocery store, if unavailable, omit.

*[2] You may also substitute green peas, peanuts or squash.

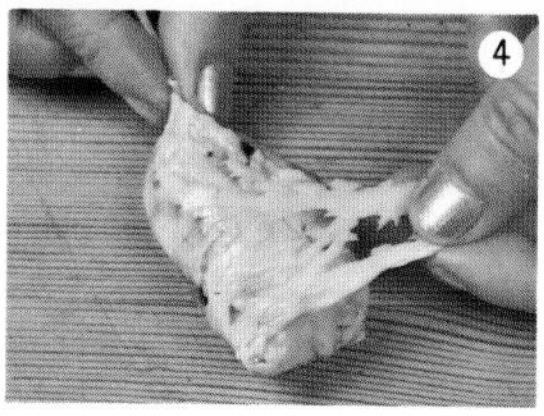

絞肉……2兩
魚漿……2兩

①
- 味精¼小匙、麻油…⅛小匙
- 糖…2小匙、酒……⅛小匙
- 胡椒⅛小匙、太白粉2小匙

②
- 洋蔥或荸薺………半杯
- 冬菇1朵、蒜末半小匙
- 紅蔥頭片(炸)…1小匙

網油……2兩
竹子……6枝
「炸油」…6杯

❶洋蔥或荸薺切碎拌少許鹽，擱約10分鐘後，擠出水份，冬菇泡軟切碎，網油切爲7公分四方(圖1)。
❷將絞肉、魚漿及①料用手攪拌均匀後，甩打多次加入②料成餡。
❸每小張網油，放入餡(1/6)，中間置竹子(圖2)，包成雞腿形狀(圖3、4)，「炸油」燒熱，以中火炸約8分鐘肉熟呈金黃色撈出即成。

■魚漿內已加鹽，故本點心鹽可免用。
■若不用網油改沾裹太白粉或麵包粉油炸也可。或用腐皮包長條油炸也可。

龍鳳腿 "Mock Chicken Legs"

材料：6枝 **Makes 6**

2 oz. chopped pork
2 oz. fish paste*[1]

①
- ¼ t. MSG, 2 t. sugar,
- ⅛ t. black pepper
- ⅛ t. sesame oil
- ⅛ t. rice wine
- 2 t. cornstarch

②
- ½ C. medium-sized onion (or water chestnut)
- 1 pre-softened Chinese black mushroom
- 1 t. minced, sauteed shallots.
- ½ t. chopped garlic

2 oz. pork net oil*[2]
6 wooden sticks
6 C. oil for frying

❶ Chop onion or water chestnuts finely; add ½t. salt and mix; let sit 10 minutes and drain. Chop black mushroom and cut por net oil into 3-inch square (Fig. 1).

❷ Mix chopped pork, fish paste and ① for 3-4 minutes, throwing mixture against inside of mixing bowl so that ingredients ar thoroughly combined; add ② ; mix well (Filling).

❸ Place one portion (1/6) of filling in the middle of pork net oil square; place stick in middle of filling (Fig. 2) and fold pork ne oil so that it encases filling (Fig. 3, 4) (as wrapping a gift). Heat oil until medium hot; deep-fry "mock chicken legs" ove medium heat for 8 minutes; remove, drain and serve.

*[1] If fish paste is unavailable, see P. 152 step ❶ , for making home made fish paste. "Store-bought" fish paste ma contain very much salt, added as a preservative; if substituting store-bought fish paste, lightly rinse onion and wat chestnut before using as directed in step ❷ .

*[2] You may substitute nori, bean curd skin or grated bread crumbs for pork net oil and use as directed.

牛肉⋯⋯⋯ 1 斤半

① 雞蛋⋯⋯⋯ 6 個
沙茶醬⋯⋯ 6 大匙
醬油⋯⋯⋯ 9 大匙

② 水⋯⋯⋯⋯ 9 杯
鹽⋯⋯⋯ 1½ 小匙
番茄（切丁）⋯ 1 個
葱段⋯⋯⋯ 6 枝
猪油⋯⋯⋯ 2 大匙

③ 豆腐⋯⋯⋯ 2 塊、唐好菜⋯⋯ 6 兩
魚丸⋯⋯⋯ 1 2 粒、菠菜⋯⋯⋯ 6 兩
大白菜⋯⋯ 1 2 兩、粉絲⋯⋯⋯ 1 把

❶將牛肉切薄片，把①料分盛6小碗內調勻，做沾食用，②料燒沸（圖1）水不夠時再補充，③料洗淨備在餐
桌上。

❷食用時依各人喜好，將③料及牛肉等邊放入②料內煮熟（圖2、3），邊沾①料供食（圖4）。

■牛肉很薄容易熟，故放到湯裏顏色一變即可食用。

■可準備一些麵，到最後時將麵放入燒煮，其味道特別鮮美。

■沙茶醬是以花生油、花生粉、炸香紅葱頭、香菜子、蒜頭粉、辣椒粉、花椒、八角、蝦米磨碎製成，向
雜貨店購買。

沙茶火鍋 Mongolian Beef Fire Pot　　　　材料：6人份 6 servings

① 2 lbs. top sirloin of beef
6 eggs
6 T. "sha cha jiang"*
9 T. soy sauce

② 9 C. water
1½ t. salt.
6 1-inch green onion sections
1 medium-size tomato
2 T. lard

③ 2 squares bean curd 、 ½ lb. spinach
12 fish balls 、 1 package bean threads
1 lb. Chinese cabbage 、 ½ lb. "tang hau tsai"

❶ Cut beef into paper-thin slices; dice bean curd and tomato; cut cabbage and spinach into bite-size pieces; pre-soften bean threads in warm water; drain. Portion ① into serving bowls; arrange ingredients of ③ on a platter and place on table near soup; pour ② mixture into a Mongolian Fire pot or electric casserole and bring liquid to a boil (Fig. 1); lower heat and allow liquid to simmer.

❷ When meat commences, using chopsticks, add beef a piece at a time and ingredients of ③ to simmering ② ; cook until tender (Fig. 2, 3). Each person, helping himself by using chopsticks, may pick out meat or ③ and then dip in sauce* before eating (Fig. 4).

The dipping sauce which may be used is called "sha cha jiang". It is a combination of peanut oil, peanut powder, green onion oil, coriander seed, garlic powder, hot pepper powder, star anise, Szechuan peppercorn, & dried shrimp mixed together to a smooth paste. It may be purchased in a Chinese grocery store. If unavailable, substitute hoisin sauce.

■Since the beef has been cut to paper-thin slices, it will cook very quickly; when color changes, remove and eat. The ingredients of ③ will require a longer cooking time; simmer until tender.

If desired, after meat and ③ have been eaten, add precooked noodles to flavorful stock for added eating.

171

小排骨‧‧‧‧‧‧‧‧‧‧ 1 斤半

① ⎰ 酒‧‧‧‧‧‧‧‧‧‧‧‧‧‧ 2 大匙
⎪ 醬油‧‧‧‧‧‧‧‧‧‧‧‧ 2 大匙
⎪ 鹽‧‧‧‧‧‧‧‧‧‧‧‧‧‧ 2 小匙
⎨ 糖‧‧‧‧‧‧‧‧‧‧‧‧‧‧ 3 大匙
⎪ 海山醬‧‧‧‧‧‧‧‧‧‧ 3 大匙
⎪ 紅腐乳‧‧‧‧‧‧‧‧‧‧ 1 塊
⎪ 五香粉‧‧‧‧‧‧‧‧‧‧ 半大匙
⎱ 蒜頭(拍破)‧‧‧‧‧‧ 5 粒

❶小排骨(圖 1)劃刀(圖 2)調入①料(圖 3)醃 1 小時 ，需時時翻拌(圖 4)，使其入味。
❷醃好的小排骨，用烤箱以 4 5 0 度烤 2 0 分鐘，至熟取出，切塊或切條，即可供食。

烤排骨 Barbecued Spareribs

材料：1 2 人份 **12 servings**

2　lbs.　spareribs

① ⎰ 2　T.　rice wine
⎪ 2　T.　soy sauce
⎪ 2　t.　salt
⎨ 3　T.　sugar
⎪ 3　T.　"hai shan jiang" (hoisin sauce)
⎪ 1　square fermented bean curd ("Chinese cheese")
⎪ ½　T.　5-spice powder
⎱ 5　cloves garlic, smashed

❶ Rinse spareribs lightly (Fig. 1); cut into individual ribs (Fig. 2) and mix with ① (Fig. 3); let soak one hour, turning occasionally (Fig. 4).
❷ Preheat oven to 450°F; place spareribs in a shallow, roasting pan. Bake 20 minutes until outside of meat is brown and inside of meat is done; cut ribs apart and serve.

里肌肉絲⋯⋯⋯⋯⋯半杯		紅蘿蔔絲⋯⋯半杯		春捲皮⋯⋯⋯１６張		麵糊	麵粉⋯２大匙
①	酒⋯⋯⋯⋯⋯１小匙	②	鹽⋯⋯⋯１小匙	③	番茄醬⋯⋯⋯１大匙		水⋯⋯２大匙
	鹽⋯⋯⋯⋯⋯⅓小匙		味精⋯⋯半小匙		黑醋⋯⋯⋯１大匙	「炸油」⋯８杯	
	太白粉⋯⋯⋯⋯１小匙		糖⋯⋯⋯１大匙		醬油⋯⋯⋯１大匙		
	綠豆芽⋯⋯⋯⋯４杯		胡椒⋯⋯¼小匙		辣豆瓣醬⋯⋯１小匙		
	韮菜黃(切２公分長)⋯１杯		麻油⋯⋯１小匙		蒜末⋯⋯⋯半小匙		

❶ 里肌肉絲調①料拌勻入油鍋炒熟盛起備用。

❷ 綠豆芽、韮菜黃、紅蘿蔔以開水川燙（１０秒）立即撈起，瀝乾水份與里肌肉絲、②料拌勻即成餡，分成
１６份。

❸ 每張春捲皮前半部邊緣沾麵糊（圖１），中間放上一份餡（圖２）包成長１２公分圓筒狀（圖３、４）。

❹ 「炸油」燒熱，中火炸４分鐘至皮脆呈金黃色撈起盛盤，食用時沾上拌勻之③料。

■ 除綠豆芽、韮菜黃、紅蘿蔔等材料外，也可用筍、包心菜、四季豆、小黃瓜、芹菜等代替。

炸春捲 Fried Egg Rolls   材料：１６條 Makes 16

	½ C. shredded pork loin		1 t. salt		1 T. tomato ketchup
	1 t. rice wine		½ t. MSG		1 T. worcestershire sauce
①	⅓ t. salt	②	1 T. sugar	③	1 T. soy sauce
	1 t. cornstarch		¼ t. black pepper		1 t. hot bean paste ("la do ban jiang")
	4 C. bean sprouts		1 t. sesame oil		½ t. chopped garlic
	1 C. Chinese chives, cut to 1-inch sections		16 egg roll skins		8 C. oil for frying
	½ C. shredded carrot			④	2 T. flour
					2 T. water

❶ Mix ① with pork loin; heat pan and 4T. oil; stir-fry pork shreds until color changes; remove and drain.

❷ Blanch bean sprouts, carrots and Chinese chives in boiling water; plunge into cold water to cool; drain. In a bowl, mix pork shreds, carrots shreds, bean sprouts and Chinese chives; add ② and toss lightly; separate into 16 equal portions.

❸ Moister a ½-inch band around the edge of the top half of the skin with ④ (Fig. 1); place a portion of filling in the middle of each skin (Fig. 2); wrap filling up like a package in egg roll skins. Rolls should be about 4-inches long (Fig. 3, 4).

❹ Heat oil for deep-frying egg rolls over medium heat for 4 minutes until golden brown; remove and drain. Combine ingredients of ③ and use as dipping sauce.

◀ The vegetables in the filling may be varied according to personal taste; you may substitute bamboo shoot, Chinese cabbage, green beans, cucumber, celery, etc.

里肌肉絲………半杯

① { 酒………1 小匙
鹽………⅓ 小匙
太白粉………1 小匙 }

② { 綠豆芽………2 杯
熟筍絲………1 杯
熟紅蘿蔔絲………半杯
五香豆干(切絲)1 杯 }

③ { 鹽………1 小匙
味精………半小匙
糖………半大匙
胡椒………¼ 小匙
麻油………1 小匙 }

香菜(略切)………1 杯
花生粉………半杯
海山醬………¼ 杯
春捲皮………1 6 張

❶里肌肉絲調①料拌勻，油4大匙燒熱，先炒里肌肉，再放入②料，並調③料炒勻，成餡盛盤備用。

❷每張春捲皮，一半邊緣塗抹少許海山醬(圖1)，中央放適量的餡及香菜、花生粉(圖2)包成長12公分的圓筒狀即成(圖3)。

■本省的習俗在尾牙(農曆12月16日)或清明節，家家戶戶都做潤餅捲過節，習慣上將所準備材料分別炒熟盛盤，也可二或三樣混合炒熟或部份青菜生吃，不止上項材料，可有蝦米、蒜白、黃瓜、唐好菜、包心菜、洋葱、乾海藻、魷魚、蘿蔔干等等，依個人喜歡夾取包著吃。

■喜食甜味者可在花生粉內加4大匙細糖。

潤餅捲 Taiwanese Egg Rolls

材料：1 6 條 **Makes 16**

½ C. shredded pork loin

① { 1 t. rice wine
⅓ t. salt
1 t. cornstarch }

② { 2 C. bean sprouts
1 C. shredded precooked bamboo shoot
½ C. shredded precooked carrot
1 C. shredded pressed beancurd }

③ { 1 t. salt
½ t. MSG
½ T. sugar
¼ t. black pepper
1 t. sesame oil }

1 C. chopped coriander
½ C. crushed peanuts*
¼ C. "hai shan jiang" (hoisin sauce)
16 egg roll skins

❶ Mix ① with pork loin; heat pan and 4T. oil; stir-fry pork shreds until color changes; add ② and ③ ; stir-fry to mix ingredients together; remove (filling).

❷ Take each skin and fold over to half; reopen to full square and rub "hai shan Jiang" on one edge of skin to help seal (Fig. 1); place ¼C. filling in middle of skin and then sprinkle coriander and crushed peanuts over all (Fig. 2). Wrap edges to form a roll 4-inches long; serve (Fig. 3).

■ Taiwanese Egg Rolls are a special holiday food eaten every year on the 16th of the 12th month to commemorate the holiday honoring the dead.

The various listed vegetables may be stir-fried in groups of 2 or 3 or served fresh. You may also substitute lettuce, dried shrimp, long garlic stalks, cucumber, green beans, celery, seaweed, squid and dried turnip, according to individual taste.

* Add 4T. sugar to the crushed peanuts for a variation in taste.

<table>
<tr><td>①</td><td>牛肉
羊肉
雞肉
豬肉</td><td>②</td><td>葱絲　　、綠豆芽
洋葱絲　、香菜
包心菜絲、番茄片
青椒絲　、菠蘿片
紅蘿蔔絲</td><td>③</td><td>蒜末　　、蝦油
紅辣椒末、糖水
醬油　　、辣油
酒　　　、麻油</td></tr>
</table>

❶將①料切成１０公分×５公分之大薄片(愈薄愈好)盛於盤上備用。

❷食用者取一中型湯碗自行夾取適量①料(圖１)，再取②料之蔬菜(圖２)，並隨個人喜好調上適量之③料(圖３、４)然後倒在燒熱之特製烤肉鐵鍋上，用一雙長筷子，迅速炒動，至肉熟盛入原碗內，端出即可食用。

蒙古烤肉 Mongolian Barbecue

①	②	③
lean, boneless beef lean, boneless leg of lamb or shoulder chicken meat pork loin	shredded green onion shredded onion shredded cabbage shredded green pepper shredded carrot bean sprouts coriander sliced tomato sliced pineapple	soy sauce rice wine shrimp oil sugar-water hot pepper oil sesame oil chopped hot red pepper chopped garlic

❶ Cut ingredients in ① into 4-inch by 2-inch paper-thin slices; arrange on platter.

❷ Each participant takes a medium-sized bowl and places ingredients from ① (Fig. 1), ② (Fig. 2), and ③ in individual bowl (may take as much or as little of each ingredients as one wishes) (Fig. 3, 4). Pour ingredients of bowl onto highly heated special"Mongolian grill"; a little water is added if necessary and ingredients are tossed lightly over high heat with long chopsticks. When meat changes color, remove and serve*.

* Mixture may be eaten plain or stuffed as a filling in "Flaky Sesame Flat Breads" P. 144

① 羊腿肉‥‥‥‥‥‥‥‥‥ 1 斤半
　 大白菜‥‥‥‥‥‥‥‥ 1 2 兩
　 青菜(菠菜或唐好菜) 1 2 兩
　 粉絲‥‥‥‥‥‥‥‥‥‥ 1 把
　 豆腐或凍豆腐‥‥‥‥‥ 2 塊

② 高湯或水‥‥‥‥‥ 6 杯
　 鹽‥‥‥‥‥‥‥‥ 1 小匙
　 味精‥‥‥‥‥‥‥ 半小匙

沾食用料：

麻油‥‥‥ 1 小匙、紅豆腐乳半大匙
蝦油‥‥‥ 半大匙、糖‥‥‥‥‥ 半小匙
辣油‥‥‥ 1 小匙、葱花‥‥‥‥ 半大匙
醬油‥‥‥ 半大匙、香菜末‥‥ 1 小匙
酒‥‥‥‥ 半小匙、韭菜花‥‥‥ 少許
醋‥‥‥‥ 半小匙、雞蛋‥‥‥‥ 1 個
味精‥‥‥ ¼小匙、

每人份

❶羊肉切長 1 0 公分，寬 5 公分極薄片(愈薄愈好)盛於盤上。
❷白菜切塊，青菜切段，粉絲泡軟，豆腐切 2 公分四方塊，盛盤備餐桌上。
❸火鍋盛②料(不夠時補充)，食用時邊放入①料煮熟(圖 1)，邊以筷子夾住肉片(圖 2)入火鍋內燙涮一下
　，見顏色變白肉熟了(圖 3)，即可沾食用料(圖 4)食之。
■沾食用料，可依個人喜歡，酌量調於小碗內，也可加雞蛋沾食。

涮羊肉 Lamb Mongolian Firepot

材料：6人份 **6 servings**

①
2　lbs. lean boneless leg of lamb or shoulder
1　lb. Chinese cabbage
1　lb. green vegetable (spinach or watercress)
1　2-oz. package bean threads
2　squares bean curd

②
6　C. stock
1　t. salt
½　t. MSG

Serving sauce:

each serving

1	t.	sesame oil	½	t.	fermented bean curd ("chinese cheese")
½	t.	shrimp oil			
1	t.	hot pepper oil	½	t.	sugar
½	t.	soy sauce	½	t.	chopped green onion
½	t.	rice wine	1	t.	chopped coriander
½	t.	worcestershire sauce	1	t.	chopped chinese chives
¼	t.	MSG	1		egg

❶ Cut meat into 4-inch by 2-inch paper-thin slices; place on platter.
❷ Cut cabbage and spinach into bite-size pieces; pre-soften bean threads in warm water; drain. Cut bean curd into 1-inch squares; arrange ingredients on a platter and place on table near soup.
❸ Pour ② into Mongolian Firepot or electric casserole; when liquid boils, add vegetables and cook until tender (Fig. 1). Prepare sauce in individual serving bowls; using chopsticks, add meat slices (Fig. 2); cook until color changes (Fig. 3). Remove meat and vegetables as desired, and dip in serving sauce (Fig. 4).
■ A raw egg may be added to sauce in serving bowls; this adds extra flavor and cools off the hot dipped ingredients faster. Ingredients of sauce may be revised according to individual taste.

紅心番薯	1 斤		麥芽糖	3 大匙
水	3 杯	①	糖	6 大匙
			醋	半大匙
			清水	2 杯
			鹽	$\frac{1}{3}$ 小匙

❶番薯去皮（圖１）洗淨，切條（圖２），加水３杯燒煮１０分鐘（圖３）取起。

❷①料燒開，放入煮過番薯，蓋鍋小火煮４０分鐘，至番薯熟，糖水成糖漿時（約半杯），將番薯置盤，淋上少許糖漿即成。

■食用時，可洒上適量花生粉，更爲可口。

蜜餞薯條 Candied Sweet Potatoes

材料：6人份 **6 servings**

1⅓ lbs. sweet potato
3 C. water

①
- ⅓ t. salt
- 3 T. honey or maltose
- 6 T. sugar
- ½ T. vinegar
- 2 C. water

❶ Pare skin from potatoes(Fig. 1); cut into long matchsticks about ½-inch thick (Fig. 2). Heat 3 C. water until boiling; cook 10 minutes over medium heat (Fig. 3); remove and drain.

❷ Bring ① mixture to a boil and add potato sticks; cover and cook for 40 minutes over low heat until potatoes are tender and sauce has thickened considerably (sauce should now equal about ½C.). Remove potato sticks and place on serving plate; pour candied sauce on top; serve.

◀ When serving, you may sprinkle a few crushed peanuts on top for extra flavor.

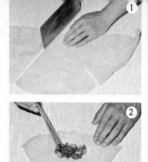

<table>
<tr><td>① {</td><td>里肌肉……………… 6 兩
蝦仁……………… 3 兩
肥肉……………… 1 兩</td></tr>
<tr><td>② {</td><td>酒…1小匙、胡椒…¼小匙
鹽…1小匙、麻油…¼小匙
味精½小匙、太白粉1小匙
糖……………… 2 小匙</td></tr>
</table>

③ {
香菜末…………… ⅓杯
葱末……………… 2 大匙

腐皮……………… 7 张
「炸油」………… 6 杯

④ {
蠔油……………… 1 大匙
味精……………… ¼小匙
糖……………… 1 小匙
太白粉………… 半大匙
水……………… 1 杯

❶將①料切丁，調入②料攪拌至有黏性，再加③料拌勻成餡。
❷將腐皮切3小張(圖1)計21張，每張上面放1大匙餡(圖2)，捲成長約6公分之春捲形狀(圖3、4)。
❸「炸油」燒熱，用中火炸4分鐘呈金黃色皮脆，撈起。
❹④料燒開，再放入炸熟之腐皮捲拌勻，燒乾水份，即可置盤供食。

蠔油腐皮捲 Stuffed Bean Skin Rolls in Oyster Sauce

材料：21捲 **Makes 21**

① {
½ lb. pork loin
¼ lb. raw, shelled shrimp
1 oz. pork fat

② {
1 t. rice wine
¼ t. black pepper
1 t. salt
¼ t. sesame oil
½ t. MSG
1 t. cornstarch
2 t. sugar

③ {
⅓ C. chopped coriander
2 T. chopped green onion

7 pre-softened bean curd skins
6 C. oil for frying

④ {
1 T. oyster sauce
¼ t. MSG
1 t. sugar
½ T. cornstarch
1 C. water

❶ Rinse shrimp and devein. Dice ingredients in ① ; add ② and throw ingredients lightly against inside of mixing bowl to combine thoroughly (filling).
❷ Cut bean curd skin into 3 pie-shaped sections (Fig. 1); spread 1 tablespoon filling over bean curd skin (Fig. 2); wrap into a 2-inch roll (Fig. 3, 4).
❸ Heat oil until medium hot; add rolls and deep-fry 4 minutes until outside is golden brown and crispy; remove and drain.
❹ Heat pan and add ④ ; heat until boiling and add fried rolls; cook over high heat until sauce is near-dry; remove and serve.

中國菜

- 393道中國菜
- 16開精裝本
- 全部彩色印刷簡單易學
- 中文、英文、中英、日文、法文

中國菜（第二冊）

- 184道中國菜
- 50種餐盤裝飾
- 16開精裝本
- 全部彩色印刷簡單易學
- 步驟圖片說明
- 中英對照版

中國餐點

- 220道中國餐點
- 16開精裝本
- 全部彩色印刷
- 有步驟圖片說明
- 中文、英文、中英、日文

中國菜（實用專輯）

- 89道中國菜
- 16開平裝本
- 全部彩色印刷簡單易學
- 10種點心，並附步驟圖片說明
- 中文、英文

愛與美插花

- 90種插花
- 16開精裝本
- 全部彩色印刷簡單易學
- 有步驟圖片說明
- 中英對照版
- 由名花道家歐幸江編著
- 中英對照版

味全

味全出版社有限公司
台北市仁愛路4段28號2樓
電話：702-1148 • 702-1149 • 704-2729
郵政劃撥：18203號　黃淑惠帳戶

味全家政班
台北市松江路125號5樓
電話：551-3564 • 521-4331

味全烹飪班美國分班
(COOKING SCHOOL AND BOOK SALES)
1434 South Atlantic Blvd.
Alhambra, CA. 91803, U.S.A.
TEL: (213) 289-8288 • 289-8289

烹飪班 Cooking Class

學習內容／

宴席菜、家常菜、中西點心。
油條、燒餅、豆漿、豆腐、春捲皮、北平烤
鴨、鹽水鴨、牛猪肉干、肉鬆、肉脯等。

Subjects:
Banquet Cuisine, Home Cuisine, Chinese and
Western Snacks.
Twisted cruller, baked cake, bean milk, bean
curd, spring roll, Peking roasted duck, spicy
salted duck, dried and seasoned beef and pork
slices, Meat fluff, and dried and seasoned meat

插花班 Flower Arrangement Class

學習內容／

初級班二個月：基本型的插法
中級班四個月：基本型應用、並列型、小品
　　　　　　　花、瓶花、下垂型。
研　究　班：寫景、非寫實、瓶花、應用型。

Subjects:
Basic course: Basic arrangement for two
months.
Middle course: Applied arrangement for four
months.
Advanced course: Comprehensive arrangement
and vase alternation for two months.

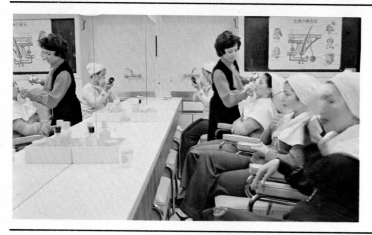

美容班 Make-up Class

學習內容／

保　養：皮膚保養　頭髮保養
化　粧：普通化粧　流行化粧

Subjects:
Maintenance:
skin care, nighttime skin care, use of face
beautifier, hair care.
Made-up:
ordinary make-up, fashion make-up.

縫紉班 Sewing Class

學習內容／

初級三個月：裙子、襯衫、長褲、洋裝、
　　　　　　裝等。
中級三個月：夾裡服裝(裙子、洋裝、套裝等)
高級三個月：自由變化、製作。

Subjects:
Basic course: skirt, shirt, trousers, Western
children's dresses for three months.
Middle course: Dress with lining (skirt, Western
dress and suit) for three months.
Advanced course: Free alterations and creation
for three months.

味全家政班
台北市松江路125號5樓
電話：(02)551-3564, 521-4331

Dept. of Home Economics Wei-Chuan Foods Corp.
5th Fl., 125, Sung Kiang Road, Taipei 104, Taiwan, Rep. of China
Tel: (02) 551-3564, 521-4331

中國餐點

味全食譜

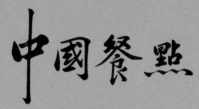

版權所有　著作權執照號碼
台內著字第6293號

編　著　黃淑惠

出版者　味全食品工業股份有限公司
附設家政短期職業補習班

發行者　黃　淑　惠
味全出版社有限公司
台北市仁愛路四段28號二樓
電話／7021148・7021149
7042729
郵政劃撥18203號

中華民國63年元月初版發行7版
中華民國65年3月創新發行第1版
中華民國71年5月創新發行A8版

中華彩色印刷公司　承印